POSTCARD HISTORY SERIES

Hampton and Hampton Beach

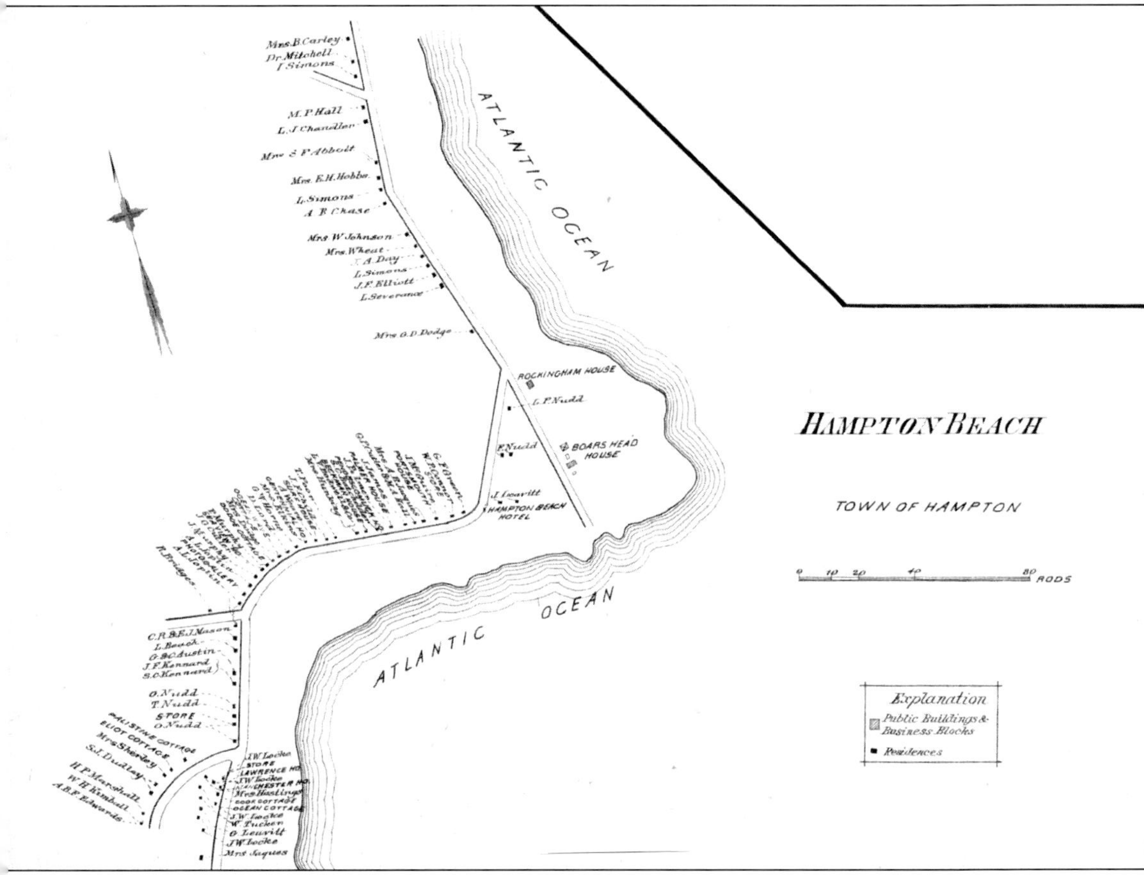

This map of the houses near Great Boar's Head at Hampton Beach was published in 1892, before the advent of the trolley and the Casino. At this time, most visitors came to stay for an extended period in one of the hotels or guesthouses. Private summer cottages had also begun to appear as seaside residences became fashionable.

POSTCARD HISTORY SERIES

Hampton and Hampton Beach

Elizabeth Aykroyd and Betty Moore

ARCADIA
PUBLISHING

ISBN 978-0-7385-3816-7

Published by Arcadia Publishing,
Charleston, South Carolina

Printed in the United States of America

Library of Congress Catalog Card Number: 2005922447

For all general information, contact Arcadia Publishing:
Telephone 843-853-2070
Fax 843-853-0044
E-mail sales@arcadiapublishing.com
For customer service and orders:
Toll-free 1-888-313-2665

Visit us on the Internet at www.arcadiapublishing.com

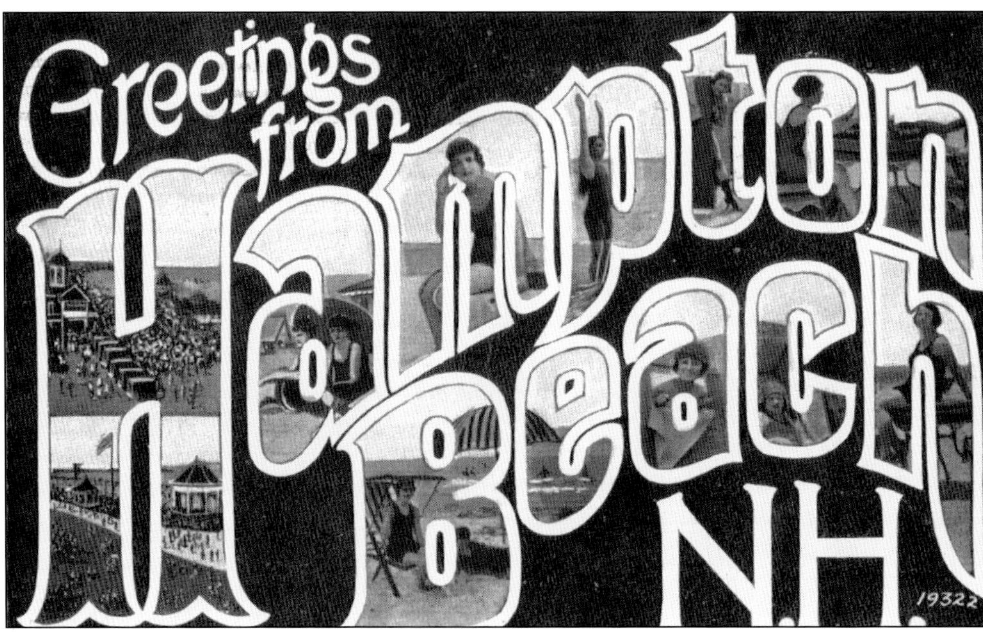

This postcard from the 1930s not only brings greetings from the beach but also gives the recipient a glimpse of a number of local attractions. Within the *H* are two views of Ocean Boulevard, while images within the other letters show people enjoying the beach.

Contents

Acknowledgments

The project of producing this postcard history was sponsored by the Hampton Historical Society and was carried out not only by the two authors but also by an enthusiastic group of volunteers, who helped with the choice of cards, lent their own postcards, researched details, and proofread the manuscript for errors. Those who met with us regularly to put this book together were Percy Annis, Nancy Coes, Carol Keating, Jerry Miller, Jody Millette, and Eleanor Young.

Almost all the postcards in this book come from the Fitzgerald, Brown, Bourgeault, and Christensen collections of the Hampton Historical Society. Special thanks go to Shirley Foote and Charlotte Preston, who not only gave us cards to use but also helped to fill in gaps in our knowledge of the beach. Roseanna Wright and Bud DesRochers were also generous with their knowledge of life in Hampton.

A major source of information about Hampton in the last century was Peter Randall's *Hampton: A Century of Town and Beach, 1888–1988.* Other resources were William Teschek's *Hampton and Hampton Beach* (in Arcadia's Images of America series) and the documents, scrapbooks, and newspaper files in the collections of the Hampton Historical Society.

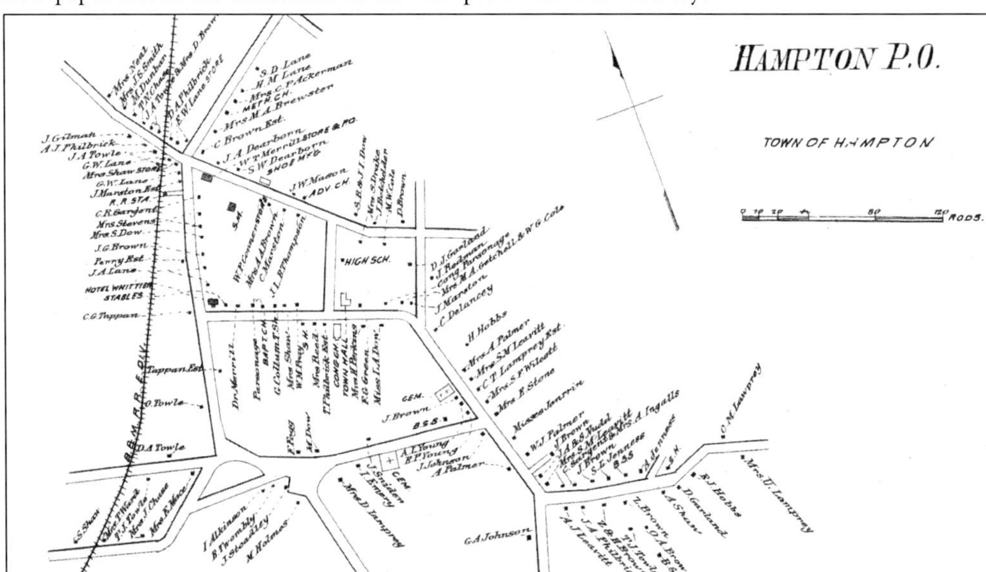

This map of the center of Hampton village in 1892 shows the growth of the business center around the depot. In the center of the map is the Meeting House Green, although by this time the meetinghouse for which it was named had disappeared. The green was the original 17th-century center of the town.

Introduction

Hampton was originally a farming and fishing community, first for Native Americans, who came in the summer from the interior of New Hampshire, and later for Englishmen, who founded a village called Winnacunnet Plantation in 1638. The town, renamed Hampton in 1639, attracted settlers who used the extensive salt marshes as grazing areas for their cattle and who found the ocean and rivers to be rich fishing grounds. The lack of a deep harbor meant that the town remained a farming village, concentrating on agriculture and the development of new settlements inland rather than on shipping and other maritime activities. This situation lasted for over 200 years until the arrival of the trains in 1840.

The coming of the railroad brought the beginnings of the tourist industry to Hampton. Until then, the seashore had been the province of fishermen, and few townspeople lived or worked there. Fishermen built shacks for their dories and fishing equipment near the end of the present High Street, and traders came there to buy their catch. In the early years of the 19th century, the Leavitt family opened what later became the first inn on the beach near the "fish houses." This building, although greatly expanded and built over, still stands.

Travel by rail brought thousands of visitors and many changes to the once quiet farming village. The center of town business moved from the landing on the creek to the area around the new depot on Lafayette Road. To take advantage of the new commercial opportunities offered by the railroad, stores and offices were opened along Lafayette Road near the train station, a large central hotel was built, and transportation services to the beach were offered for early tourists. Dozens of hotels were opened along the once deserted shore, soon to be joined by the summer cottages of a new type of citizen: the summer resident.

Although train travel played a major role in the development of Hampton Beach as a seaside attraction, it was the street railway, or trolley, and later the automobile, that caused the explosive growth of the tourist business in Hampton. In 1897, the Exeter, Hampton, and Amesbury Street Railway began service to the beach from the surrounding towns, allowing people to travel to the sea for a stay of a day or only a few hours. Although trolley service ended in 1926, the growth of automobile travel meant that visitors continued to come by the thousands, as they do today.

An important part of a tourist's stay in Hampton was a souvenir. Items ranging from wooden plaques to teacups were printed with beach scenes and sold in the thousands. No item, however, was more reminiscent of Hampton than the postcard. Postcards featuring Hampton scenes, both of the beach and of the town center, began to appear around 1900 and provided an opportunity for visitors to send an inexpensive reminder of their stay here to friends and neighbors back home. Local merchants, such as E. G. Cole or Dudley and White, were quick to publish a large selection of photographic postcards, which they offered for sale in their stores.

Postcards are evocative not only of Hampton at an earlier time but also of a scene that is rapidly changing. Buildings burn, are torn down, or are completely remodeled over the years, and often the only documentation of how a place appeared 50 or even 20 years ago is a postcard purchased by a visitor. Hotels and other entertainment establishments are constantly changing to meet new fashions and new needs, and postcards chart these changes by documenting the history of the building. This is particularly true of Hampton Beach, which has been the focus of the majority of the postcards published in the last 100 years. As a new master plan for the beach is being implemented, more changes are likely to alter the appearance of the area, increasing the importance of the information offered to us by the simple postcard.

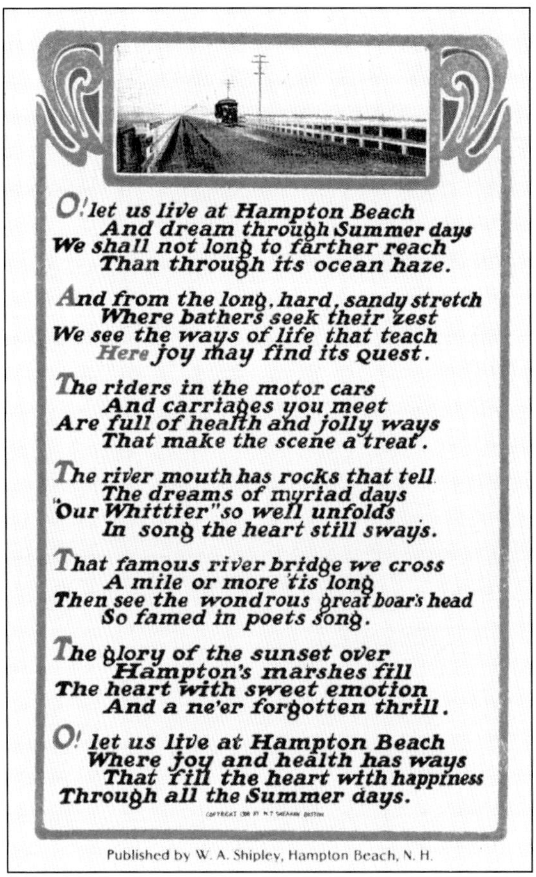

A poem to extol the delights to be found by those visiting Hampton Beach was published by local businessman Wilbur Shipley in 1908. The image shows a trolley crossing "the famous river bridge."

One

The Changing Landscape

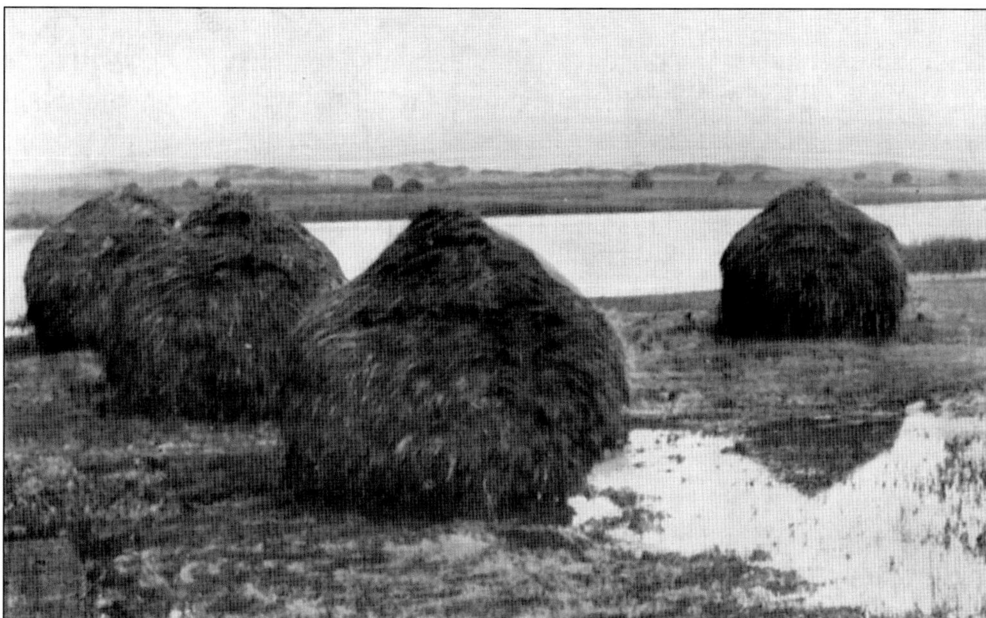

Marsh Scene, Hampton Beach, N. H. 1

In the 1630s, when the first Englishmen explored the area now known as Hampton, they were immediately attracted by the broad expanse of salt marsh. Extending several miles inland from the narrow strip of beach, it was covered by a thick growth of salt hay and made an ideal pasture for cows and oxen. Native Americans, too, had found the region a good place to live; they fished in the river and planted their corn on the upland. Cleared fields marked their summer dwelling places, but most of these clearings were deserted after the epidemics that killed thousands of Native Americans in the early 17th century.

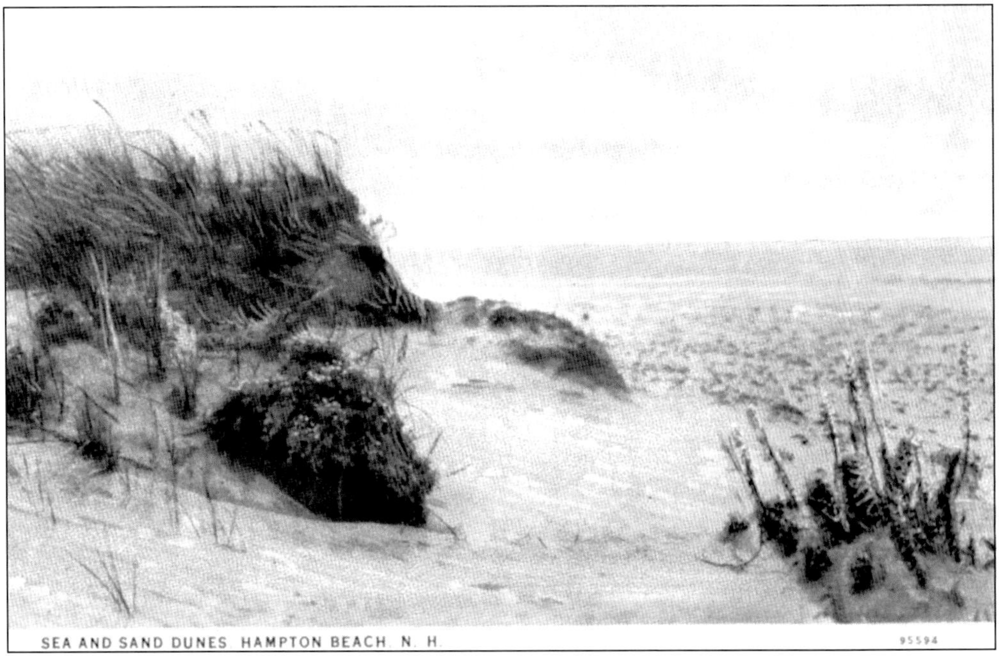

Neither the early Native Americans nor the English took much interest in the seashore of Hampton. The barren rocky coast of the north beach contrasted with the sandy dunes of the south beach, shown here. The beach was separated from the village by the vast salt marsh and was inhabited by only a few fishermen. These dunes have mostly vanished now, leveled by later development.

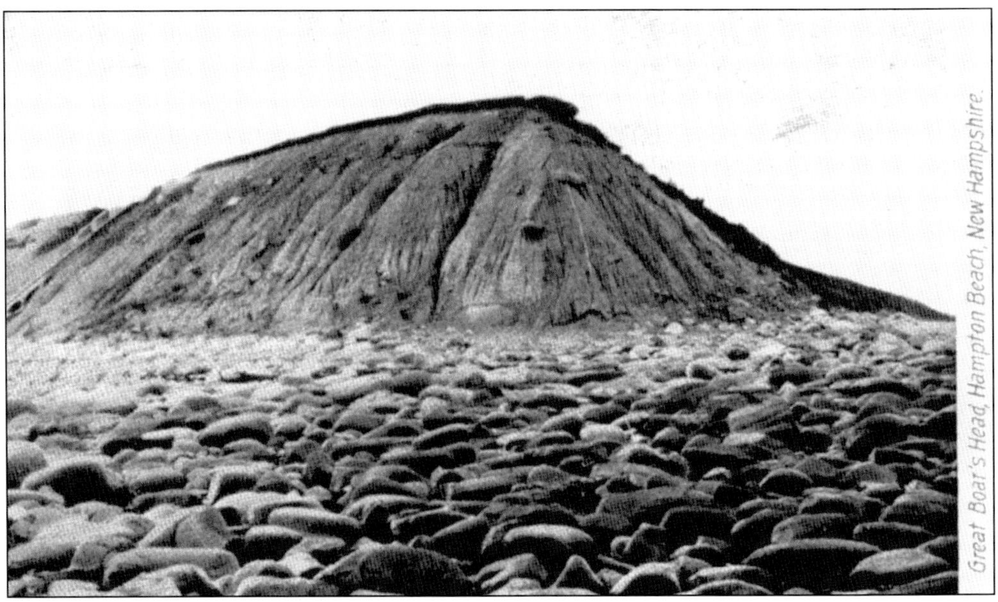

The dividing line between the north and south beaches is the striking promontory called Great Boar's Head. During the first two centuries of settlement, this rocky glacial deposit, or drumlin, was part of the Great Ox Common, a valuable grazing area. Although a few houses were built at the base of the cliff to serve fishermen in the 19th century, it was only in the 20th century that the land was divided into house lots and sold for development.

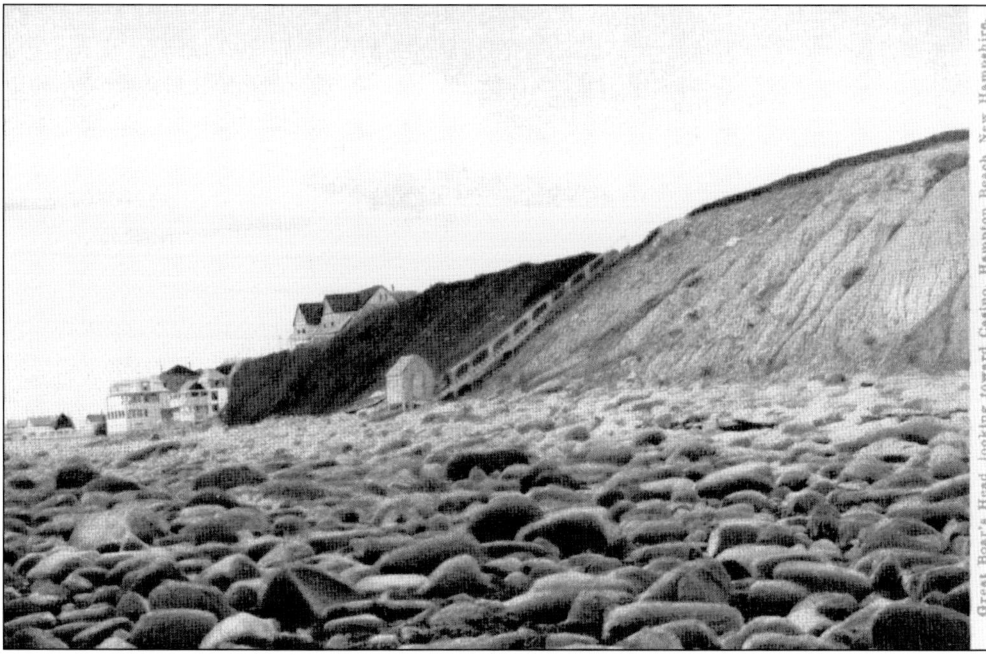

The long flight of 50 wooden steps leading from the top of Great Boar's Head to the fish house and landing at the bottom were public property. Local hunters came in the fall to shoot migrating sea fowl like coots and sea brants, and fishermen used the fish house and boat landing year-round. As tourism increased, so did the use of the stairs, which were eventually removed because of safety concerns.

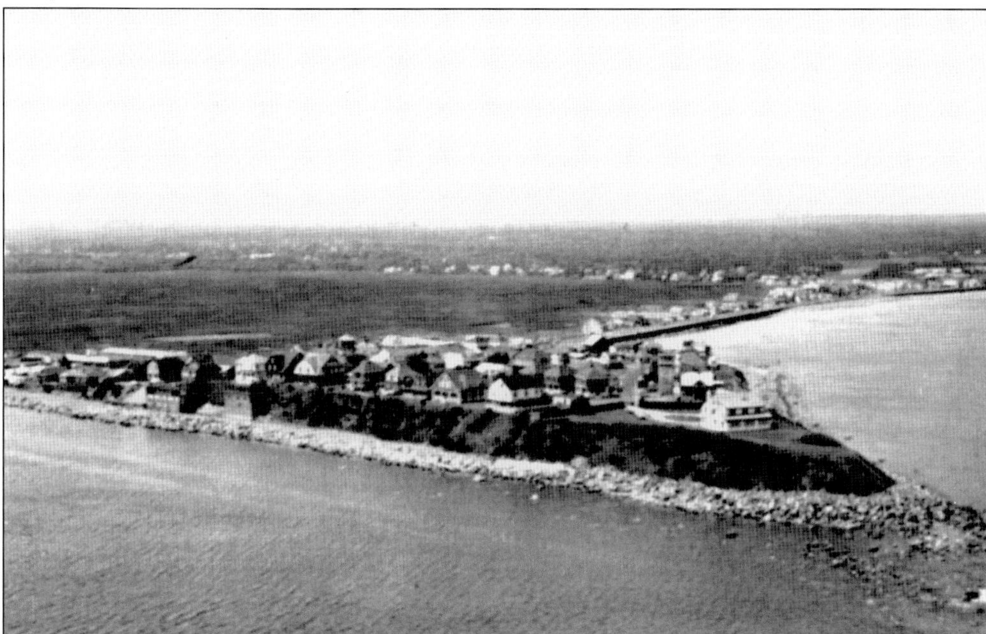

This more modern view clearly delineates the distinctive shape of Boar's Head. In the distance stretches the vast marshy plain known as the Great Ox Common. In the 17th and 18th centuries, this land was held in common by farmers who used it exclusively as pasture for their oxen.

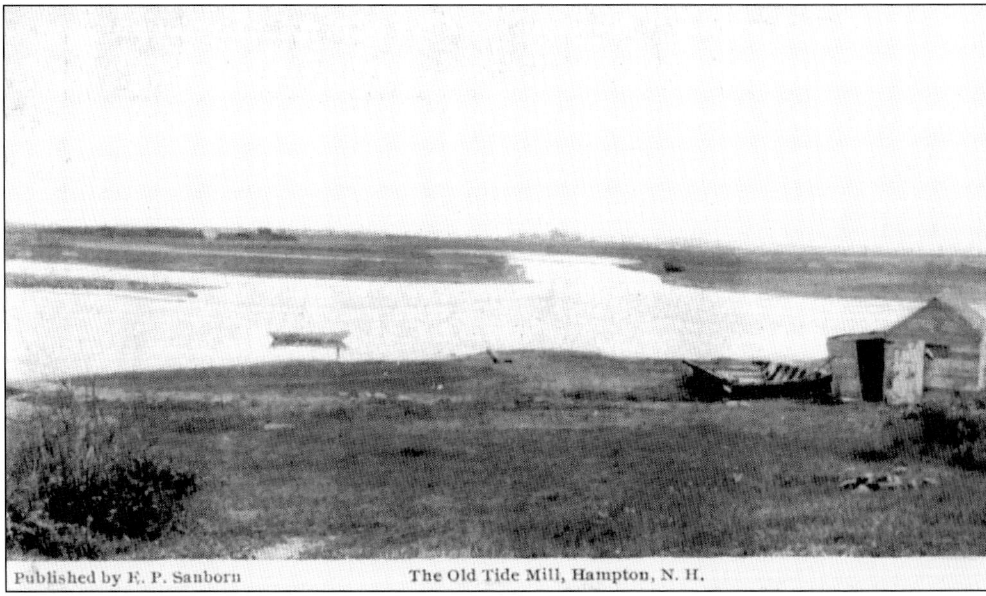

The tidal Hampton River meanders through the salt marsh to the sea. The twice-daily rise and fall of the tides prompted local citizens to build a gristmill operated solely by the tides. However, the town vote specified that the mill could not be operated when the marsh hay was being cut. The mill was abandoned in the late 19th century and was later demolished. Although this card shows the site of the mill on the marsh, the building in the image is part of the old wharf that stood just south of the tide mill.

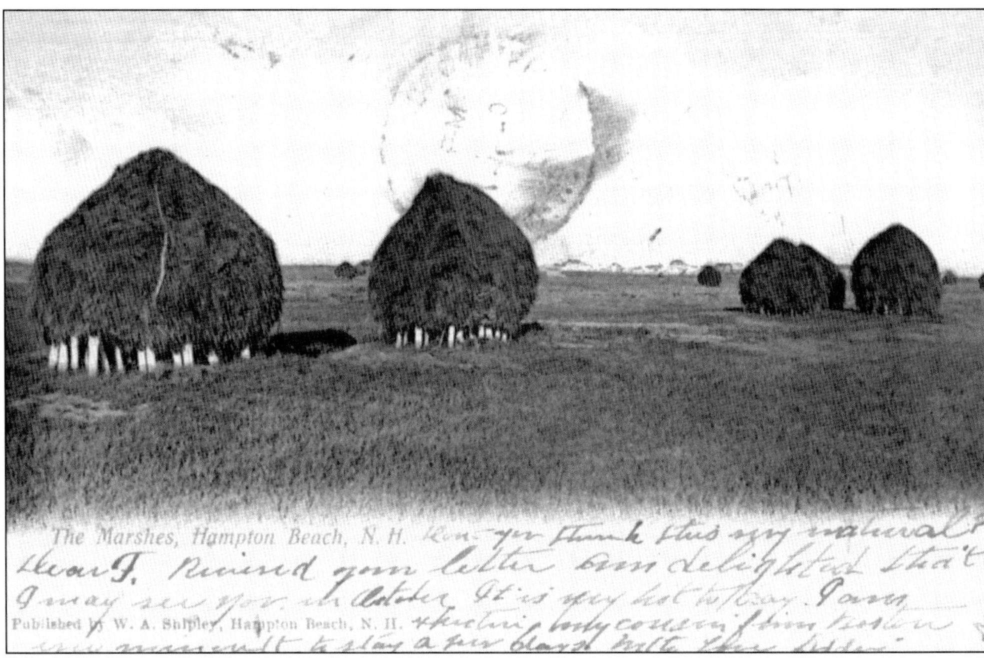

This 1906 postcard shows the harvested hay piled high on stakes, or "staddles," right on the marsh. These haystacks were a common sight in New England marshes and were a favorite subject of painters and photographers. Haying the marshes ceased in the 1920s, but some staddles can still be seen on the marshes today.

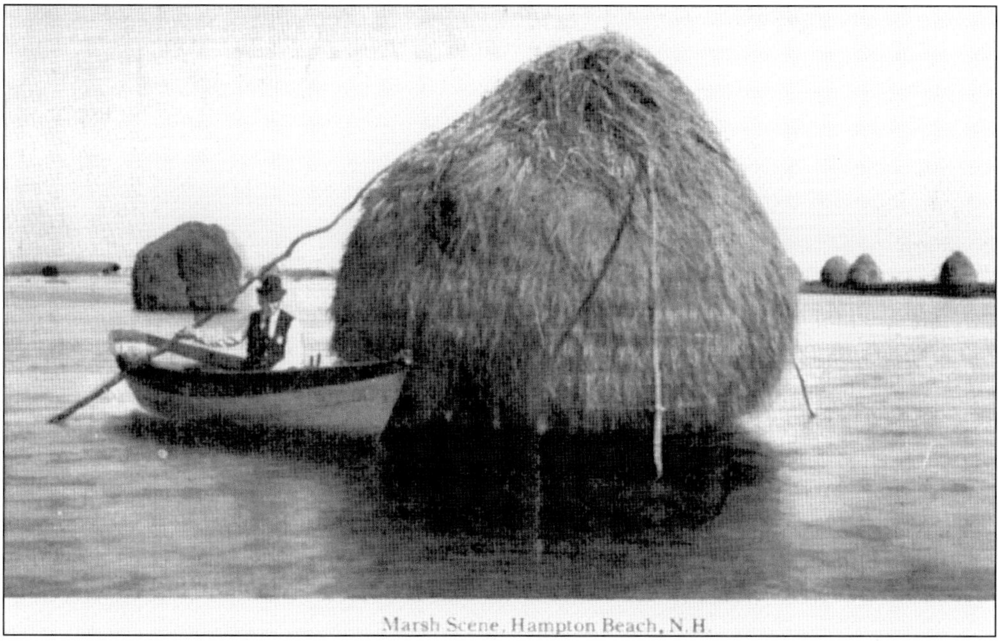

Hay was piled on staddles tall enough to keep the hay dry at high tide. The marsh hay was cut by hand with a scythe or by a horse-drawn mower. Piling the hay onto the staddles was backbreaking work performed by men armed with long hay poles and hay forks. In this image, a farmer has rowed out to check his haystacks at flood tide. Note that he has donned his best top hat especially for the photograph.

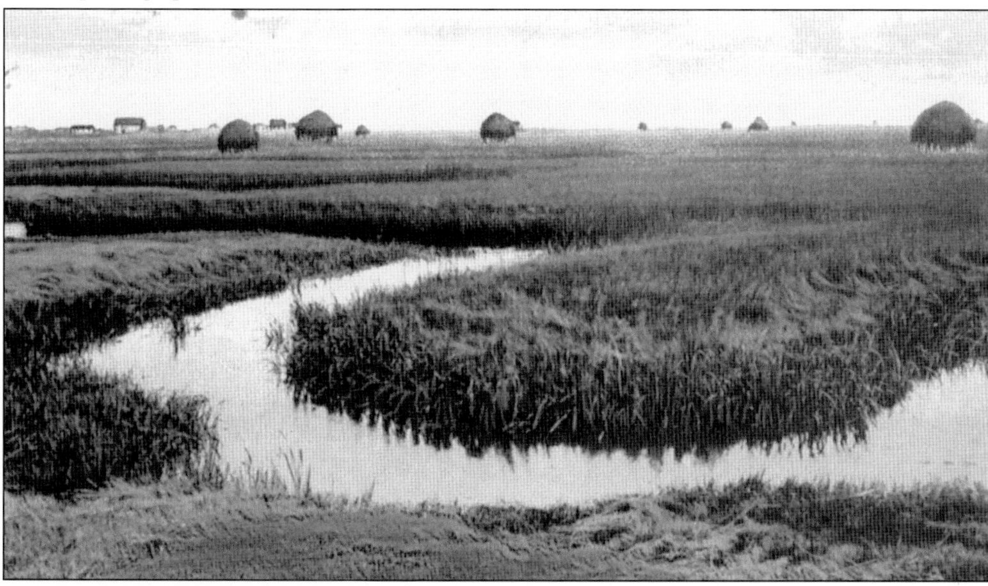

This view of the marshes, from the first decade of the 20th century, shows the beach in the background and the river winding between the haystacks in the foreground. Until recent years, almost all the marshes were in private hands, a legacy of the days when ownership of marshland was a valuable asset for a farmer. Proposals to develop part of the marshes in the 1960s resulted in a campaign for their conservation led by activist Ruth Stimson. As a result, so many lots were placed in a protected status that any plans to build on the marsh effectively ended.

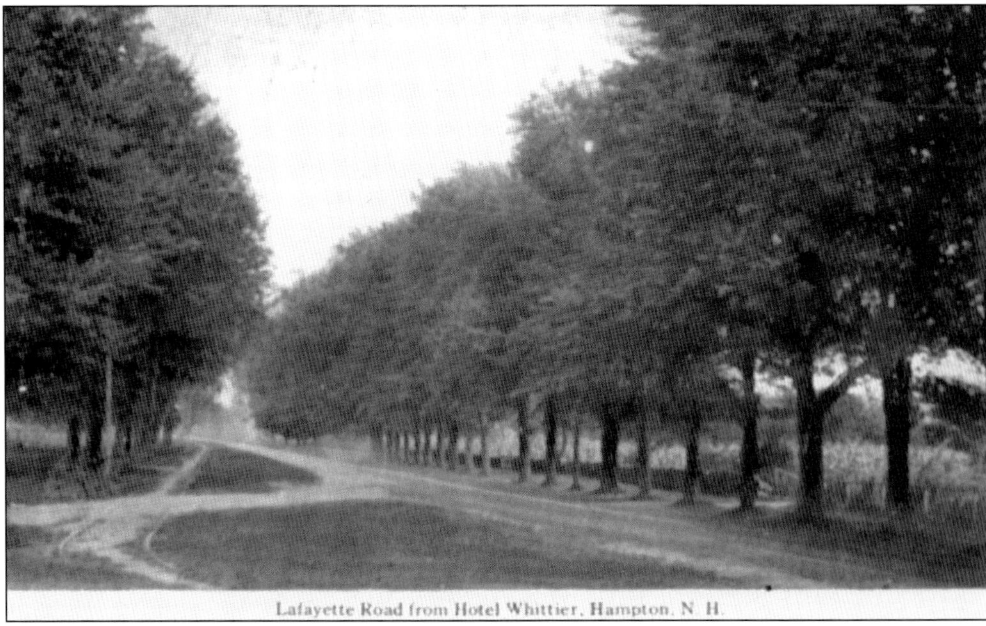

This *c.* 1900 view of Lafayette Road from just south of Winnacunnet Road belies the busy commercial street that we see today. The agricultural aspect of Hampton's townscape is well represented by the corn field behind the stone wall across the street. The magnificent row of maple trees disappeared in the 1950s. Note the tracks for the street railway in the foreground.

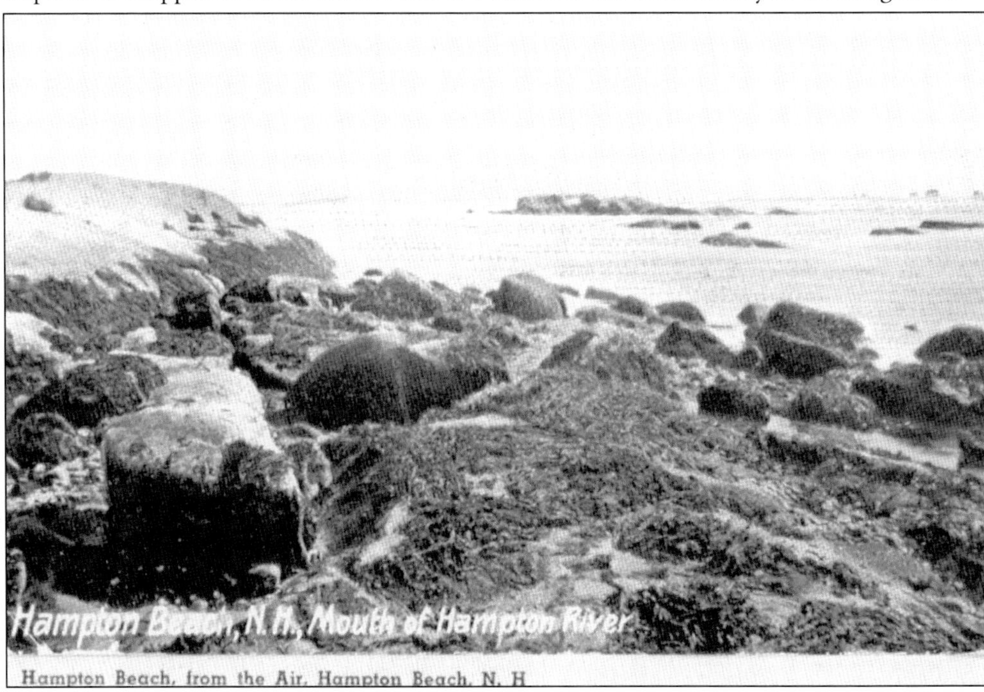

In the past 100 years, the southern end of Hampton Beach has changed more than any other area of the town. The sands at the mouth of the Hampton River have shifted several times, altering the course of the river substantially. The rocky shore seen here has disappeared under an area that was filled in during the 1930s to form a new state beach.

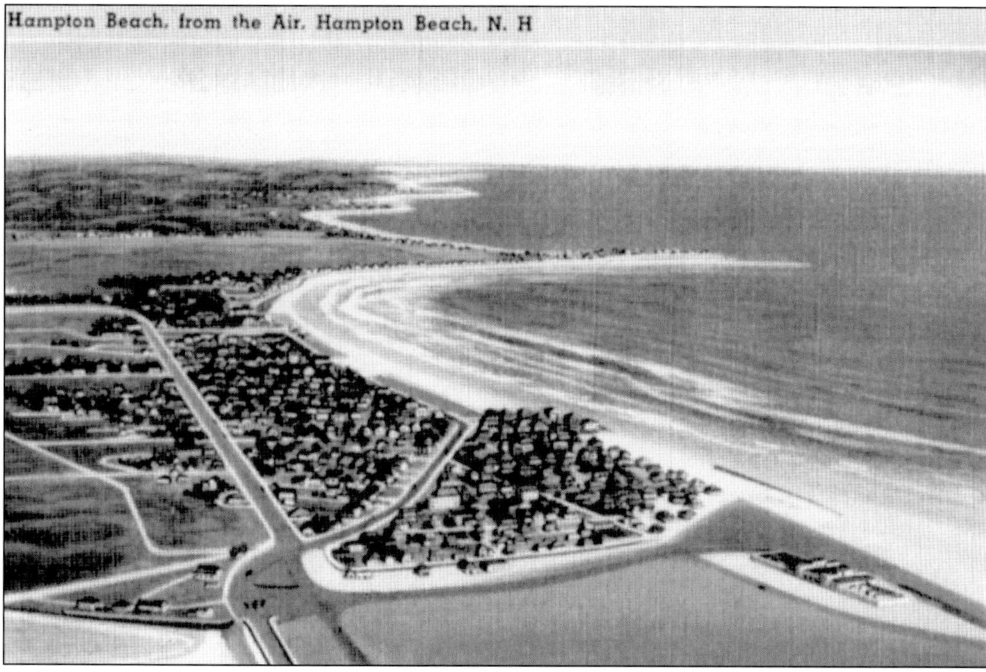

In this *c.* 1945 postcard, all the area in the foreground is filled land. The line of cottages represents the old natural limit of the south beach. In 1934, some 50 acres of new land were formed by fill dredged from the harbor, and the Hampton Beach State Park was established on this new beach.

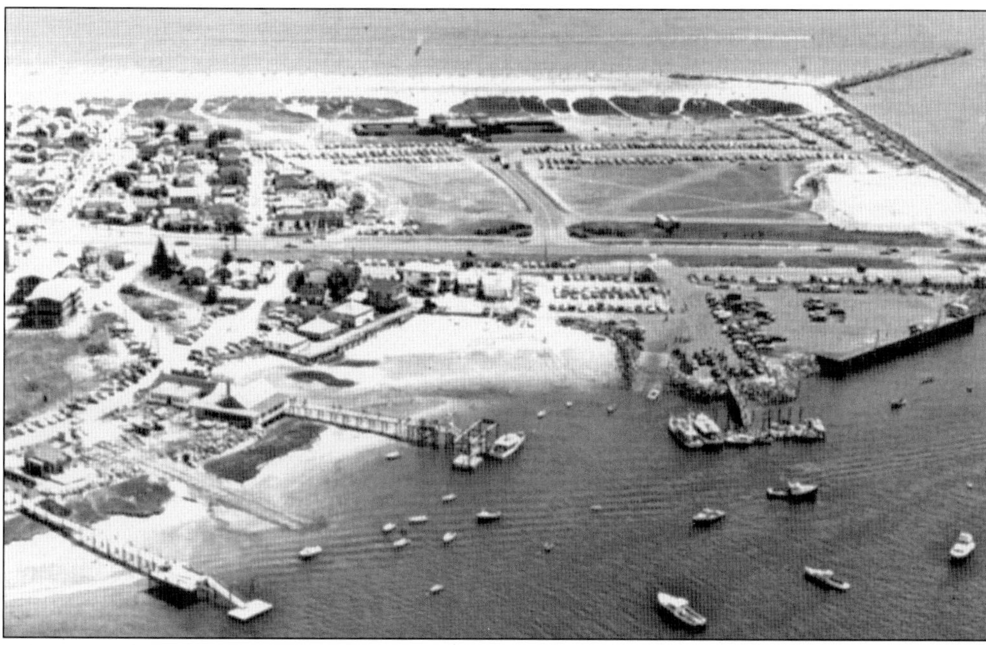

A later view of the same area clearly shows the jetty built in 1935 (at the top of the image) and Hampton Harbor (at the bottom). The small cottages and fishing piers of this card have, in many cases, given way to large condominium complexes. The shallows near the piers demonstrate the continually shifting sandy bottom of the river.

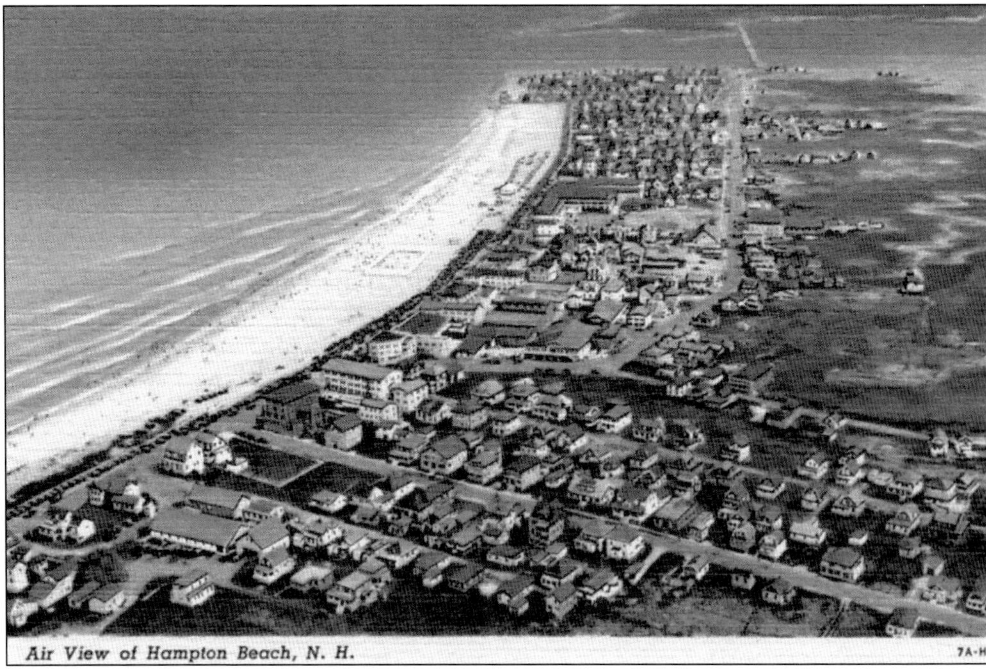

This aerial view of Hampton Beach was taken before the land was filled in for the state park in 1935. The broad sweep of the sandy beach is clearly seen, as well as the hotels and hundreds of cottages that had been built since the end of the 19th century. The white square in the sand near the top was a children's playground, which was built on the sand in 1927.

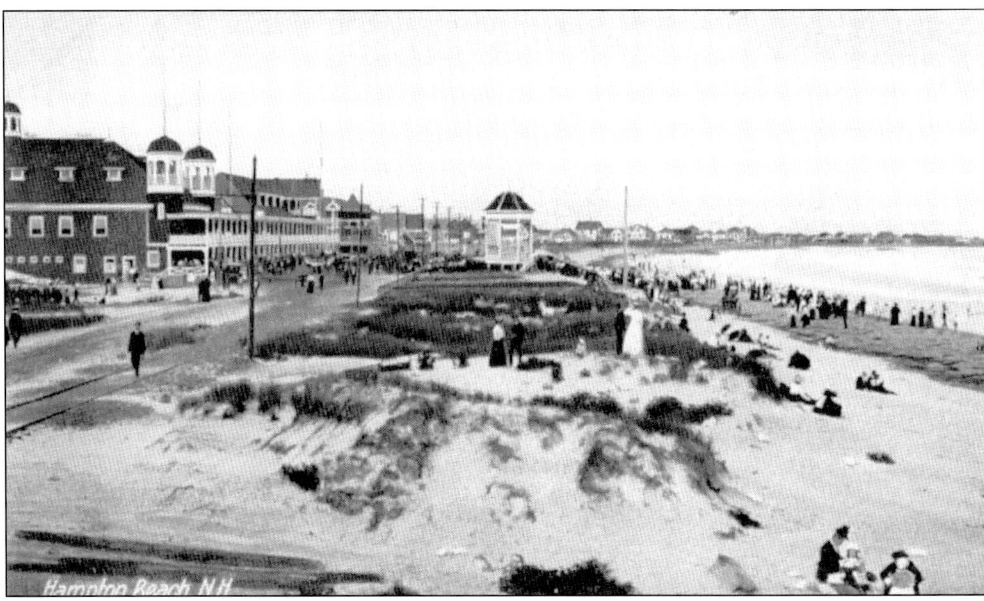

This postcard of the beach south of the Casino is dated *c.* 1901. Here, the sand dunes that were characteristic of the whole beach are still in place below the bandstand. The protection from storm damage that the dunes afforded the buildings disappeared when the dunes were leveled for development. Hampton Beach is, in effect, a large sandy island, and today steel-reinforced concrete sea walls are needed for shelter from the storms of winter.

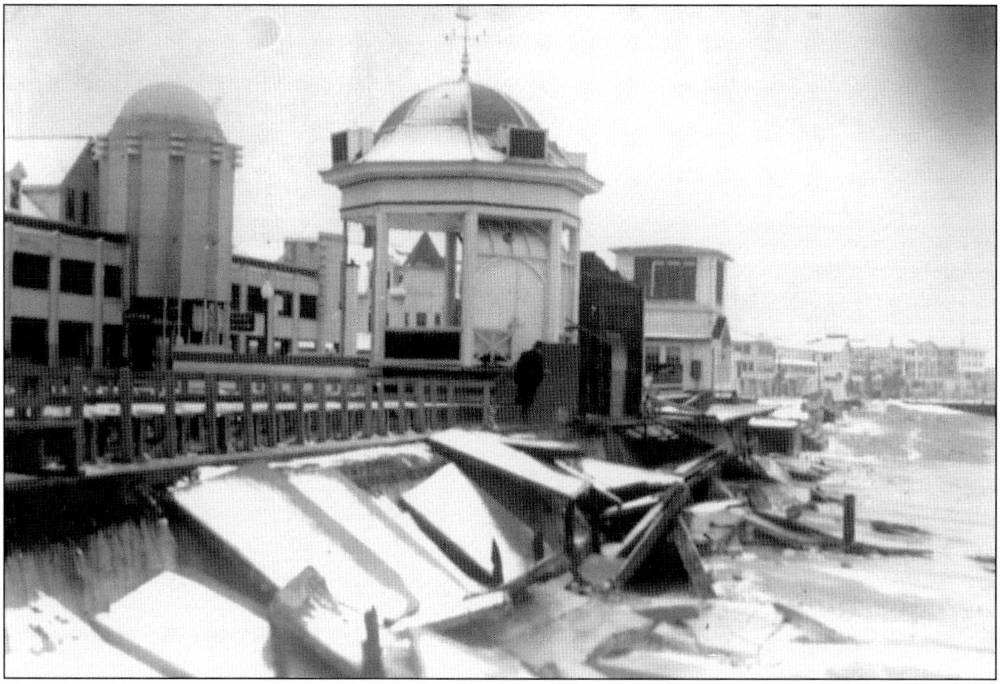

Beach erosion and damage continue despite the sea walls. This postcard, published after a big storm in 1939, clearly illustrates the destructive power of the surf during a northeaster.

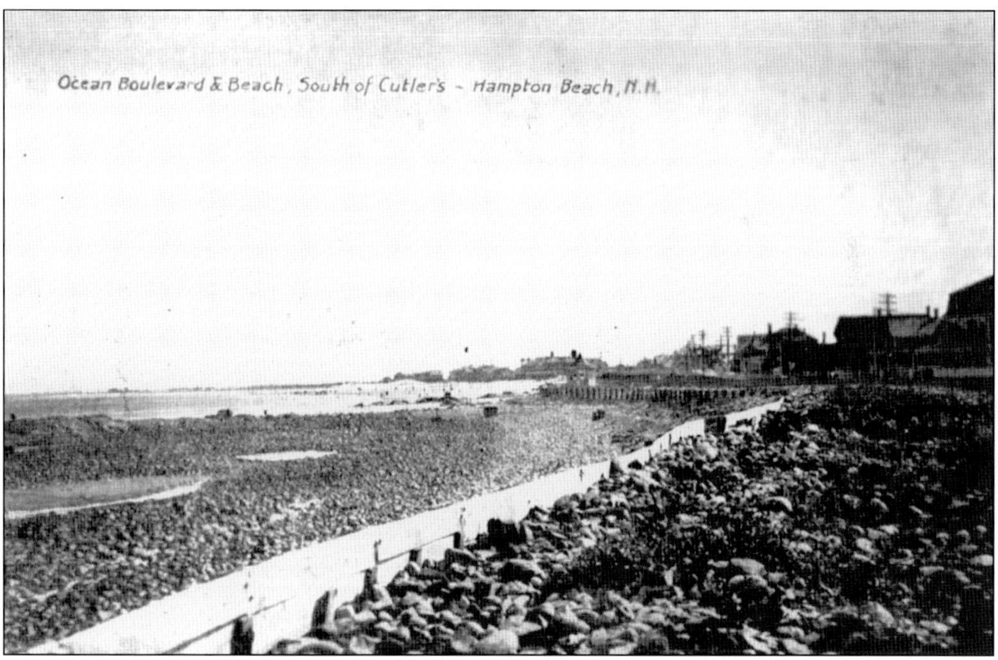

The rocky shore near Great Boar's Head especially needed a sea wall. This wooden breakwater was built in the 1890s, but it was eventually destroyed by the relentless pounding of the surf during the storms that hit the beach every year.

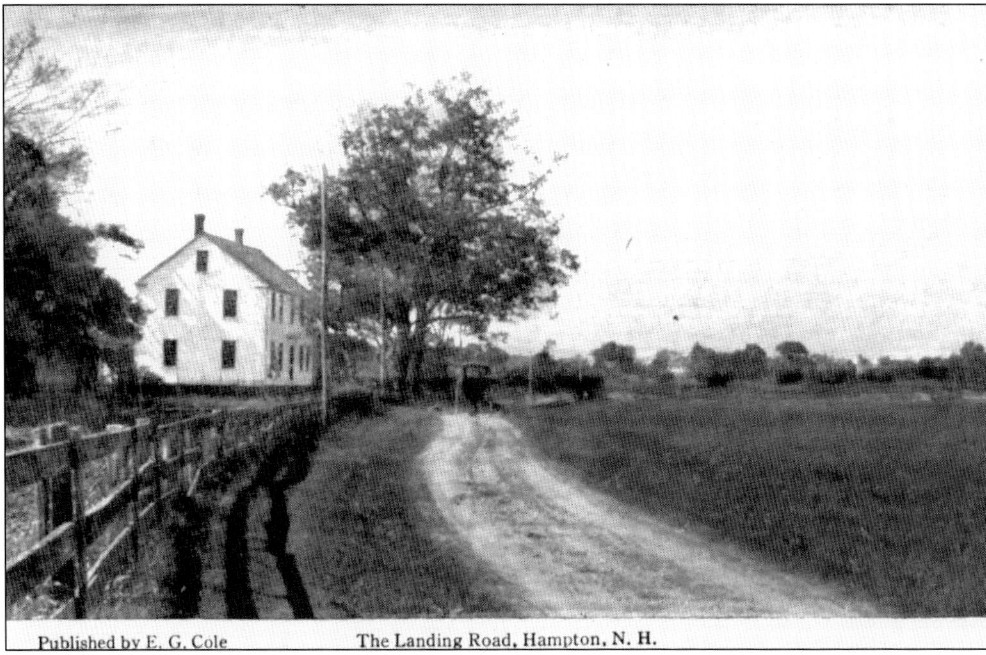

This card from the late 19th century shows the earliest road in Hampton, which led from the first settlers' landing place on the river to the green in the center of town. In 1961, this road was cut into two separate sections by the new state highway that ran across the marsh to the beach. The playing fields of Winnacunnet High School cover one segment of the old road.

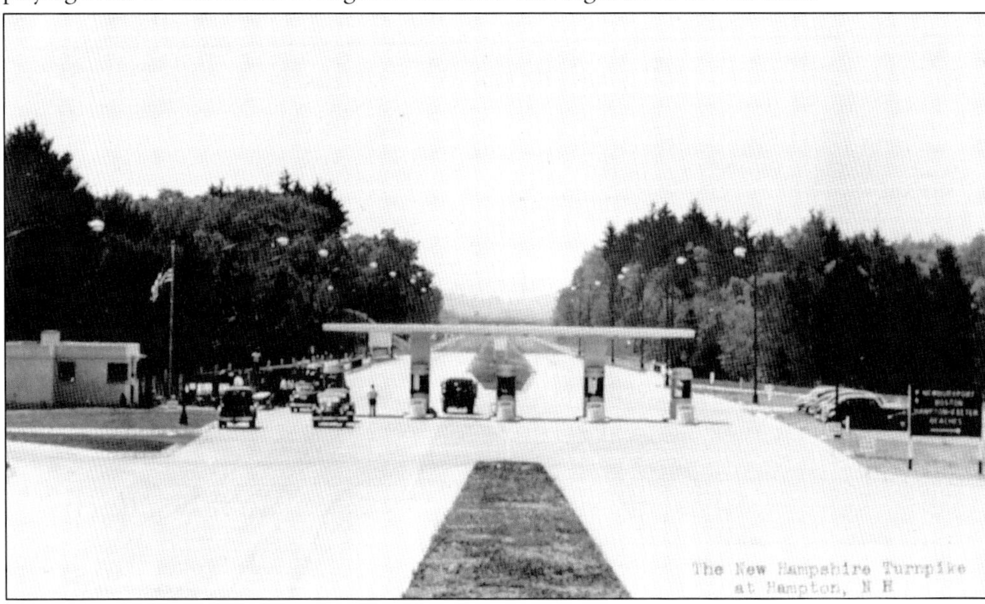

Despite the many changes that had taken place in the town since its founding in 1638, it was the construction of the New Hampshire Turnpike (later part of Route 95) that contributed most to the fundamental shift in Hampton's townscape after World War II. The advent of a swift route to Boston brought new residents to the town, as well as to the rest of the Seacoast. What had been a small, rather isolated farming village with a seasonal beach resort became a suburban bedroom community with an increasingly year-round beach population.

Two

PLAICE COVE TO GREAT BOAR'S HEAD

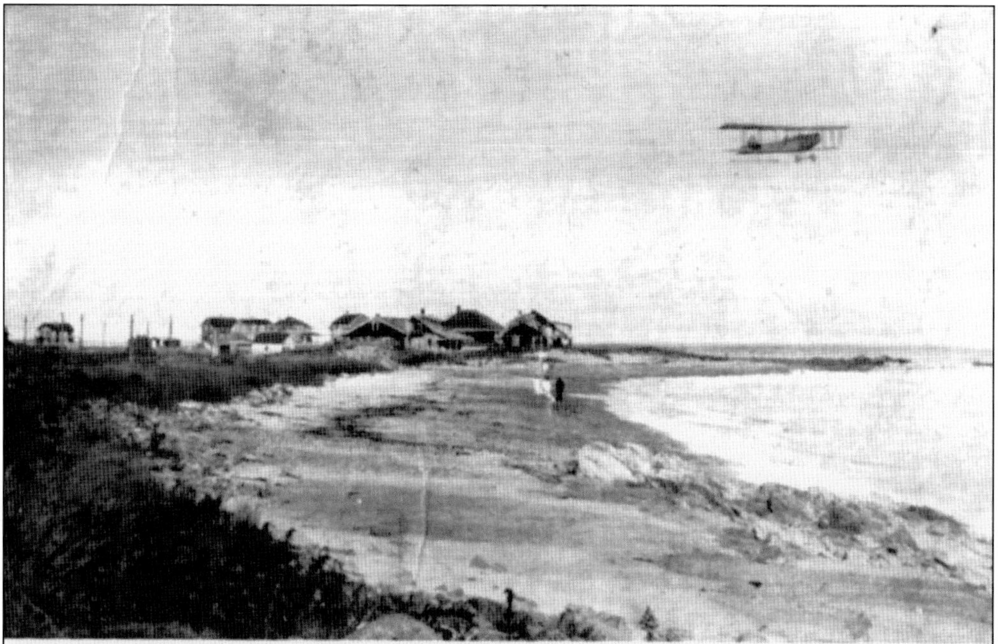

Published by E. G. Cole   Place Cove, North Beach, Hampton, N. H.

Plaice Cove, located at the northern end of Hampton's coastline, was the first area of the beach to host any activity. The early fishermen put their boats out to sea from here and named the cove after the flat fish that they caught in great quantities. Several sightseeing planes flew out of the airfield on Winnacunnet Road in the 1920s and 1930s. Longtime resident Ansell Palmer remembers that the pilots would take some of the local children up for the first run of the day before landing on the beach to pick up paying customers. Note the misspelled name on the card.

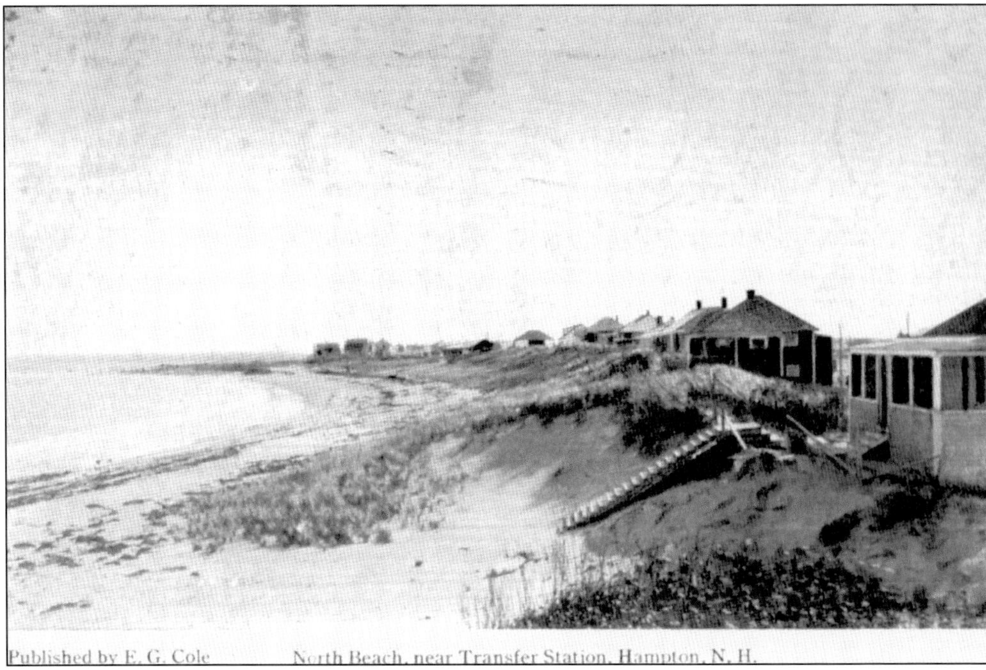

This photograph of the cottages at Plaice Cove, taken from the north, shows the steps built by homeowners to allow access over the dunes to the beach. These small cottages were intended for summer use only. Their foundations were only piers driven into the sandy ground.

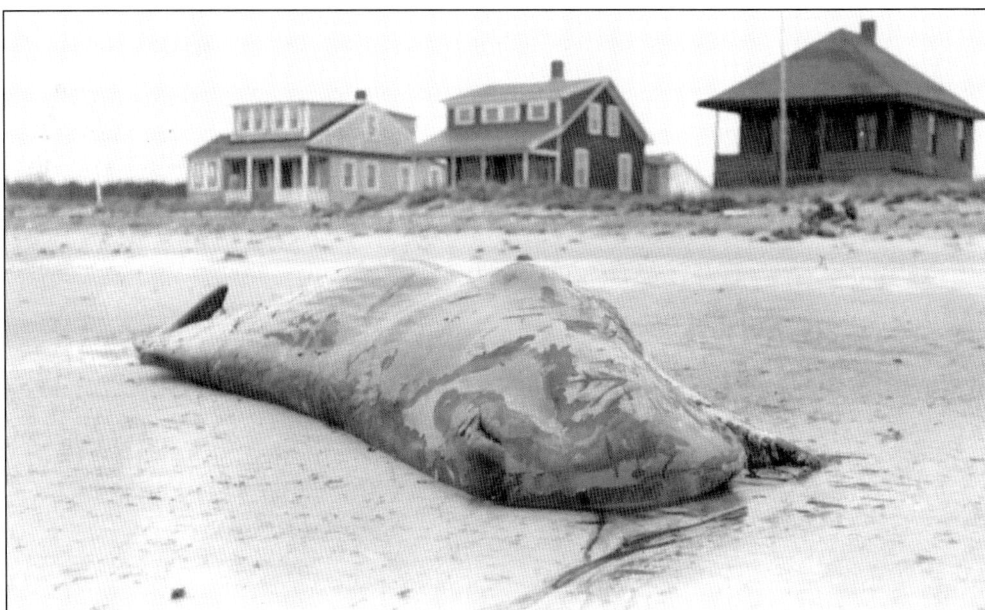

Photographers were quick to seize on interesting local events, such as fires or marine disasters, and produce a limited quantity of special postcards. Such was the case with this card of a 34-foot sperm whale that washed ashore at Plaice Cove in February 1942.

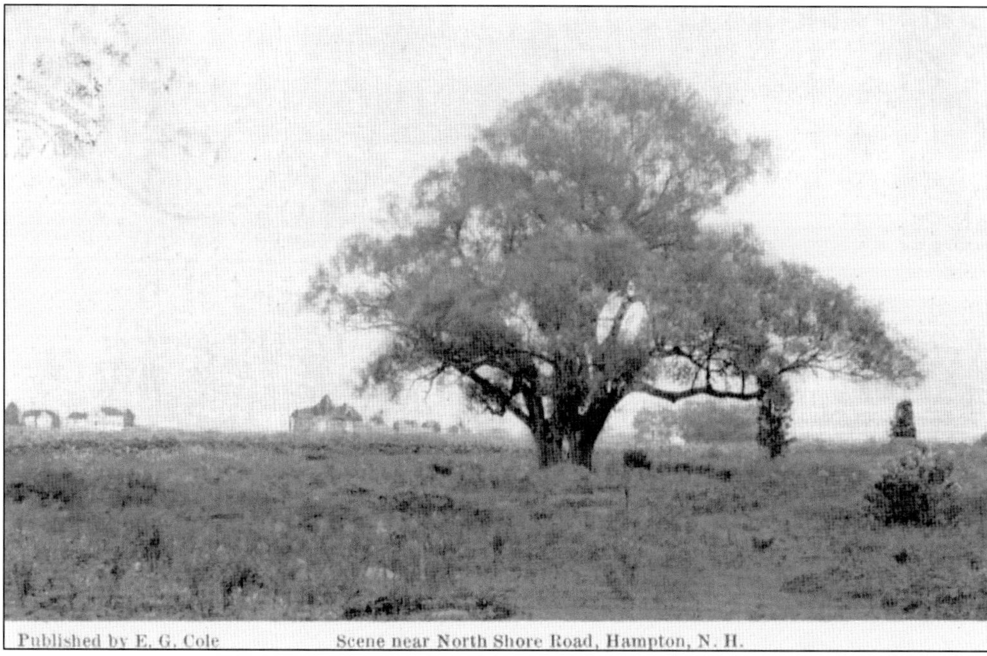

Today, Route 1A runs along the coastline, and condominiums have replaced this pastoral field. In the distance may be seen the fish houses and the lifesaving station that stood south of Plaice Cove.

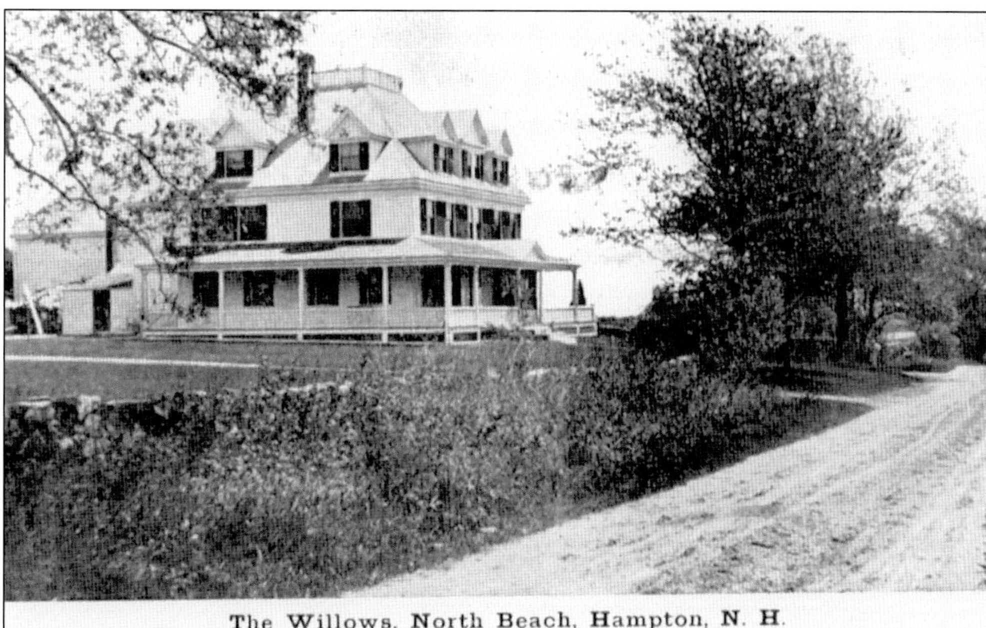

Some of the earliest lodging places were at the north end of the beach. First intended to provide fishermen and fish traders with food and drink, the inns quickly came to accommodate a new type of customer: the tourist. The Willows, which was located on what is now Cusack Road, was one of the early boardinghouses designed especially for the new visitors.

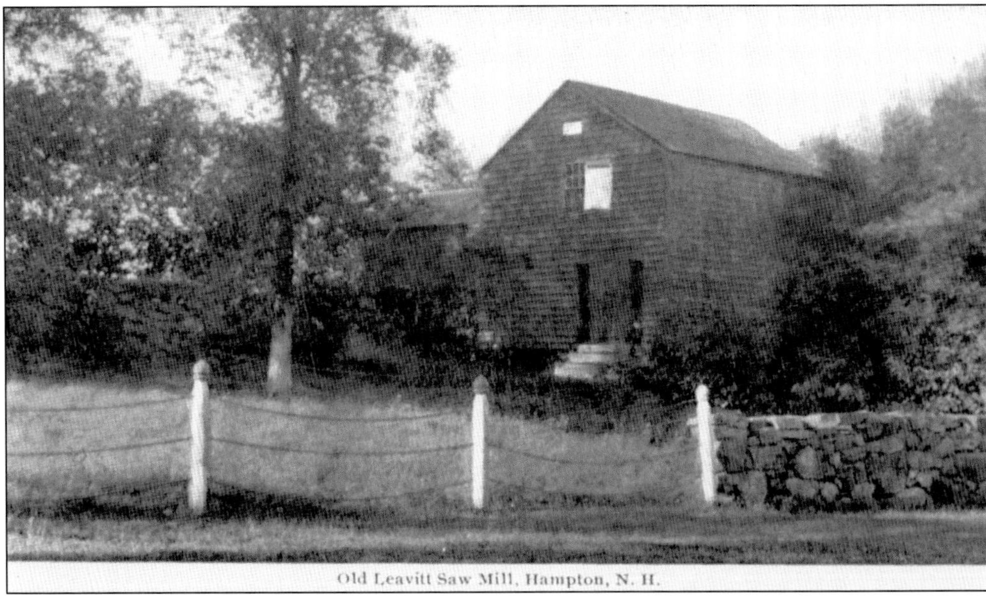

Although this card is titled "Old Leavitt Saw Mill," the mill was in fact a gristmill for grain. A mill has stood on this site on lower High Street since 1686, when Deacon John Tuck was granted the privilege of constructing a gristmill on the Nilus Brook. This building, although heavily restored, dates from 1815, when Moses Leavitt purchased the mill and replaced the old structure. A silent witness to the agricultural past of the neighborhood, it now belongs to the town of Hampton.

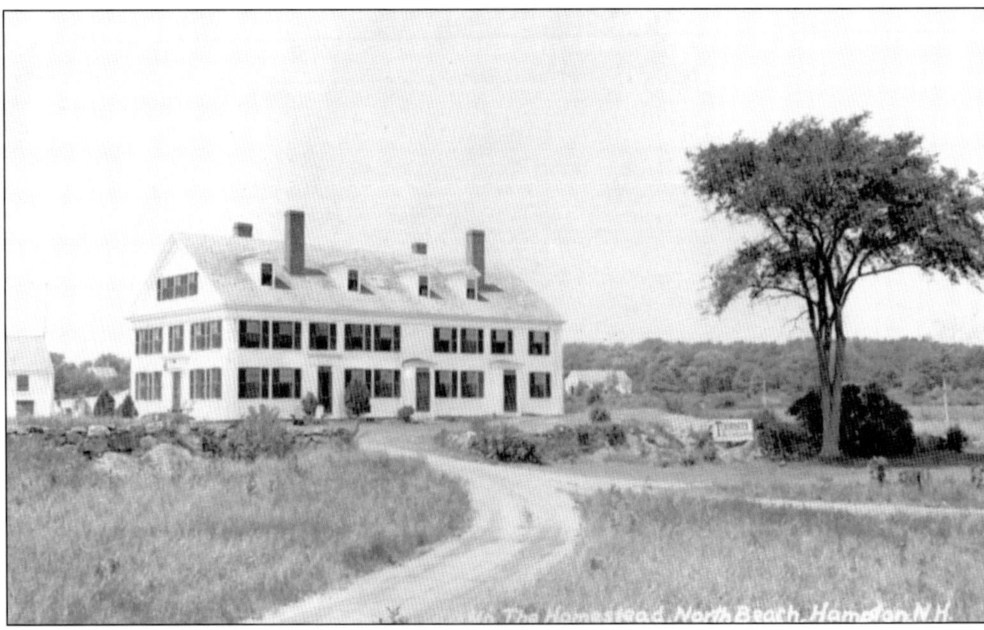

This "homestead," although rebuilt and enlarged, is the oldest building still standing at Hampton Beach. It was built at the end of Nook Lane (now High Street) around 1800 by John Elkins. Bought by the Leavitt family, it became an inn later in the 19th century, first for fishermen and later for tourists. Known as Leavitt's Homestead, it served thousands of tourists over 100 years. Today it is the Windjammer Motel, at the corner of High Street and Ocean Boulevard.

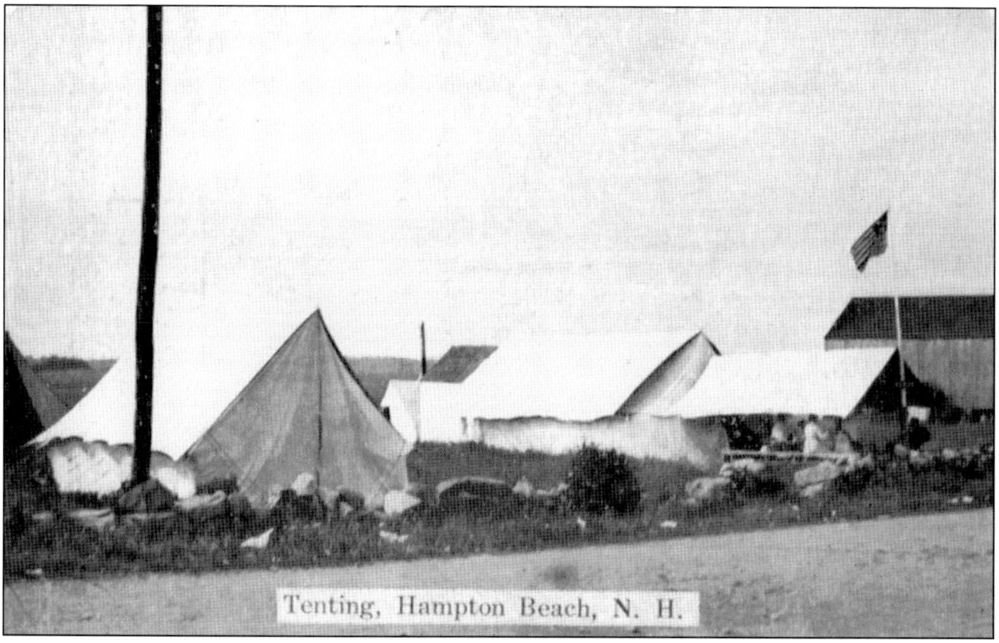

Camping at the beach was a popular pastime, not only for hunters or fishermen in pursuit of the sea fowl or flounder but also for vacationers wishing to enjoy the seashore. In 1867, the poet John Greenleaf Whittier published a collection of poems entitled *The Tent on the Beach*, which included legends of Hampton, as well as descriptions of the magnificent beach scenery.

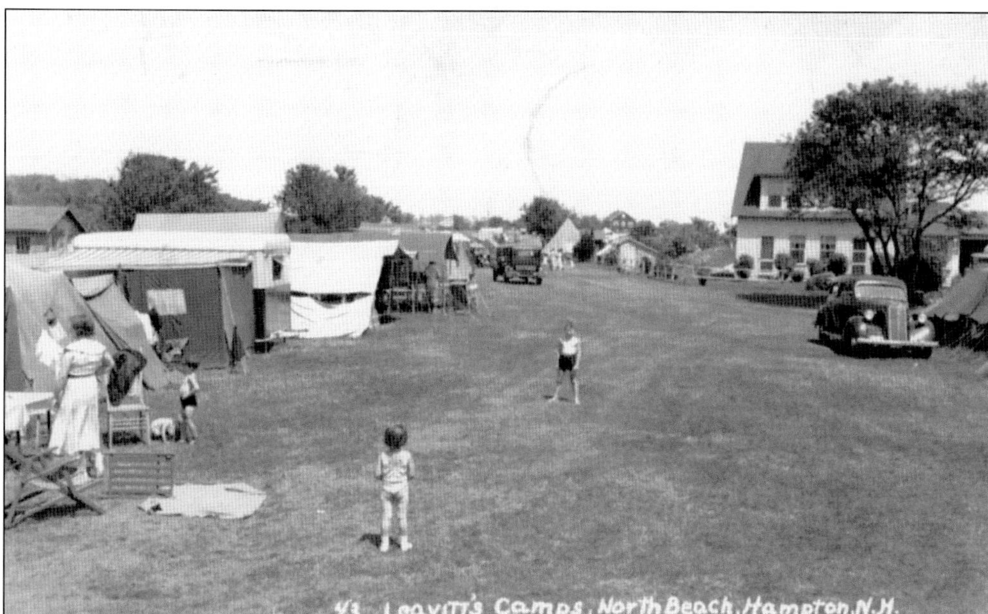

Near Leavitt's Homestead were Leavitt's Camps, which catered to tourists who preferred their own tents to more expensive hotel rooms. This 1930s view of the campground shows the informal arrangement of tents and camping trailers. The campground was north of Leavitt's Homestead, at the end of Leavitt Avenue off Ocean Boulevard.

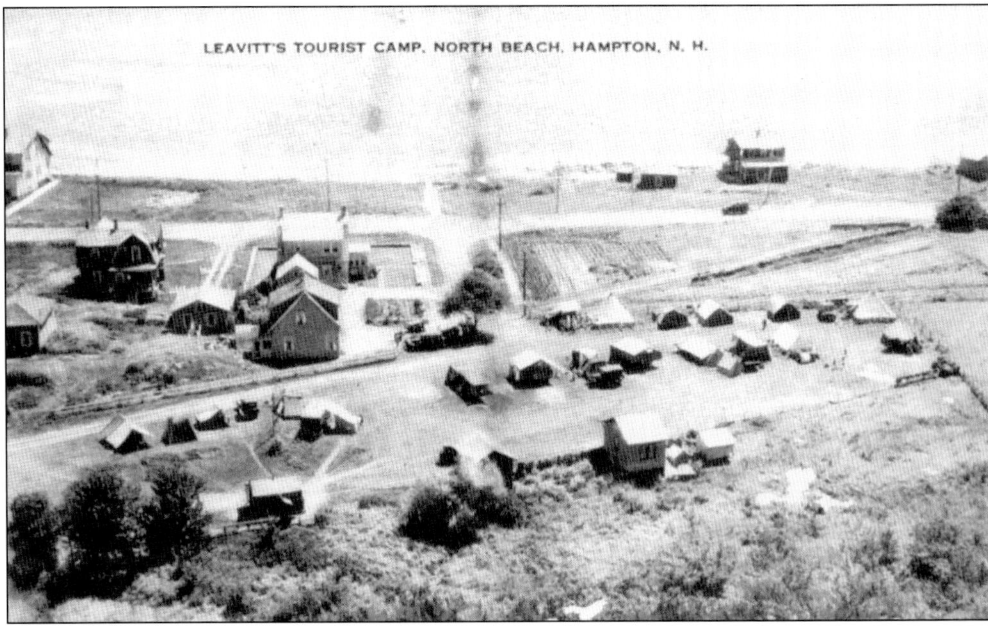

This aerial photograph of Leavitt's Camps shows tents and trailers scattered around what was essentially a rural area. Now this same ground is covered by private cottages, some of which are occupied year-round.

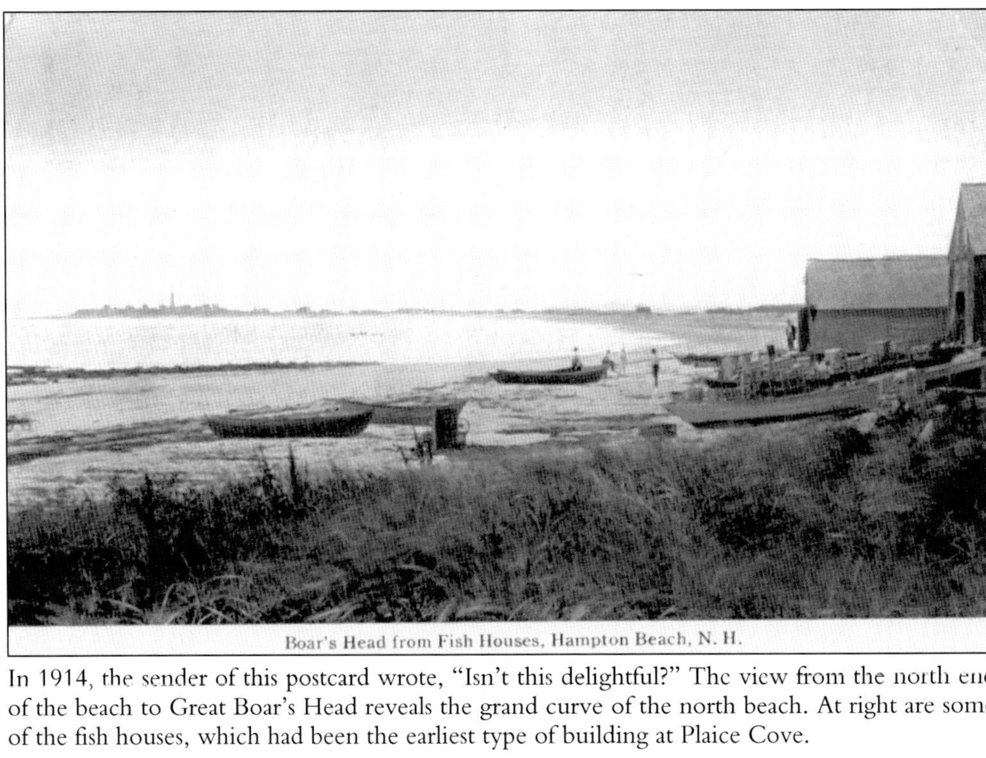

In 1914, the sender of this postcard wrote, "Isn't this delightful?" The view from the north end of the beach to Great Boar's Head reveals the grand curve of the north beach. At right are some of the fish houses, which had been the earliest type of building at Plaice Cove.

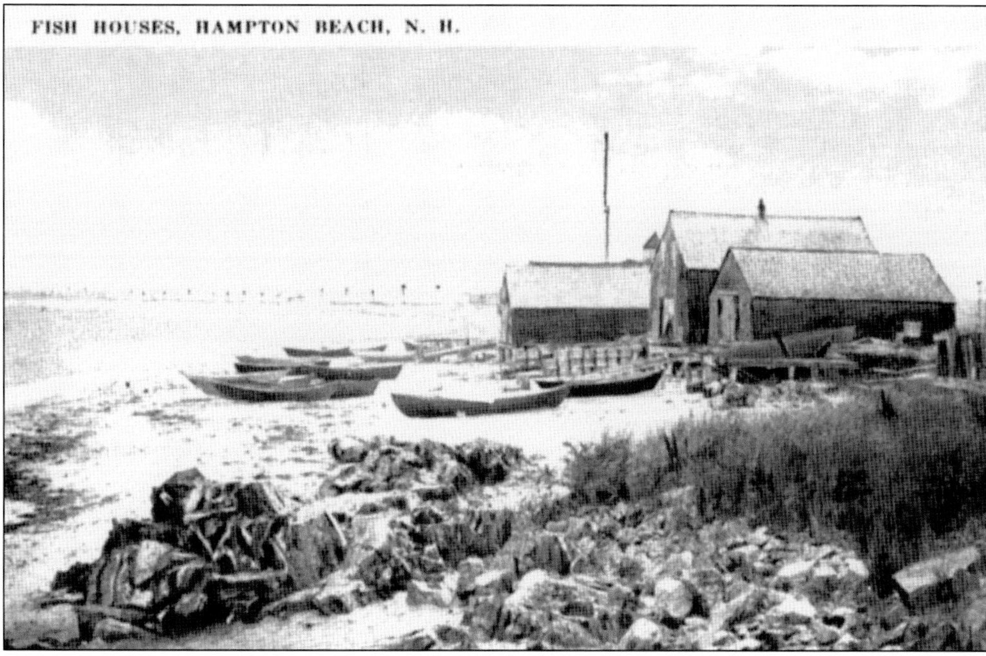

From the earliest settlement, fishermen used the beach and cove as a landing place for their dories. Fishing by a hand line in an open dory was a hard life, but the rich catch was worth the danger. The fishermen built small structures, called "fish houses," on the beach to store their gear and prepare their fish for market. The dories were pulled up on the shore in front of the houses. Roland Sawyer, the early-20th-century Hampton historian, remembered with relish "the red cod unloaded from Hampton whaleboats, drawn up before the fish houses."

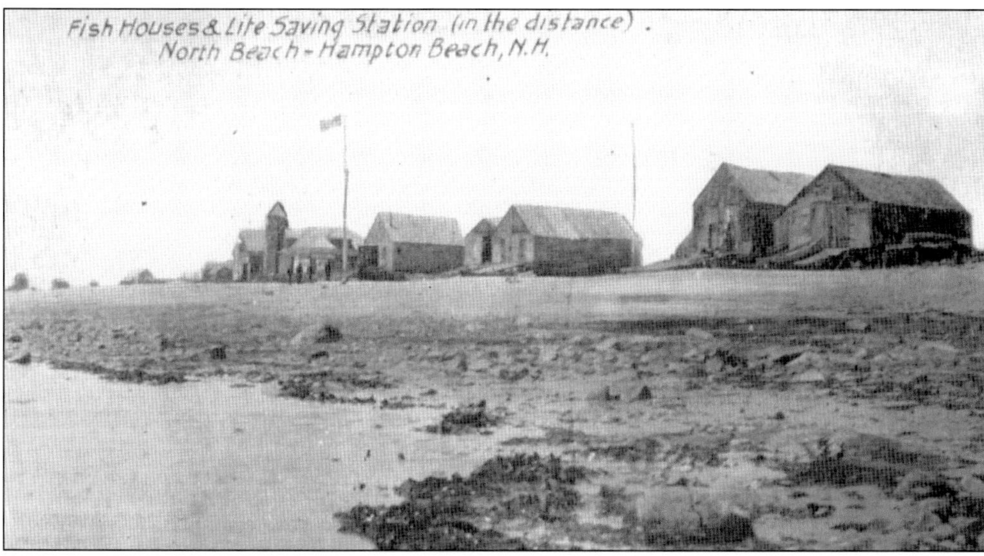

The 1806 map of Hampton shows 16 fish houses. In 1950, 13 remained, although some of the buildings were replacements. Ten years later, following an acrimonious court battle over ownership of the land beneath the buildings, all but two of the houses were removed. One fish house has been given to the town, but the other is still in private hands. The site opposite the end of High Street is now designated as Ruth Stimson Park in honor of Hampton's leading conservationist.

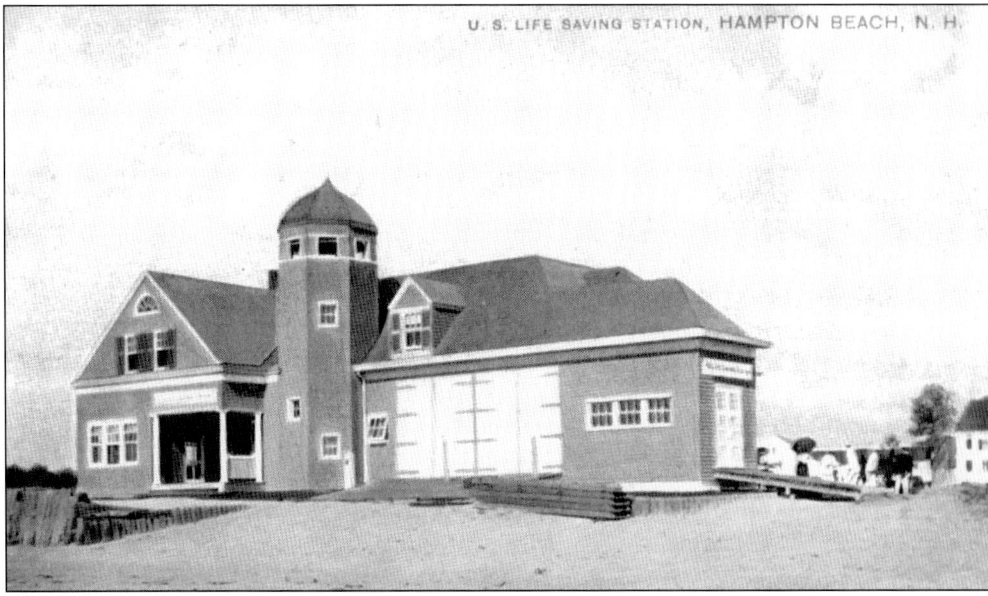

The lifesaving station opened in 1899 after a number of spectacular shipwrecks had occurred on the Hampton shore a few years earlier. The U.S. Life-Saving Service, later a part of the Coast Guard, operated out of this building until 1966. This card was produced not long after the building was first erected; the protective breakwater of logs is still under construction.

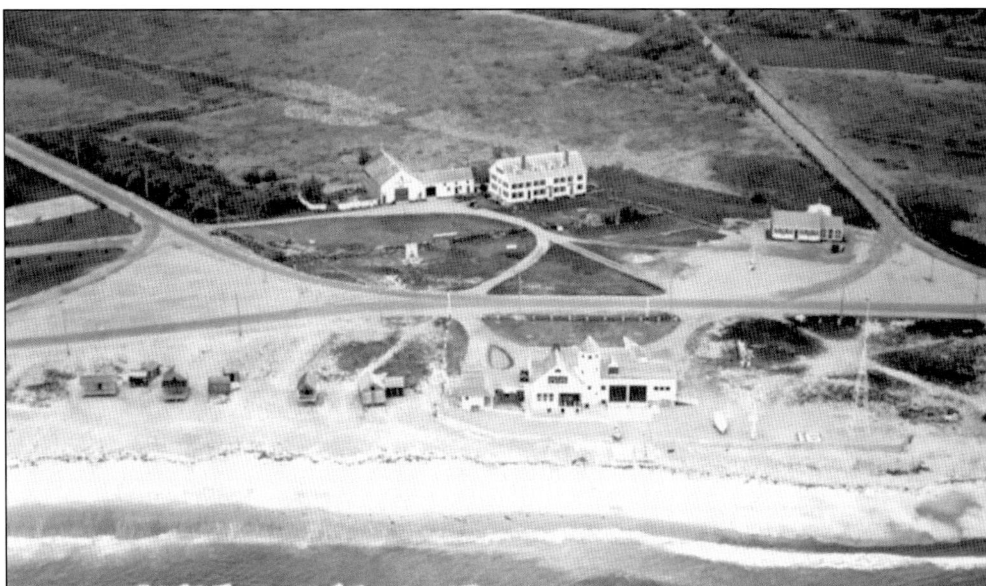

This 1940s aerial view shows the Coast Guard station at the center, opposite the end of High Street, and Leavitt's Homestead at the top. The large barn at Leavitt's, once used as a theater, no longer stands, and the old station was burned down in a practice firefighting drill in 1973. Bicentennial Park now occupies the site.

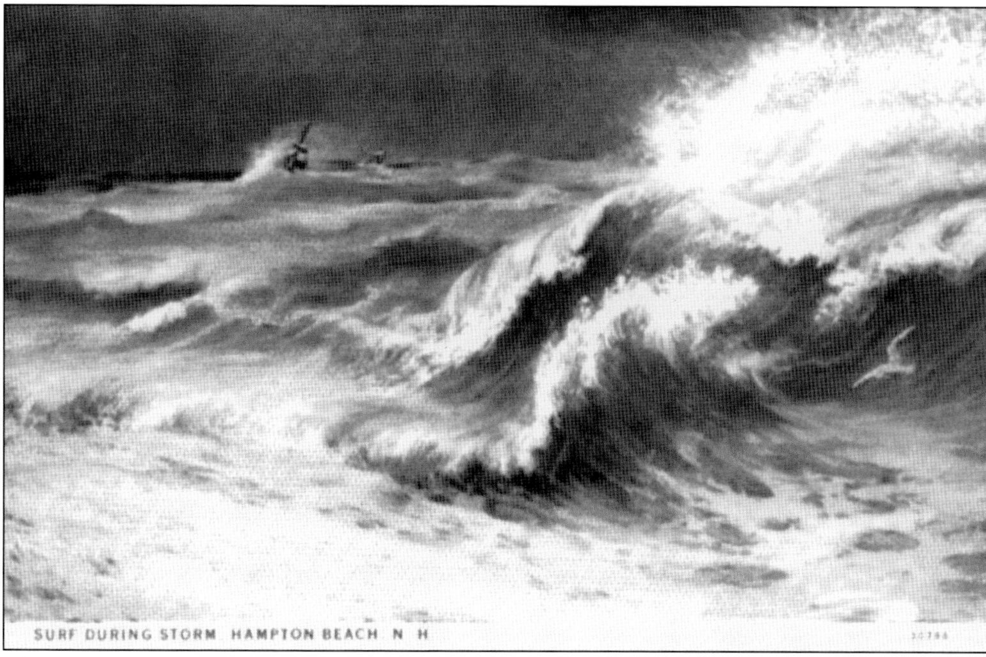

This card of surf breaking on Hampton Beach during a storm vividly illustrates the dangers that awaited the fishermen and sailors who navigated the New Hampshire coastline. Note the ship rolling in the waves in the background. It was the frequent occurrence of storms like this one that encouraged the stationing of a lifesaving crew in Hampton.

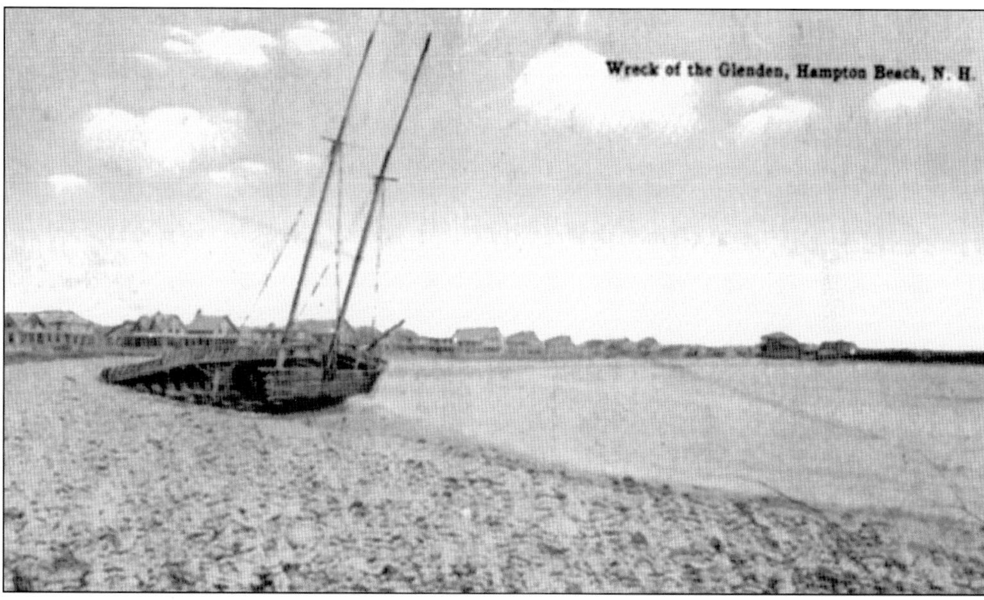

The schooner *Glendon* foundered on the shore just south of Great Boar's Head in February 1896. Crews from Rye responded to the distress call from Hampton. Aided by local volunteers, they managed to get a line out to the wreck and run a breeches buoy to bring the crew ashore. The wrecked hull of the *Glendon* was visible for a number of years on the beach and quickly became a subject of postcards and souvenirs. It was this storm, in particular, that prompted the building of the lifesaving station.

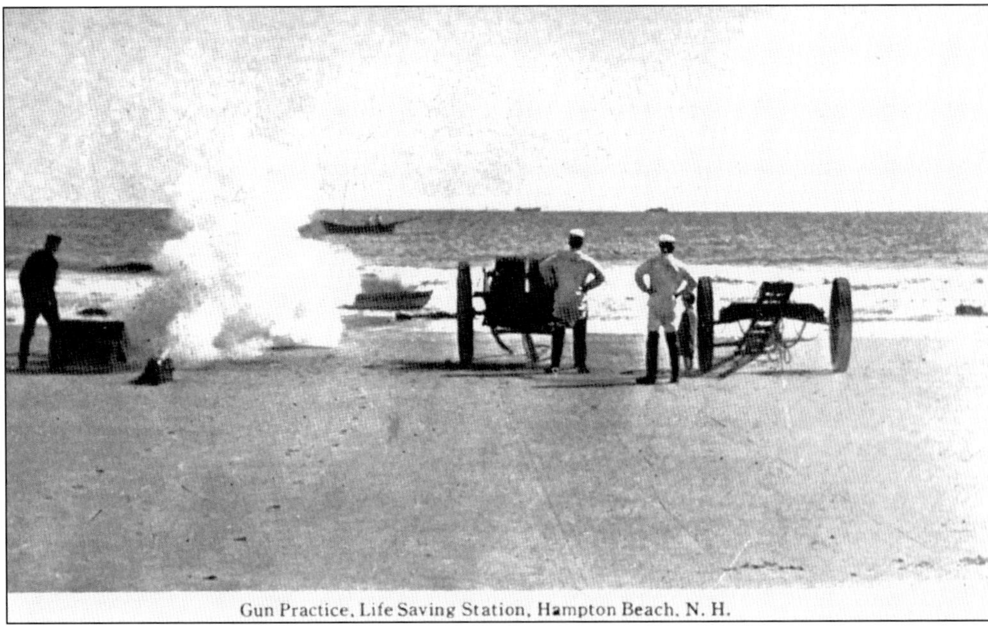

In this *c.* 1910 lifesaving drill, a line has been fired from the Lyle gun on shore to the ship offshore. Once the line was secured to the mast, a breeches buoy was hauled out to bring the endangered crew ashore one by one. These frequent practices were popular events for the locals and tourists. (Note the small boy standing at the right.) Resident Eleanor Young recalls that, as a child, she participated in the land-based breeches buoy drill by allowing herself to be hauled across a cable from one tower to another.

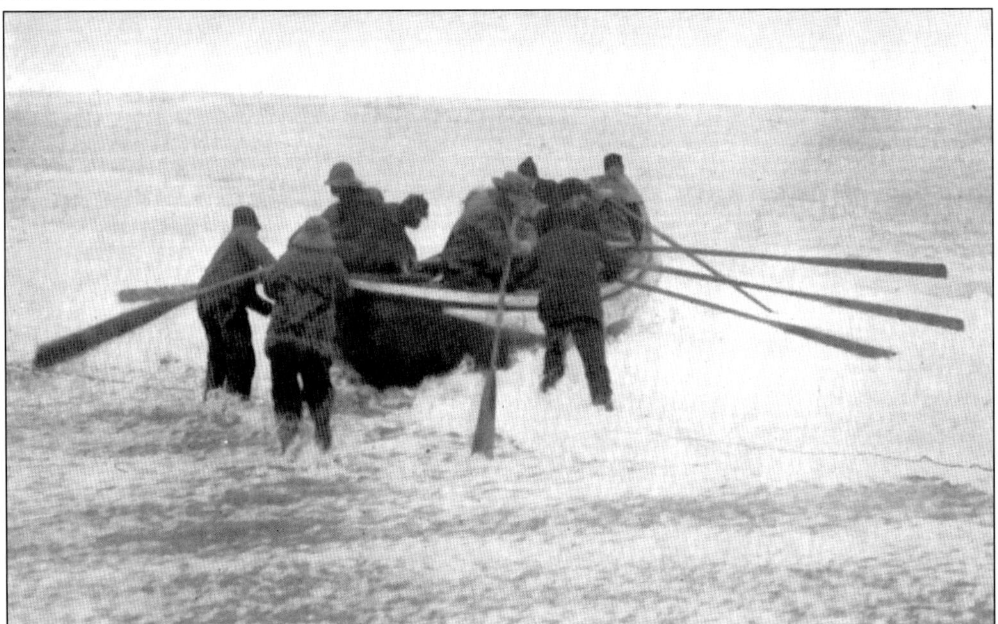

The crew of the lifesaving station was equipped with a lifeboat powered by three sets of oars. Kept in the station boathouse, the lifeboat could be launched quickly by its well-trained crew. The gun and breeches buoy were used only when the boat could not be safely launched.

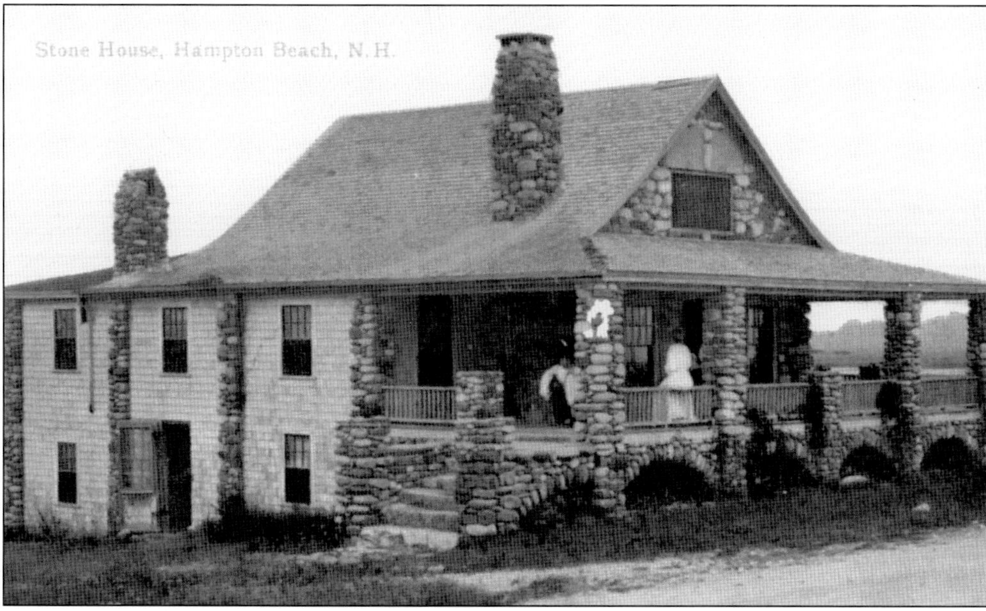

Hampton Beach attracted its share of wealthy summer residents. Mary Aiken of Franklin, formerly of Hampton Falls, built this well-known cottage in 1894, incorporating beach stones into its façade. The house, at 555 Ocean Boulevard, is still a beach landmark today.

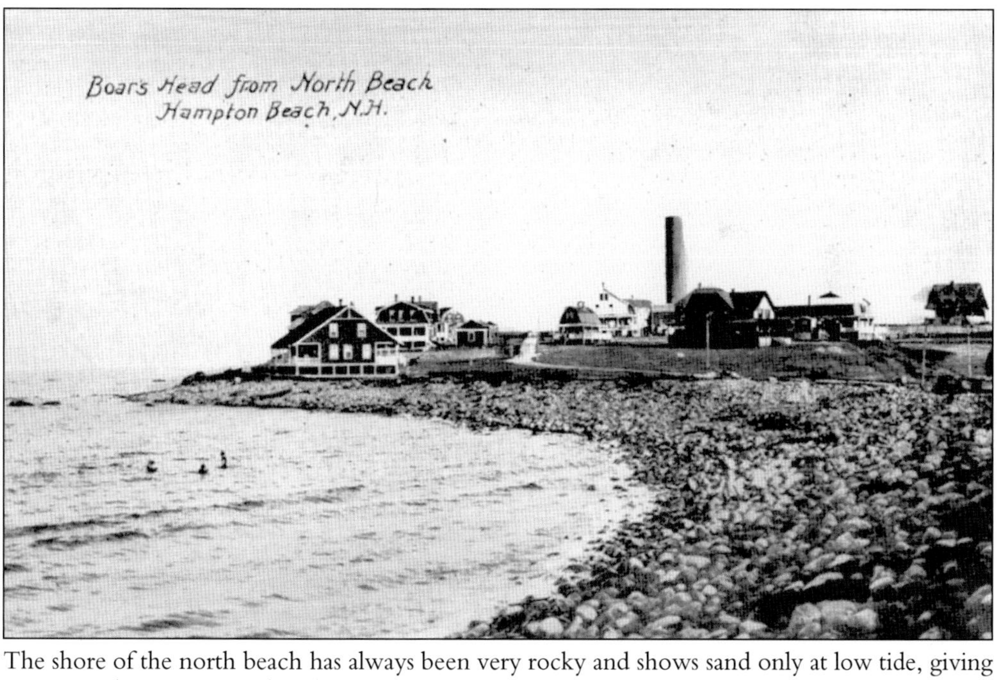

The shore of the north beach has always been very rocky and shows sand only at low tide, giving rise to its designation as the "low-tide beach." The shore curves up to the north side of Great Boar's Head. This *c.* 1910 card shows the first cottages to be built on Boar's Head after the first sale of house lots in 1904. The water standpipe was added in 1907.

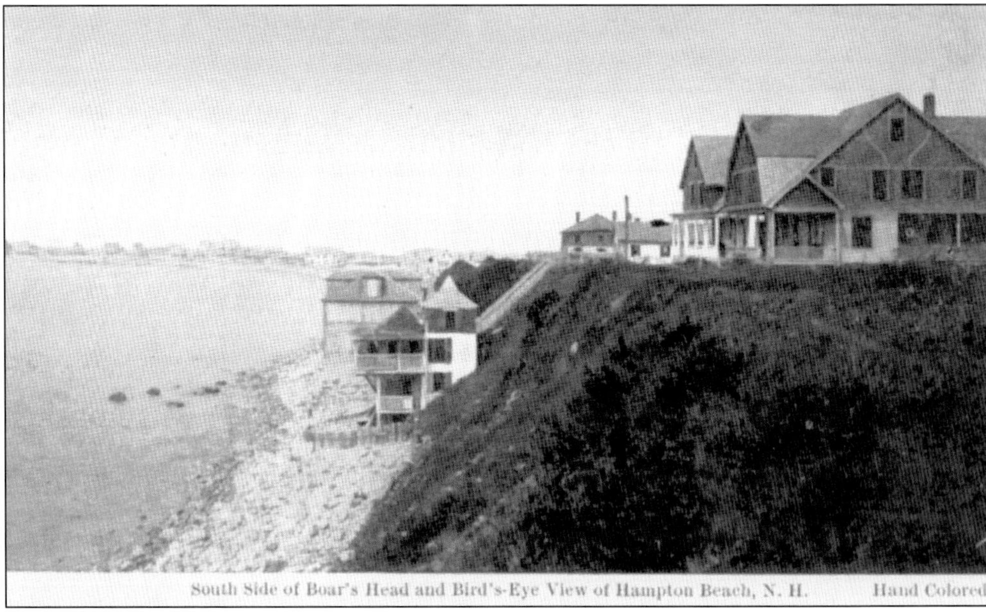

This is another view of the early cottages on the south side of Boar's Head. The cottage that appears to be clinging to the side of the cliff was appropriately named the Barnacle when it was built in 1899.

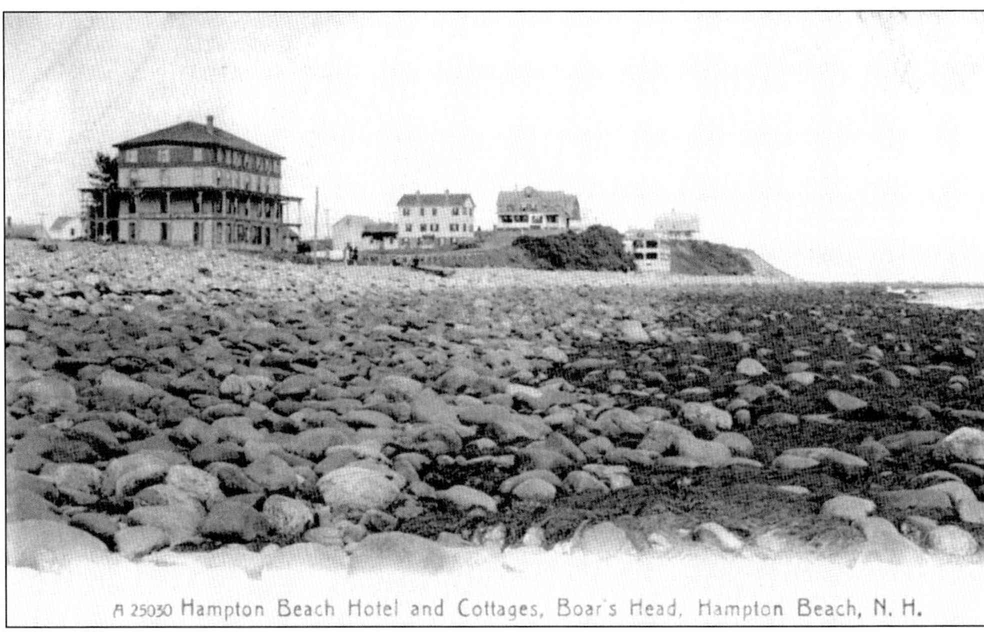

This *c.* 1905 postcard shows how the view of Boar's Head from the south was dominated by Leavitt's Hampton Beach Hotel, which served guests for nearly 50 years. It stood at the base of Boar's Head at a place called Rocky Bend.

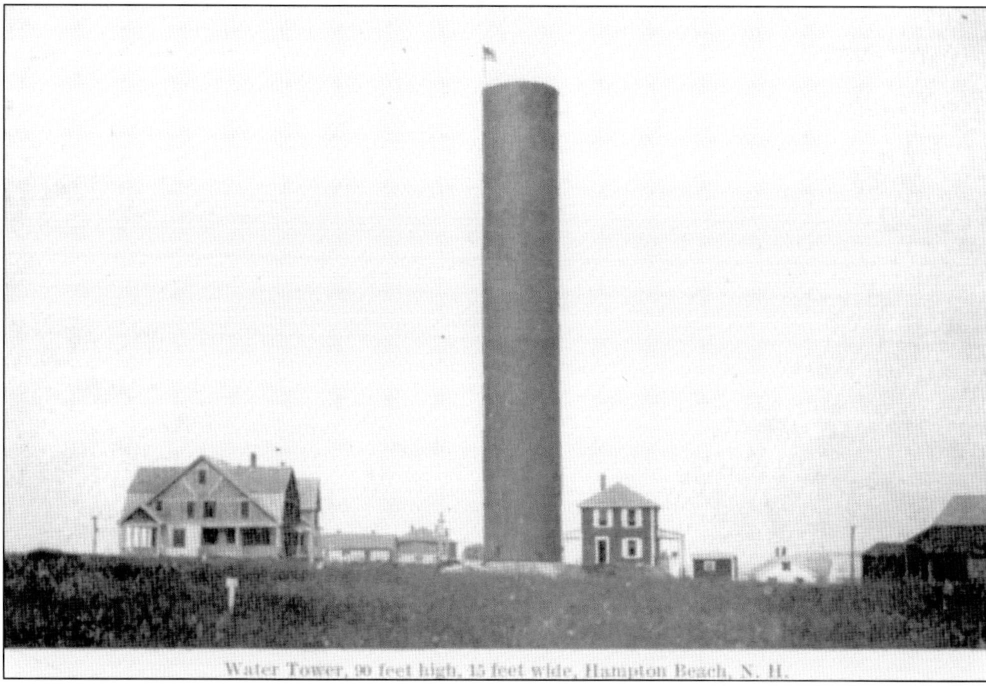

The Boar's Head water tower, or standpipe, was a noted beach landmark from its construction in 1907 to its eventual removal in 1966. The newly formed Hampton Water Works Company brought running water to Boar's Head residents for the first time. The standpipe, along with new mains from Winnacunnet Road to the Casino, was the first municipal waterworks in the town.

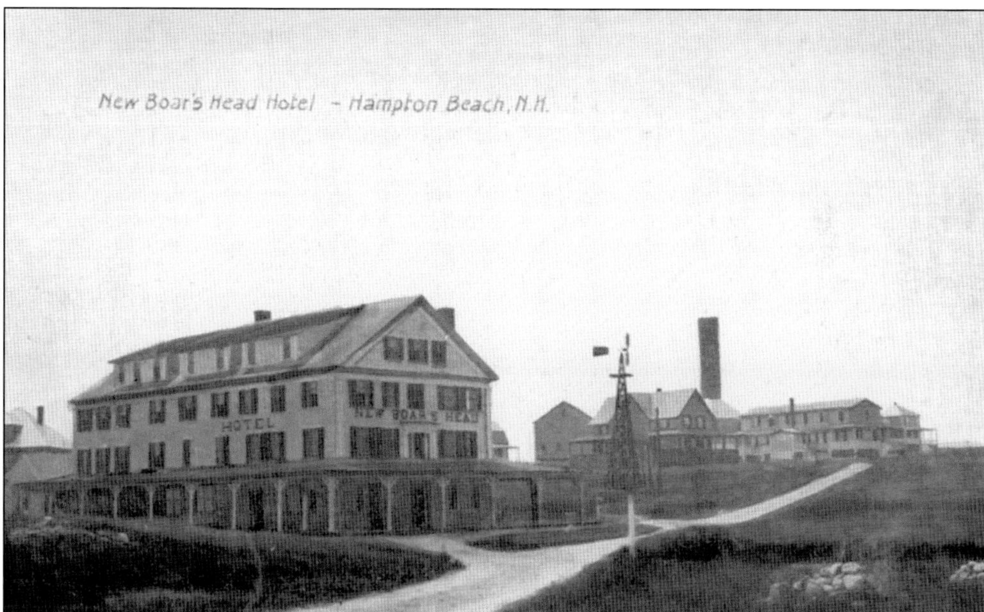

In 1893, the large hotel on the summit of Boar's Head burned. The owner, S. H. Dumas, decided not to rebuild and instead renamed his smaller hotel at the base the New Boar's Head Hotel. This, in turn, burned in 1908, and it was not replaced. Boar's Head today is largely residential.

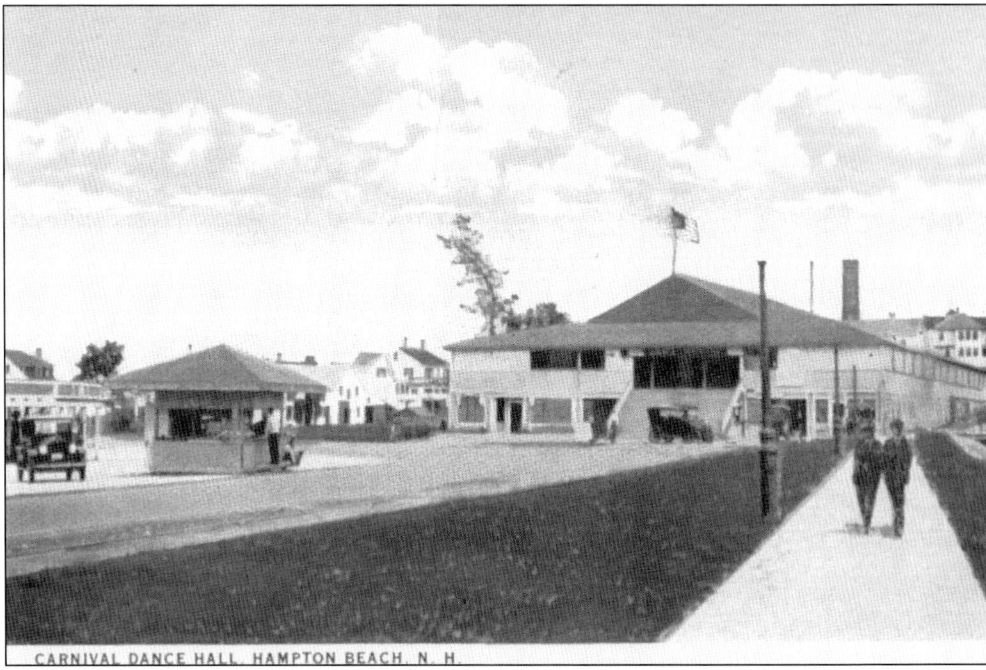

The Dance Carnival, which replaced the Hampton Beach Hotel at Rocky Bend, opened in 1921. The large hall was a popular spot for summer tourists. Its amenities included a bowling alley and a seaside café run by Leroy and Ella Woods. The Dance Carnival lost some of its popularity when the Casino Ballroom opened in 1927. When the Dance Carnival burned in 1929, no attempt was made to revive the business.

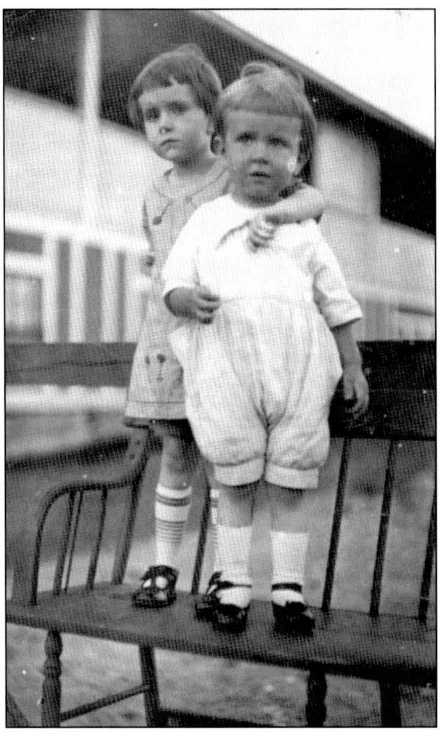

Ella Woods was famous for her pies, and tourists could enjoy them on the deck outside the Dance Carnival. In this 1922 photograph, Woods's grandchildren Eleanor Palmer Dennett Young and Arnold "Bud" Palmer pose together on the deck, or pavilion, as it was usually called.

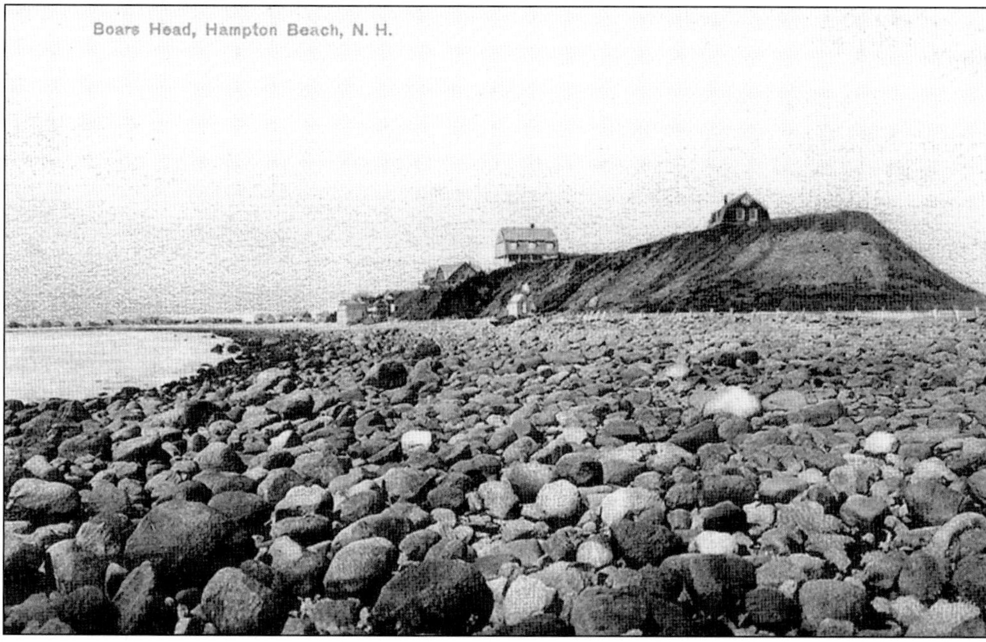

In this *c.* 1905 card, the photographer is looking back at Great Boar's Head from the rocks off the point. There are only a few houses, and the standpipe has yet to be built.

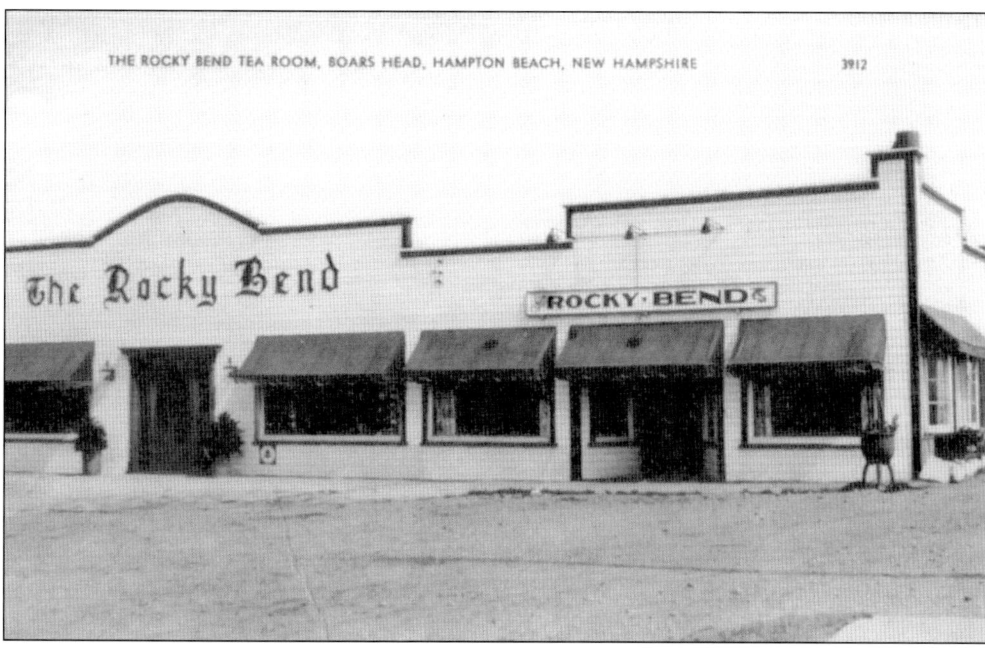

After the Dance Carnival burned, a new tearoom, the Rocky Bend, opened on the same site. As the north end of the beach became increasingly residential, this business gave way to the Rocky Bend Condominiums in 1976.

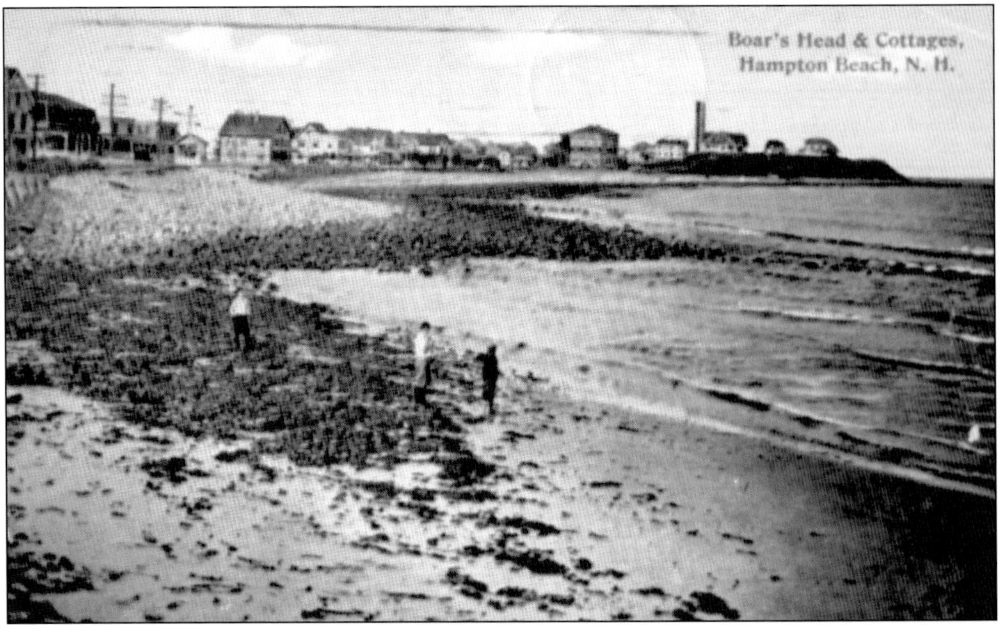

This *c.* 1915 photograph of the beach leading to the south side of Great Boar's Head shows the early wooden breakwater at the edge of the beach. When the sand dunes were leveled to provide space for roads and parking, the natural protection against the surf was lost. Although this wall has been replaced by the concrete structure that is familiar today, constant repairs are still needed after winter storms.

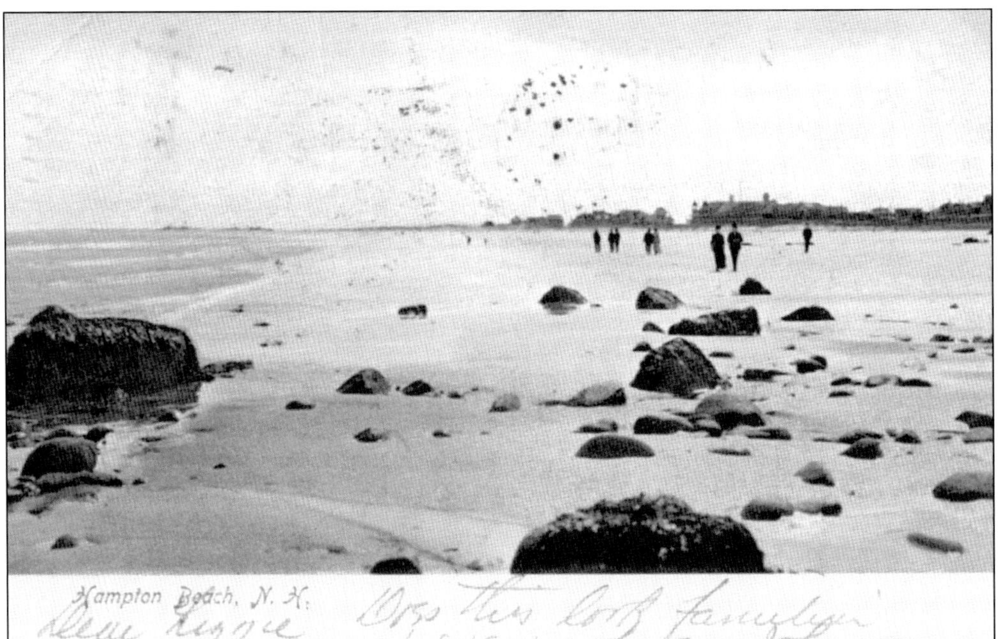

This postcard, mailed in 1906, shows the broad sweep of beach south of Great Boar's Head. In the distance, the roofline of the Casino is discernible. Note that walking on the beach was as popular a pastime then as it is now.

Three

The Main Beach and the Casino

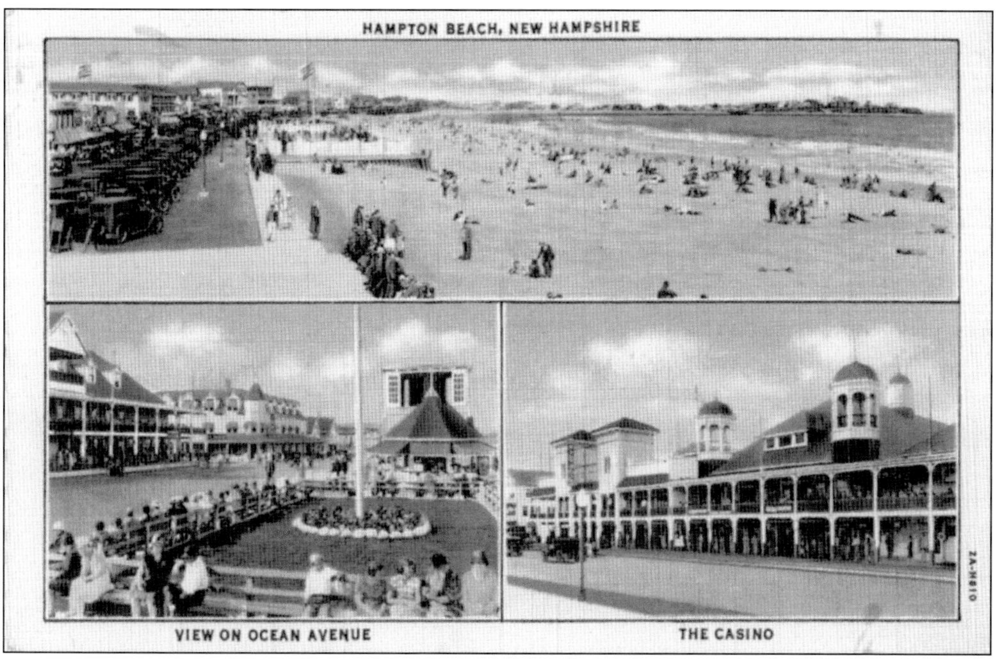

This postcard summarizes what symbolized Hampton Beach to its visitors in the 1930s and 1940s. At the top can be seen the broad sands of the main beach, which accommodated thousands of sun worshipers. The Casino appears at the bottom right. On the left is a small grassy park that was just across from the Casino. This park has long since disappeared.

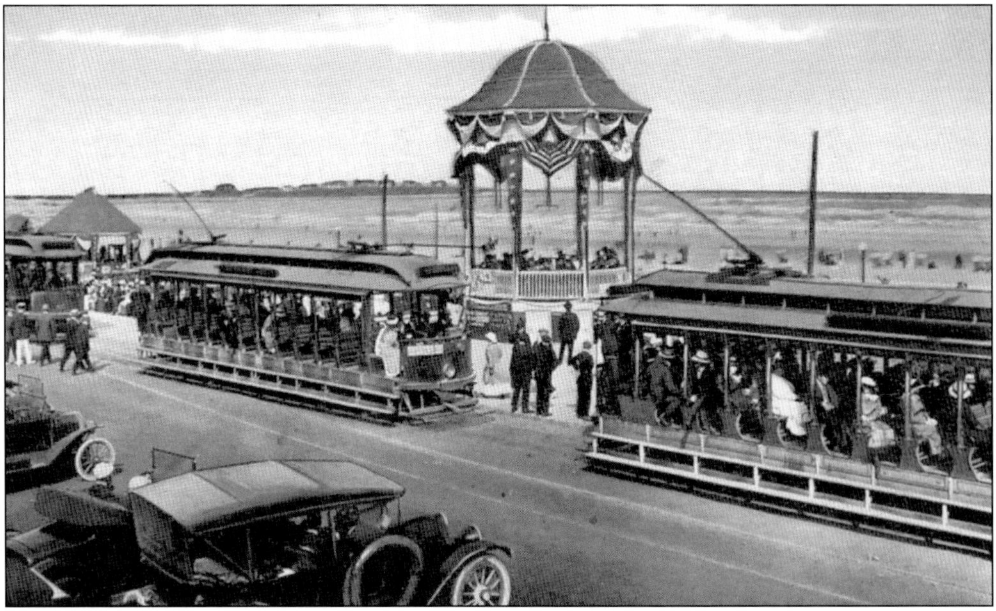

The Exeter, Hampton, and Amesbury Street Railway brought the biggest change to the sandy island that became the Hampton Beach resort. Beginning in July 1897, the railway brought thousands of visitors to the beach from the Hampton depot and from Exeter. Eventually the network connected to other street railway routes, allowing people to travel from as far away as Lawrence and Lowell, Massachusetts. The main beach stop was at the southern end of the beach near the bandstand and Casino. Here, three trolleys have arrived at the stop near the Casino. Note the second set of tracks to accommodate more trolley traffic.

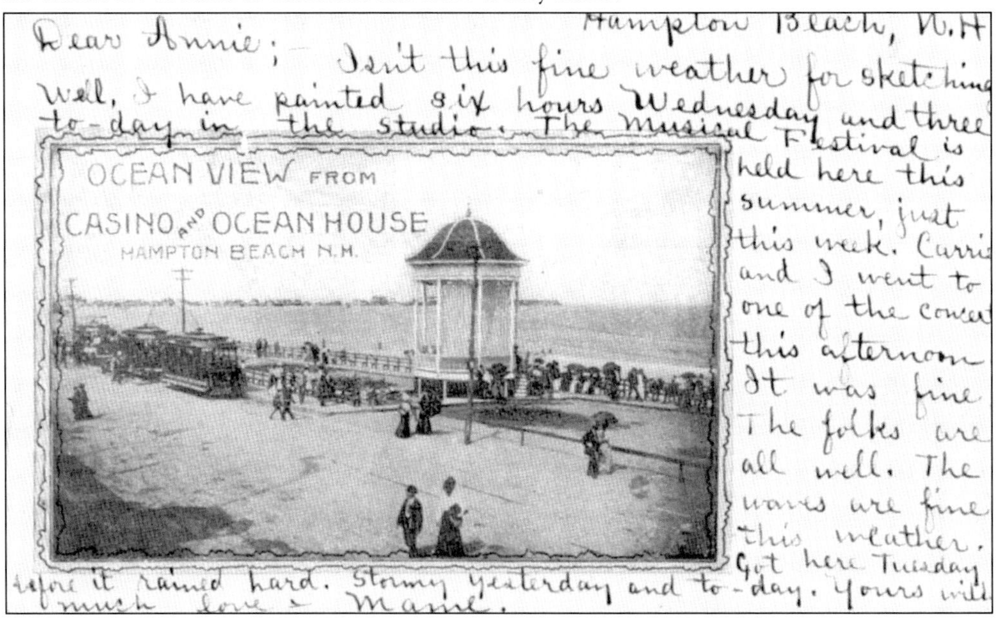

The bandstand, built in 1901 by the owners of the Casino across the street, was the center of outdoor entertainment at the beach for over 50 years. The trolley stopped here, and there was a boardwalk for promenades. Refreshments were also available. The writer of this card in 1903 noted that there was a music festival the week she visited the beach.

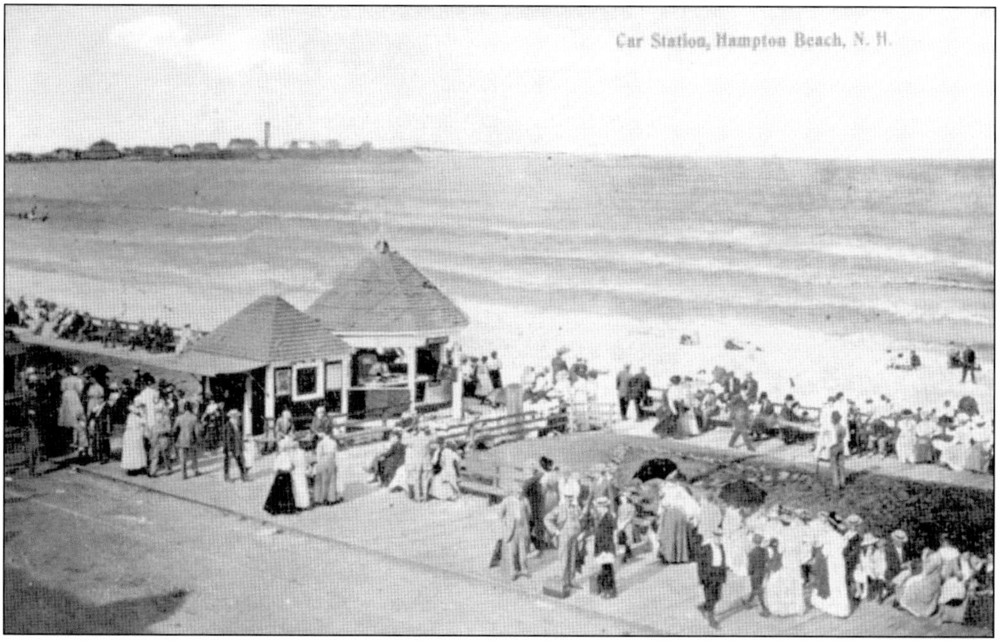

Just north of the bandstand was the ticket office for the trolley, as well as a large popcorn stand that was operated by the trolley company. This *c.* 1911 card shows a stream of elegantly dressed tourists strolling on the boardwalk, while only a few people have chosen to sit on the sand.

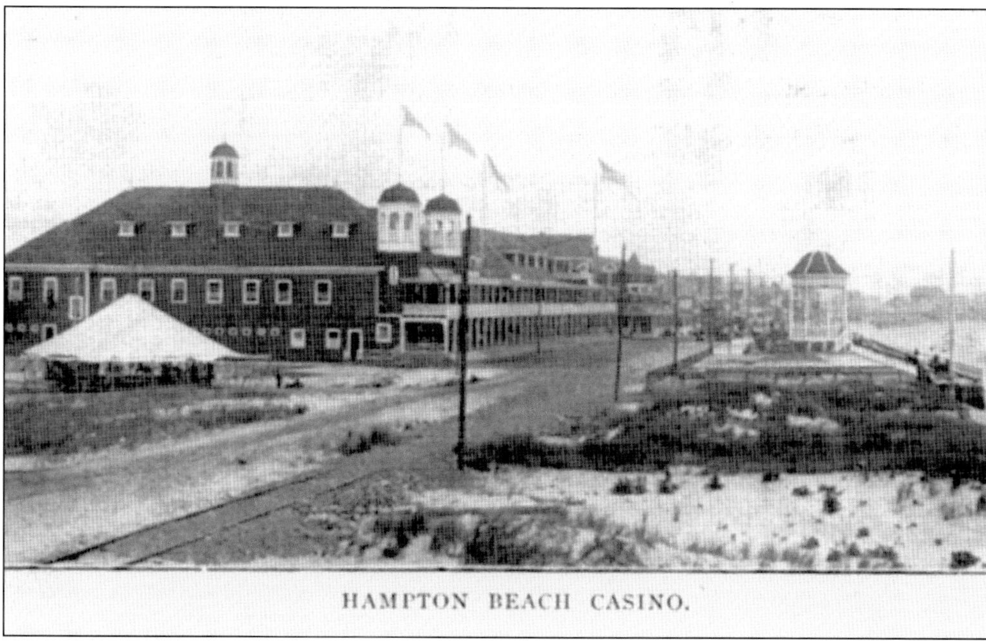

In order to persuade tourists to travel to the beach by trolley, Wallace Lovell (the founder of the Exeter, Hampton, and Amesbury Street Railway) built a large entertainment hall called the Casino at the southern end of the beach. Originally erected in 1899, the Casino was expanded in 1901 by the addition of the Opera House, recognizable here by its distinctive towers. This card is a private mailing card, a type that was replaced by the familiar postal card in 1902, thus dating this particular issue to the year 1901.

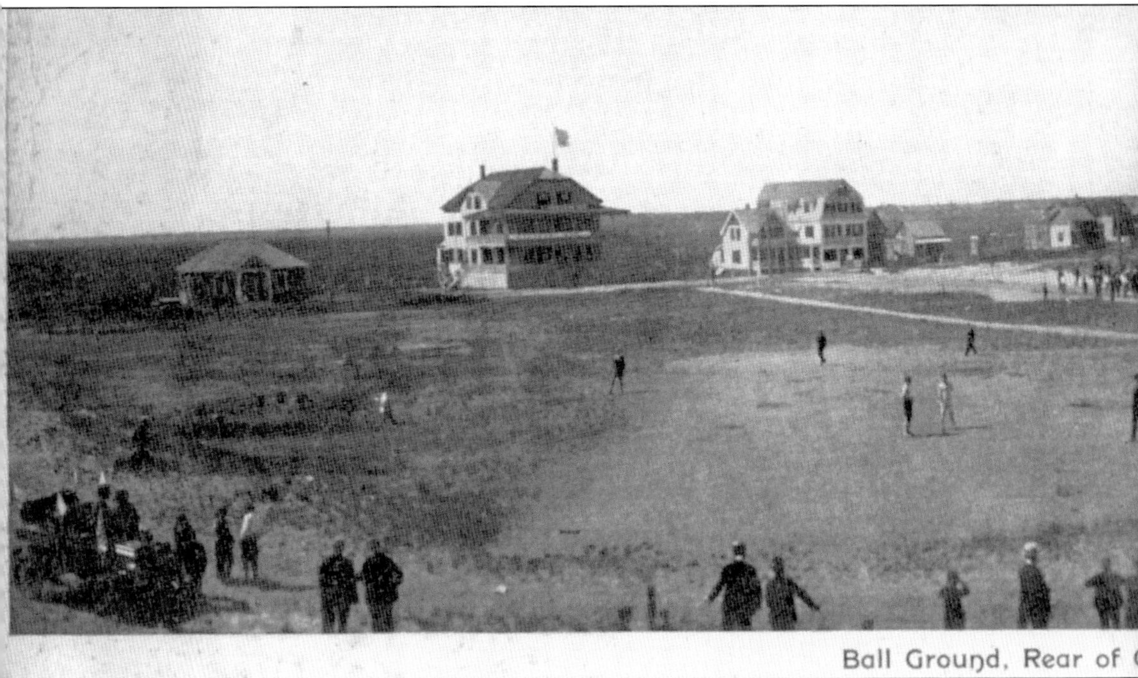

Behind the Casino, a large playing field offered space for a number of sports. On this early-20th-century card, a baseball game is in progress. Note the cottages that have begun to appear on the streets around the Casino. Some were built as private homes, while others were built by the

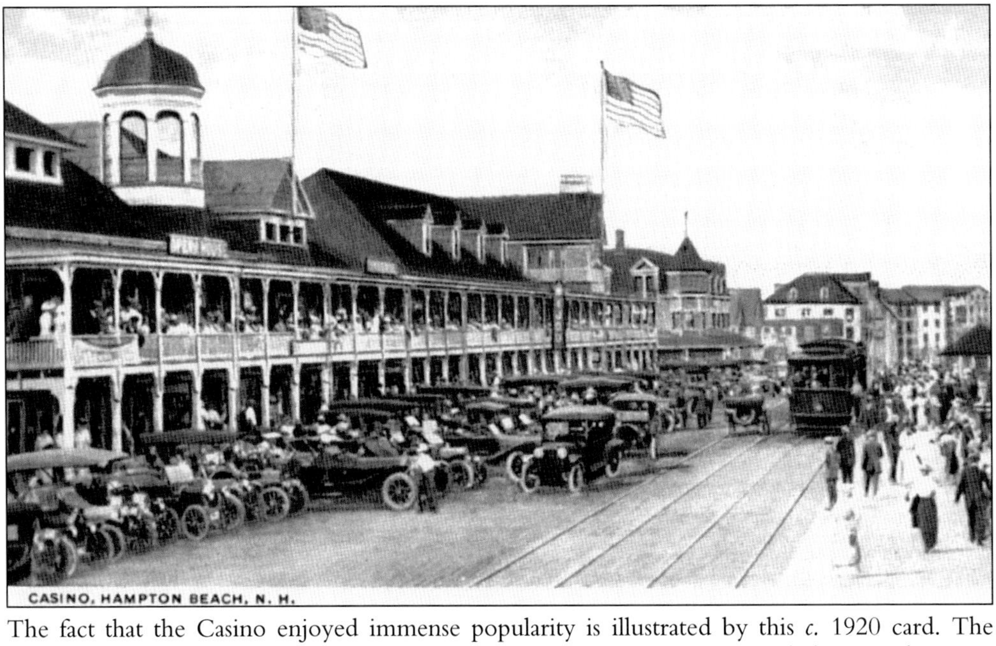

The fact that the Casino enjoyed immense popularity is illustrated by this *c.* 1920 card. The second-floor porches, or piazzas, are filled with visitors observing the scene below. At this time, the automobile was becoming a popular method of travel, as can be seen on this crowded street, where the trolleys are forced to share the tracks with cars. The police required drivers to back into the parking spaces in front of the Casino in order to conserve space.

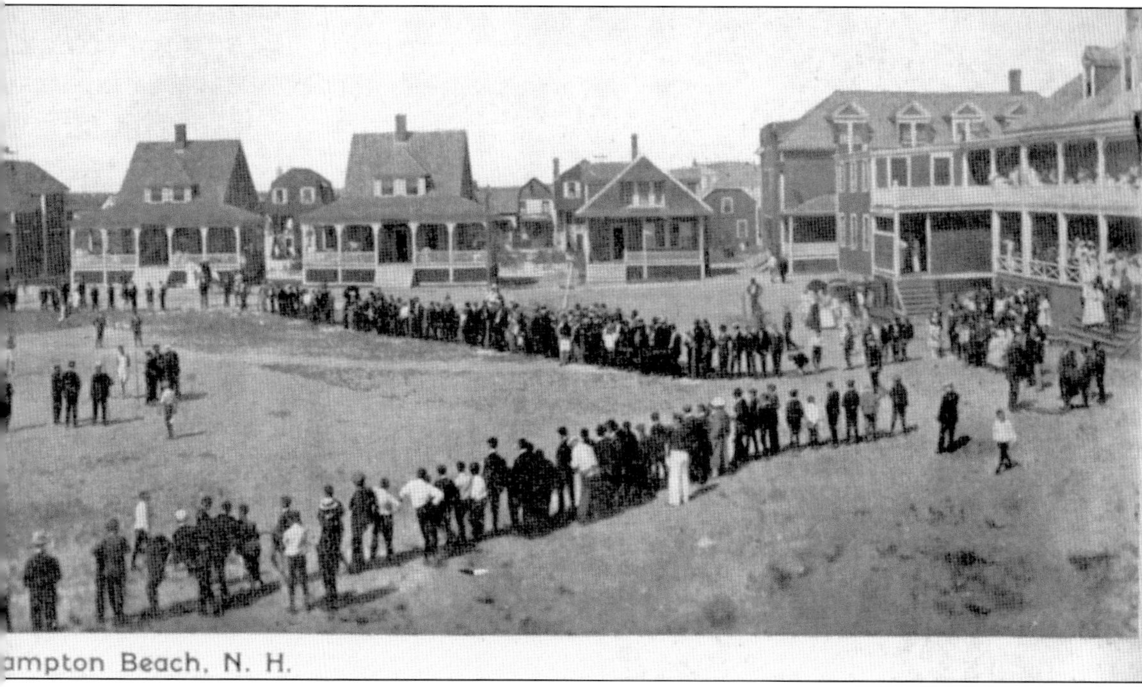

Casino proprietors to be rented out to vacationers. The building with the flag is the Hampton Inn, which was located where the Janmere Motel now stands.

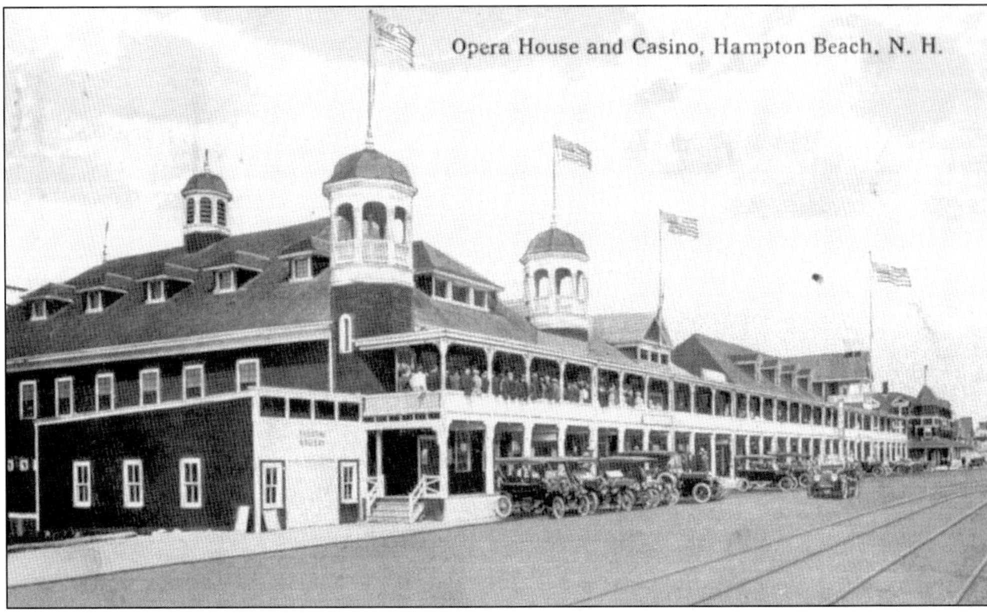

Among the entertainments provided by the Casino was a gallery for shooting clay pigeons. This small building was built next to the Opera House after 1910 on a site covered by the new ballroom in 1927.

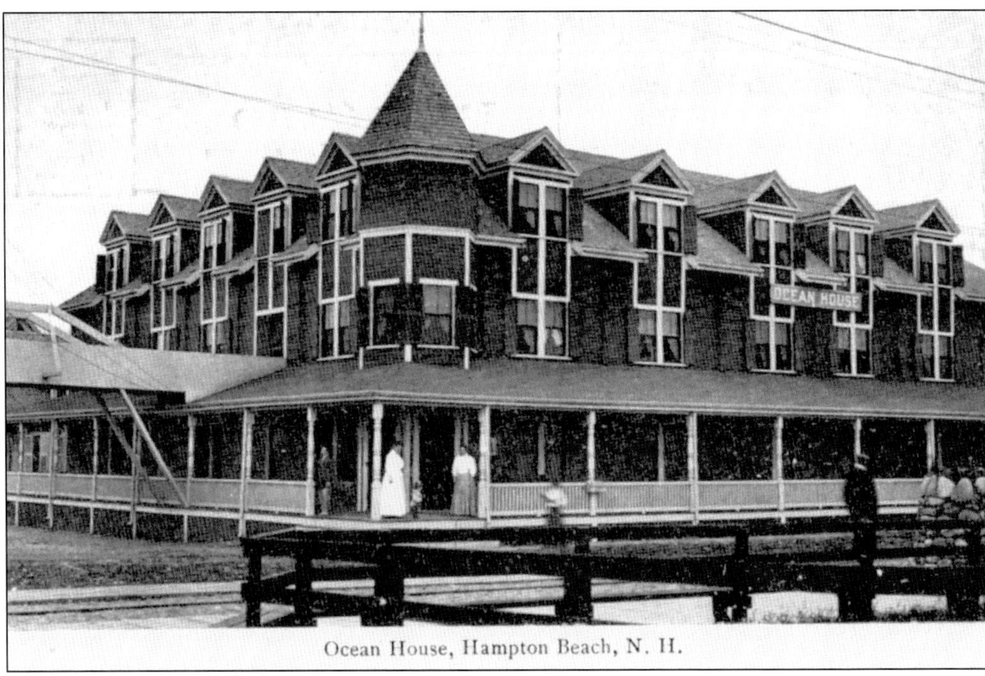

In order to encourage vacationers to stay longer at the beach, in 1901 Wallace Lovell built the Ocean House, a 57-room hotel connected to the Casino by a walkway. The hotel, on the corner of D Street, boasted both running water and electric lights. Note at the left of the card a portion of the suspended walkway over D Street. The walkway was removed before 1915.

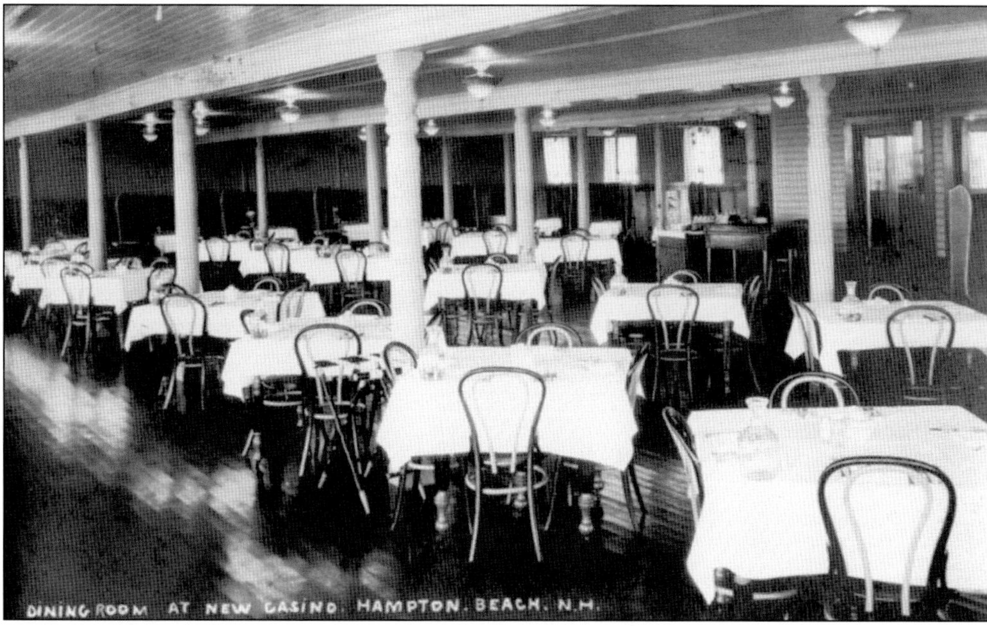

As the beach became a tourist destination, good dining facilities were important. This pre-1920 card shows one of the public dining rooms in the Casino. The owners advertised the availability of both public and private dining rooms.

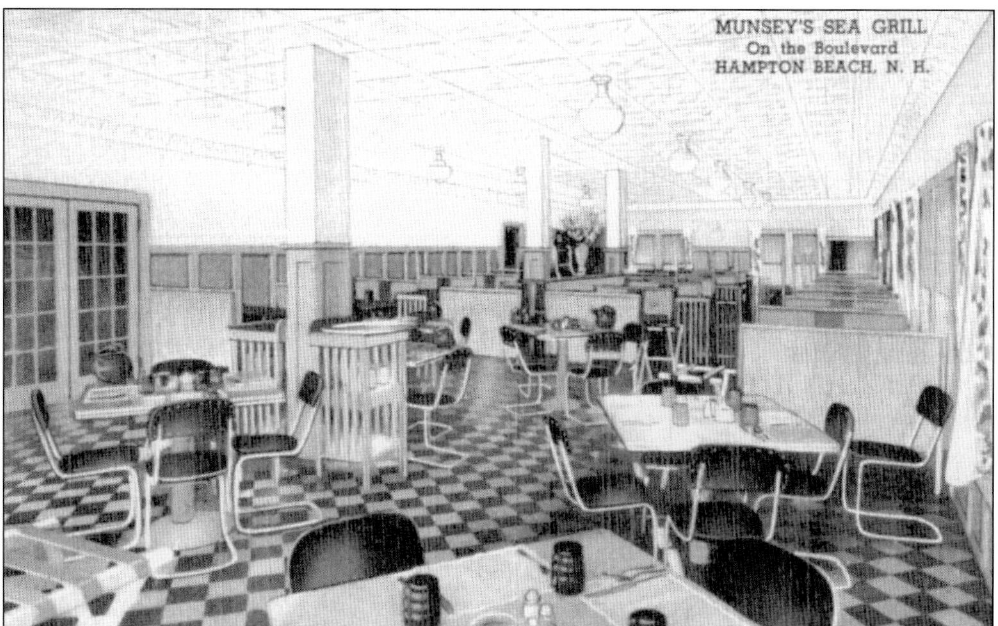

Munsey's Sea Grill advertised itself in 1935 as "one of the oldest established businesses at Hampton Beach . . . where discriminating autoists dine." Located on the corner of A Street and Ocean Boulevard in the Janvrin Hotel, it was run by Florence Munsey, an important businesswoman in the early years of the beach's development.

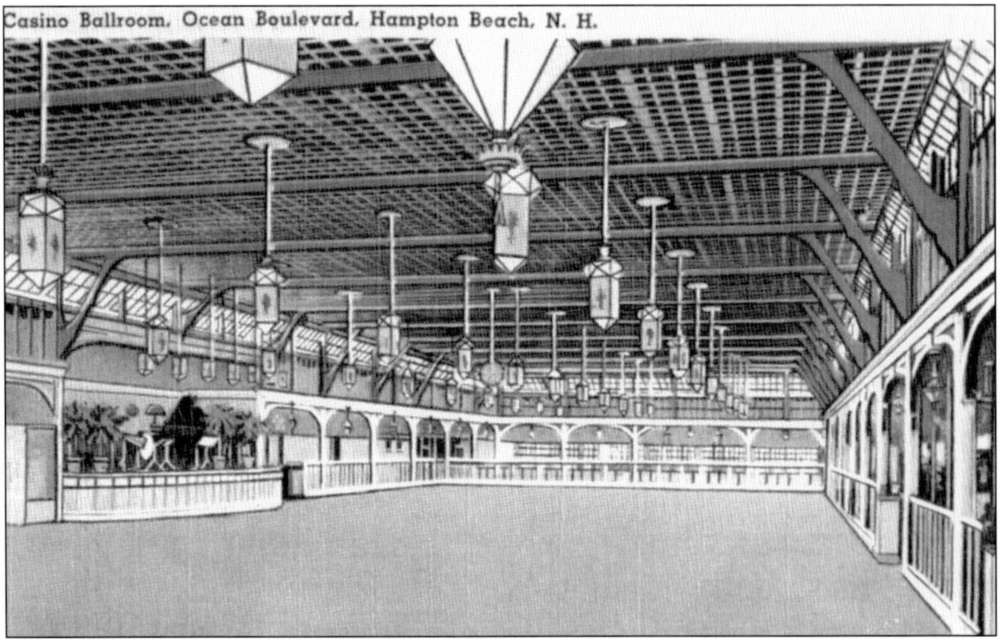

The Casino continued to expand despite several changes in ownership. In 1927, a large ballroom was added to the south end next to the Opera House. Lavishly decorated, it was immediately popular, attracting as many as 20,000 customers each week. It has remained the main entertainment venue at the beach for nearly 80 years.

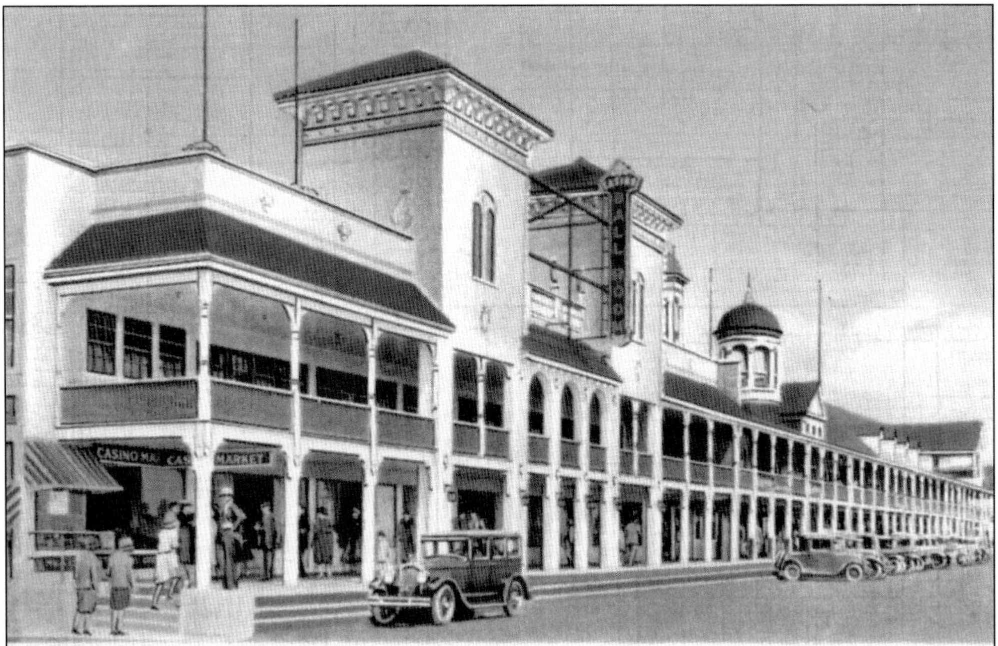

The Casino has dominated the main beach in Hampton, continually adapting its entertainment offerings to suit changing tastes. Even its architecture has followed fashion. In this 1930 card, the 1927 ballroom flaunts Italianate towers, which overshadow the Victorian front of the adjoining Opera House. It was at this time that the building was painted white.

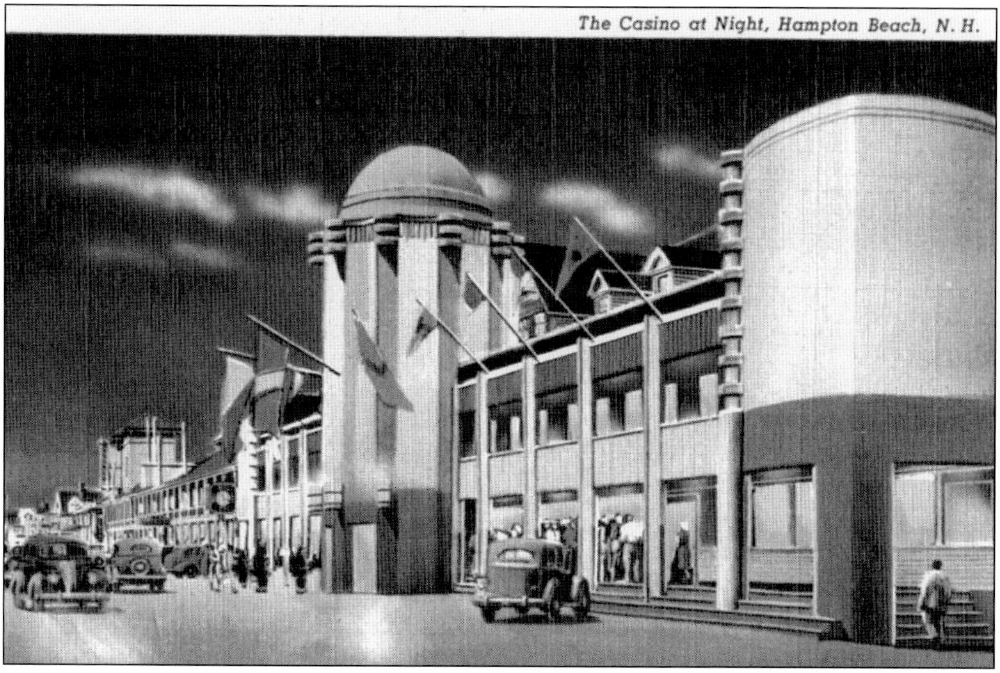

By 1939, parts of the Casino's façade had been reclad in an Art Deco style, complete with a futuristic tower on the north end. Note that the Opera House's cupolas have been removed.

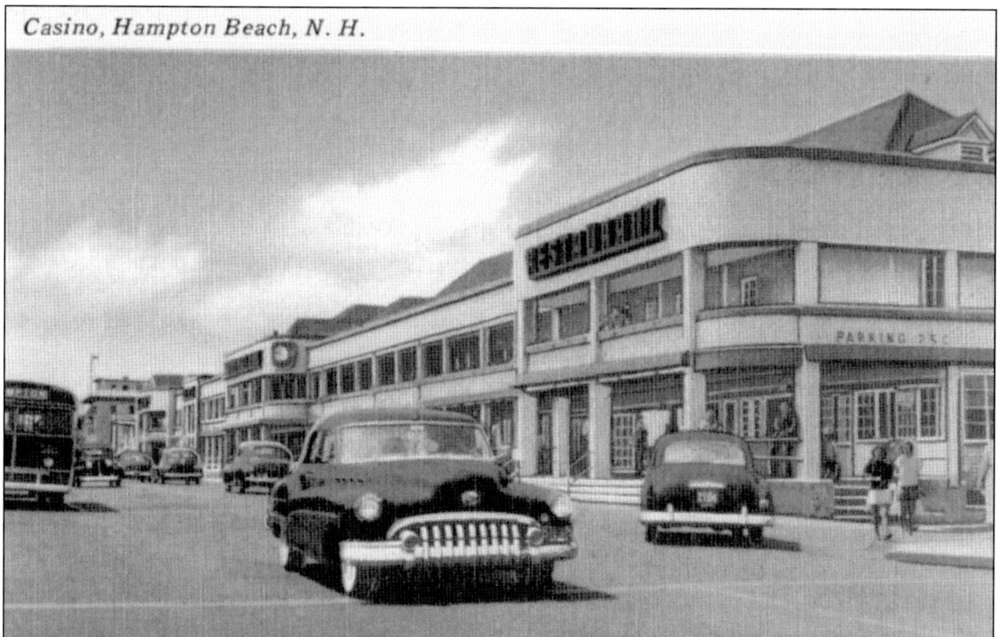

After World War II, the Casino was remodeled again, this time in the prevailing Art Moderne style. In this *c.* 1950 image, the façade has been unified by strong horizontal panels. The various towers and dormers have disappeared, replaced by smooth surfaces with curved corners.

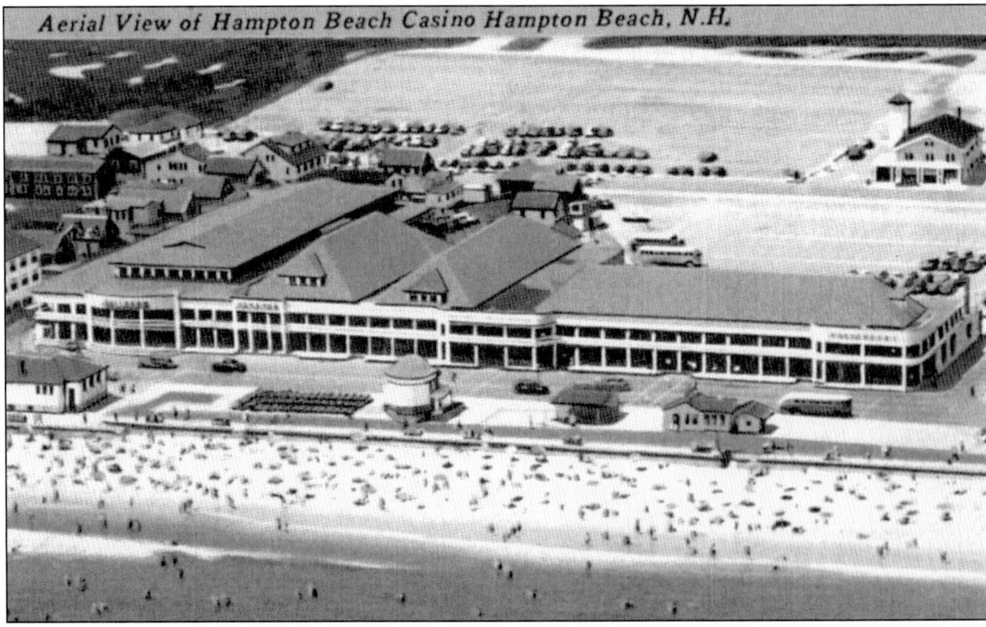

This aerial view from the late 1950s illustrates the dominant position of the Casino on the beach. Note that the playing field behind the Casino has given way to a parking lot. The buildings seen here on the edge of the beach now have all disappeared, replaced by the Sea Shell, built in 1962. In the background at the right is the fire station.

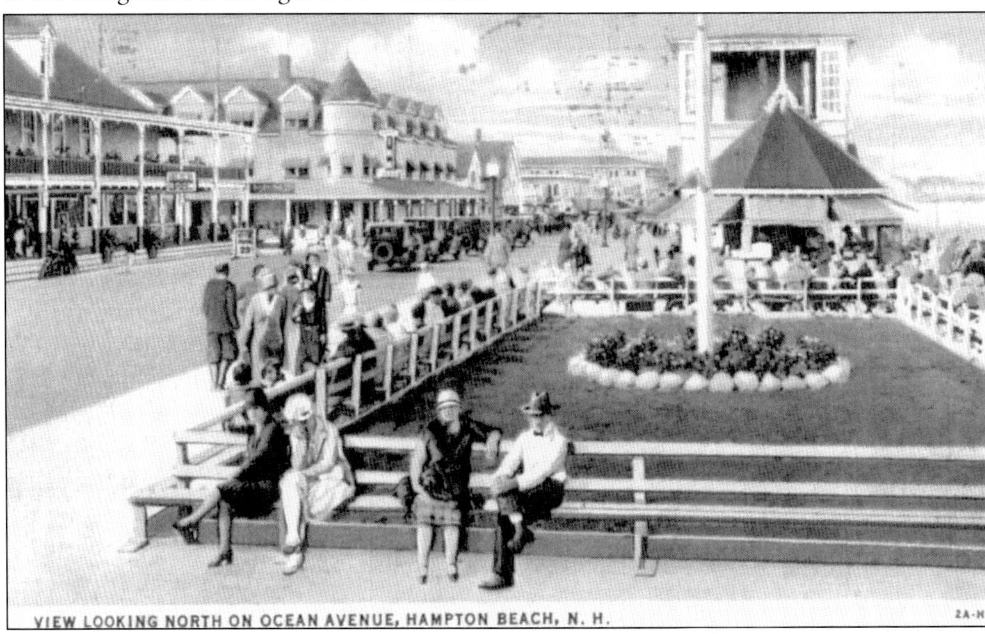

This 1930s photograph of the beachfront was taken from the bandstand. The north end of the Casino and the Ocean House are at the left, while at the right is the popcorn stand with the tall chamber of commerce building behind it. The Hampton Beach Area Chamber of Commerce evolved from the board of trade, which was organized in 1915 by local businessmen to promote the beach. As the trolley business declined, the work of the chamber became very important in the development of the beach.

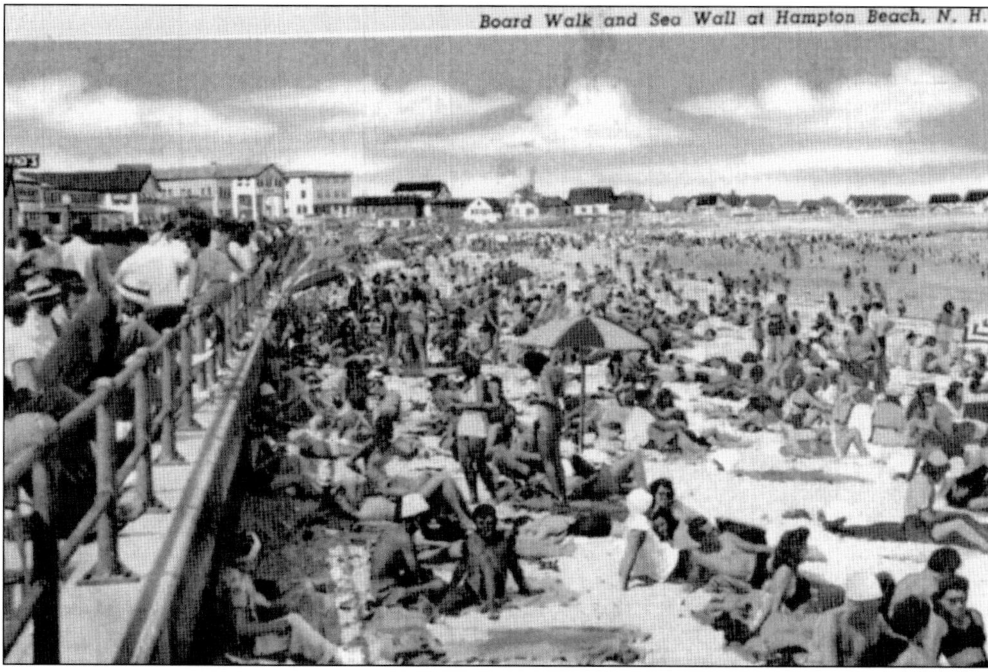

A crowded beachfront has been the hallmark of warm summer days in Hampton for over 70 years. The beach was an especially popular destination during World War II, when gasoline rationing limited travel. In July 1943, the hotels were so full that some tourists slept on the sand.

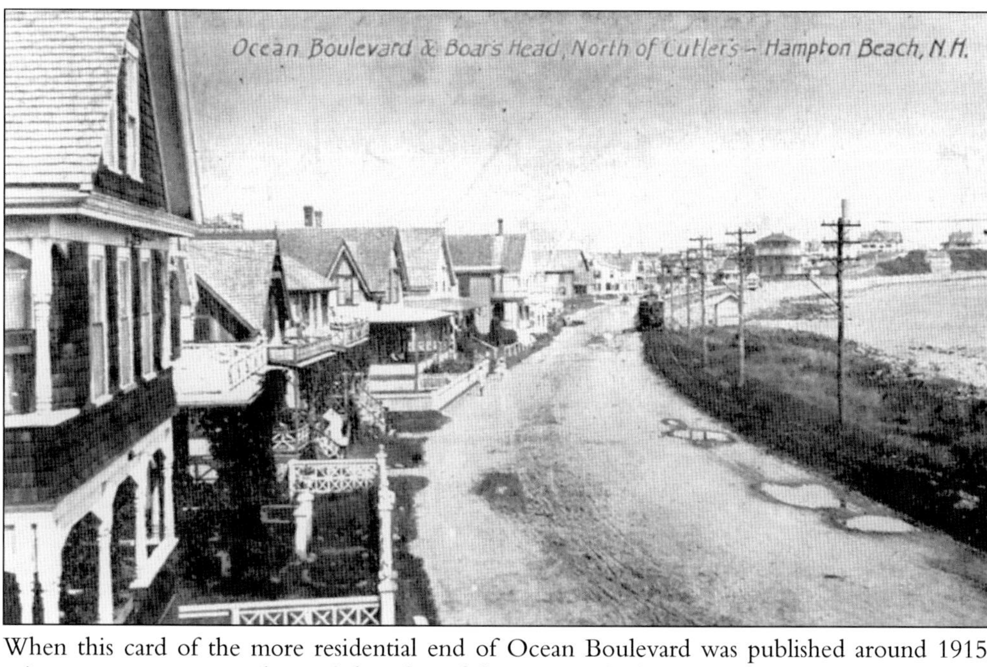

When this card of the more residential end of Ocean Boulevard was published around 1915, private summer cottages hugged the edge of the street, which was no more than a sandy track. Note the trolley approaching on the right through the sea grass. In the background, the water standpipe may be seen on Great Boar's Head.

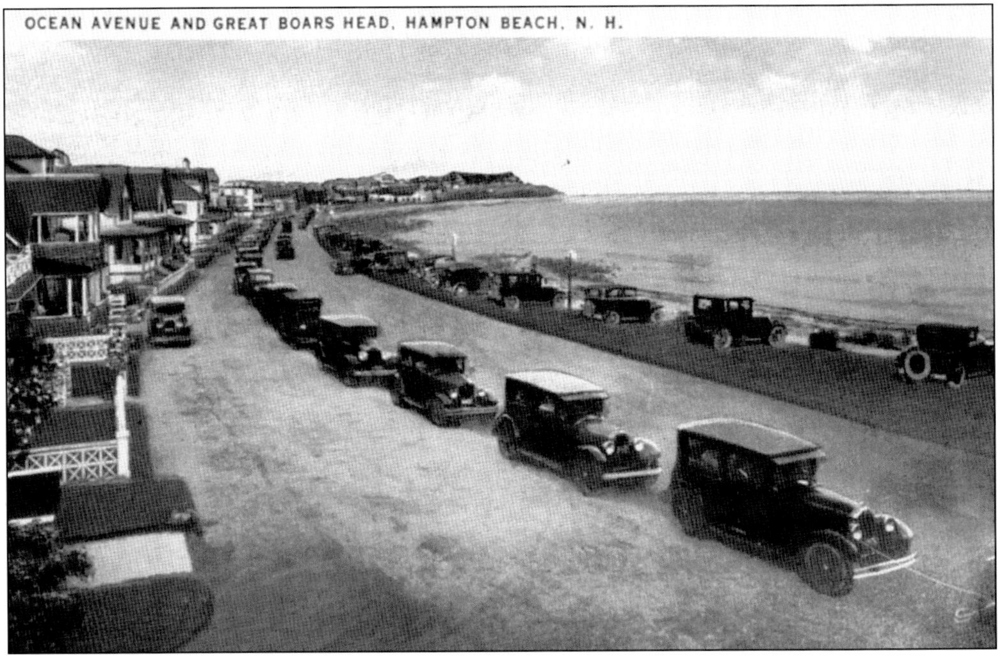

This *c.* 1930 view of Ocean Boulevard shows the lawns in front of the houses and the grassy strip on the edge of the beach where the sea wall now stands. The cars in the center are actually parked on the median between the lanes of traffic.

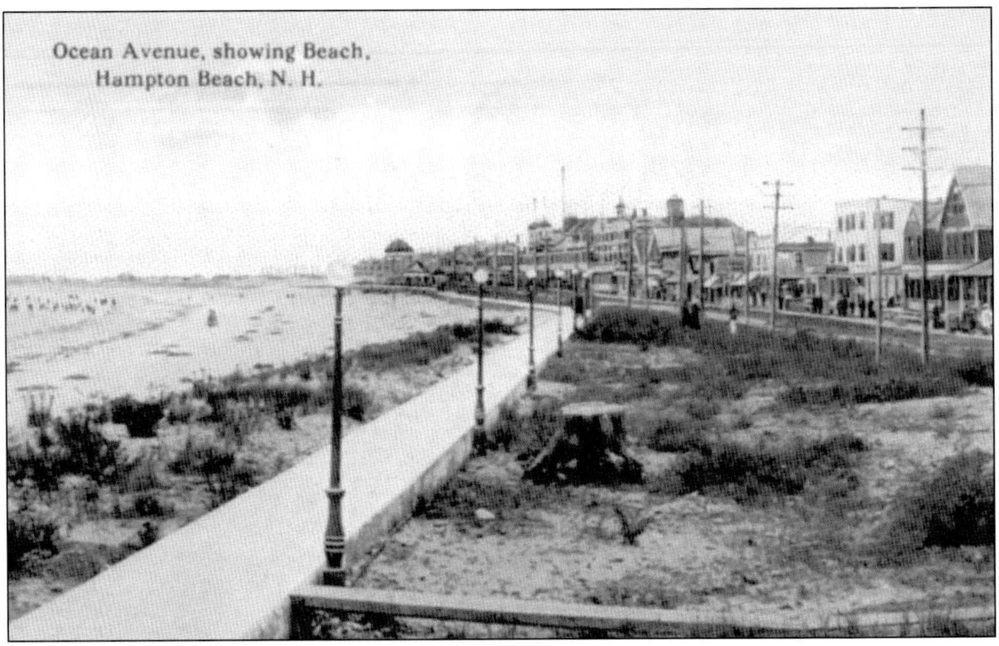

When the Casino was built in 1899, it stood isolated at the southern end of the beach. By the time this card was published less than 15 years later, development had reached the area. Hotels and cottages lined the approach to the Casino and the bandstand, and sidewalks had been installed. A tourist noted on a postcard in 1912 that "new cement walks and Harvard Bridge electric lights along the beach are new to us."

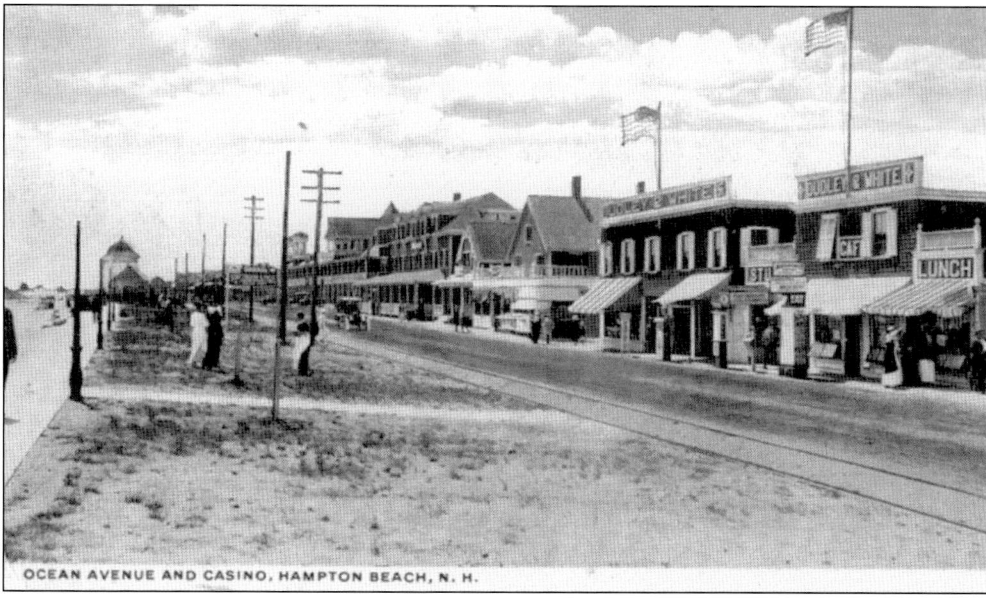

Joseph Dudley and John White were some of the earliest entrepreneurs to build up a business in the area of the Casino. They leased a lot at C Street from the Hampton Beach Improvement Company (HBIC), a private corporation that obtained from the town a 99-year lease for the property between what is now Ocean Boulevard and Ashworth Avenue. Even the Casino's land was leased from the HBIC. Dudley and White's store and café was a beach landmark for many years, serving visitors and residents alike.

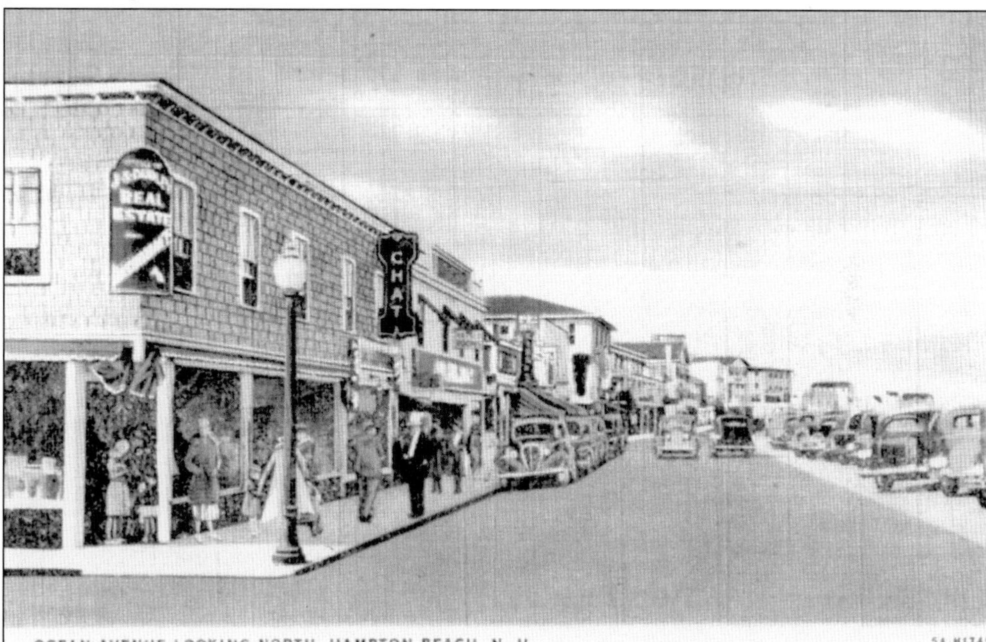

This building was the successor to the Dudley and White block seen in the previous image. John White died in 1927, and Joseph Dudley carried on through the 1930s, when this store was constructed. It burned in 1950 along with the Playland Arcade next door, but it has been rebuilt. There is still a Dudley's store at the site.

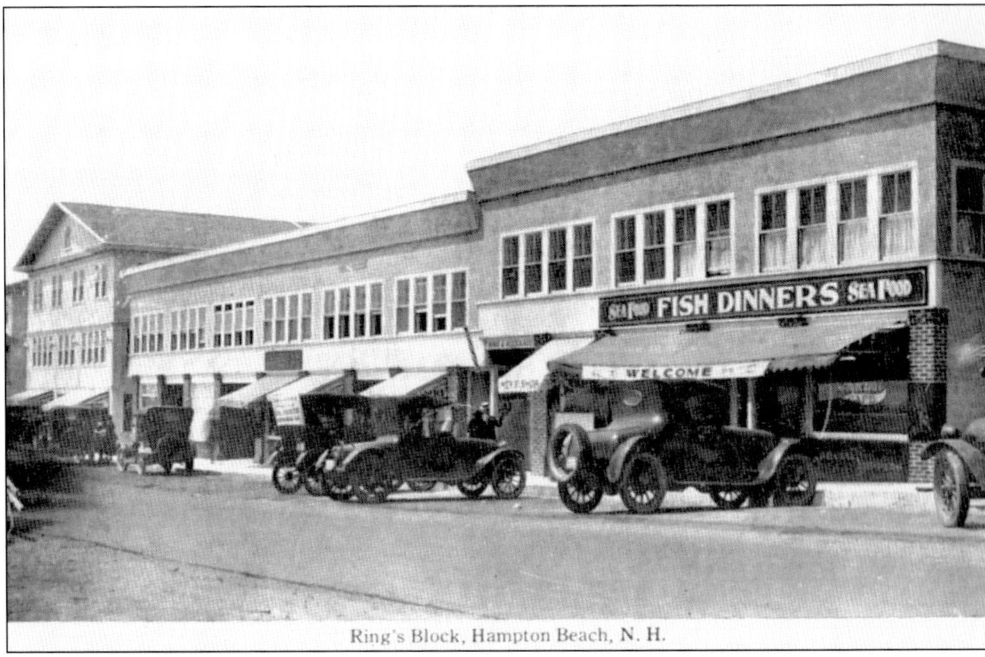

Ring's Block was the property of Lemuel C. Ring, who was one of the most active early entrepreneurs at the beach. He came to town from Haverhill, Massachusetts, and built a cottage on B Street. He built a number of businesses and hotels, including the Ashworth. Although he lost his buildings to fire more than once, he was undeterred and promptly rebuilt. He was also active in town affairs as a fire chief and a selectman.

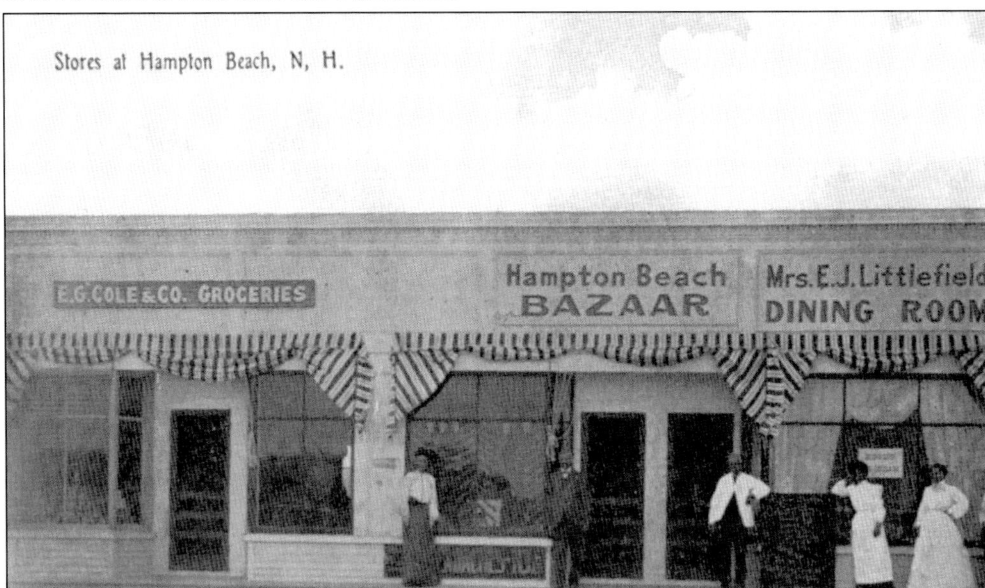

This 1909 postcard illustrates three businesses on Ocean Boulevard. The Hampton Beach Bazaar and Mrs. E. J. Littlefield's Dining Room catered to tourists, while E. G. Cole's grocery supplied the cottages. Cole had a large store in the center of Hampton village, and this was a branch shop that operated only in the summer.

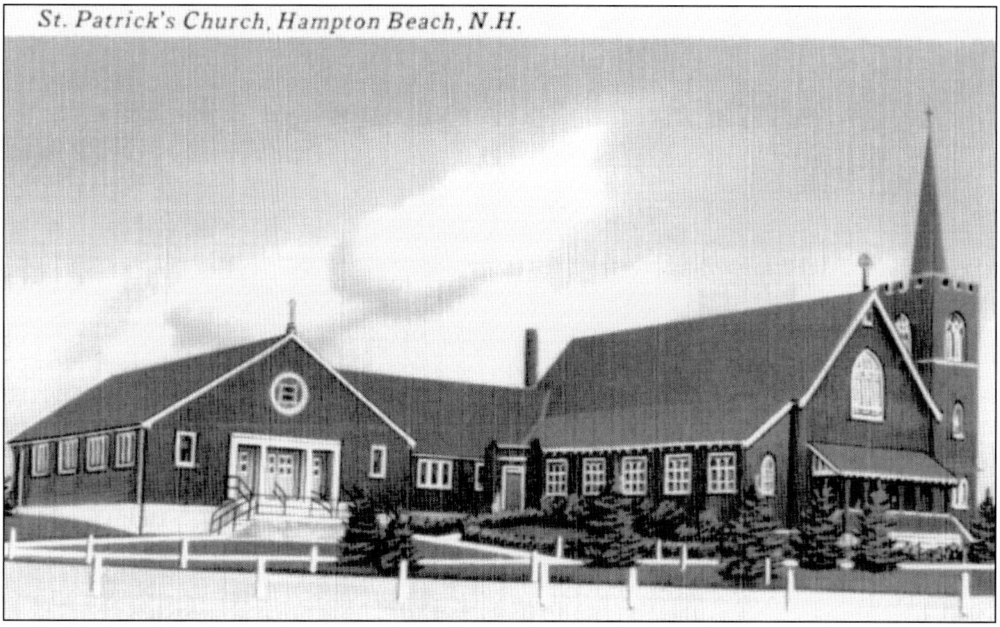

As people began to spend vacations at Hampton Beach, churches were built for summer visitors. The first church at the beach, St. Peter's Episcopal, was built in 1912, but it was destroyed in the 1915 fire and was not rebuilt. St. Patrick's Catholic Church on Church Street was founded in 1914 to serve the growing number of Catholic visitors. It was unheated at first, but the addition in 1937 of a chapel with a heating system allowed services to be held there year-round until 1948, when the Catholic church in the center of town was built.

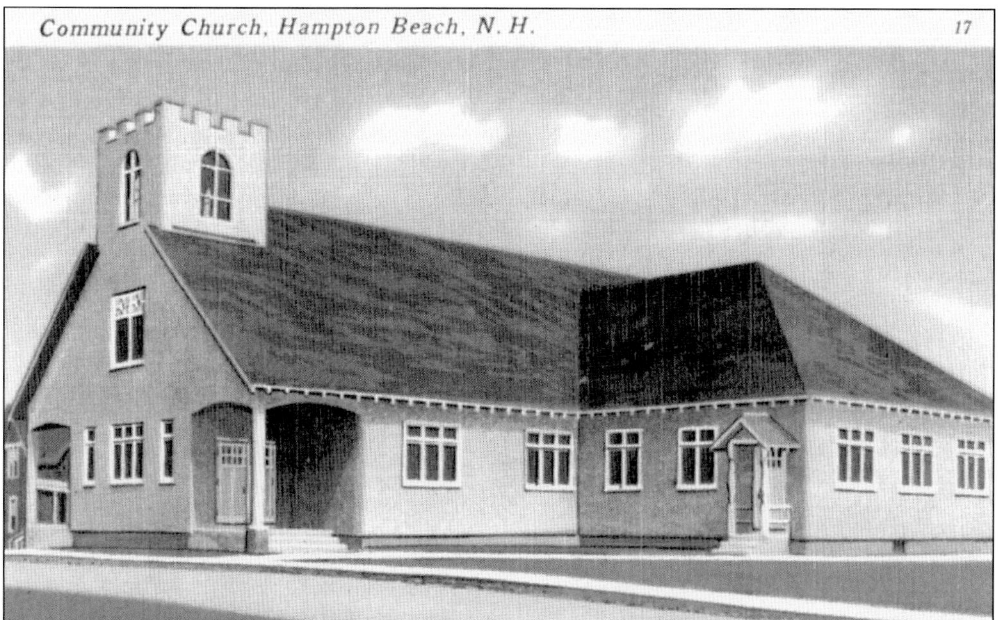

The Hampton Beach Community Church stands on D Street on a lot donated by the Casino. The church was the work of Lemuel C. Ring and opened for services in 1925. Since the 1930s, it has had the reputation of being a "singing church," and it has a busy summer season each year.

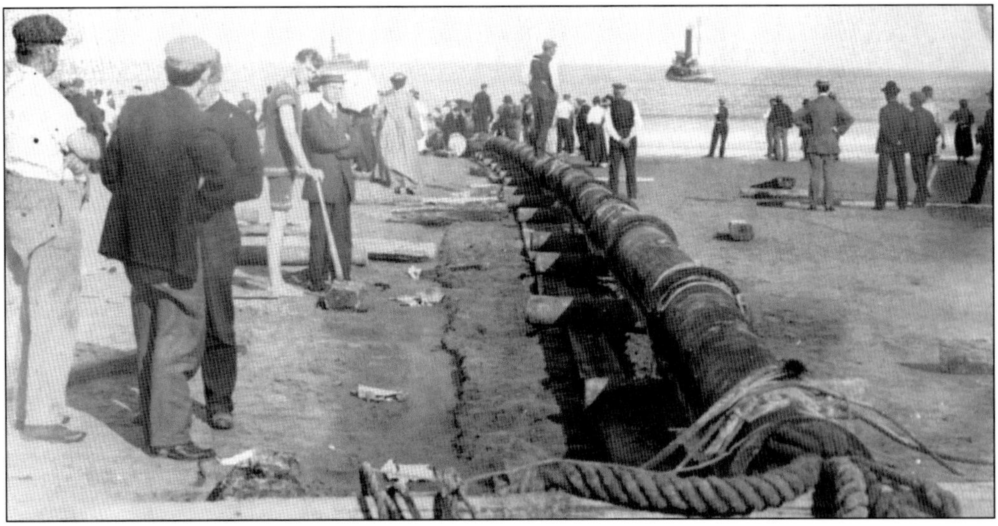

The influx of tourists meant that the disposal of raw sewage became an urgent issue. Delay in solving this problem was one of the reasons for the establishment, in 1907, of the Hampton Beach Village District (the Beach Precinct) by beach businessmen who felt that their concerns were not being heard by the town. The construction of a sewage discharge pipe in 1908 was one of the Beach Precinct's first accomplishments. Discharge from this pipe opposite Church Street continued until 1934, when Hampton became the first town in New Hampshire to build a wastewater-treatment plant.

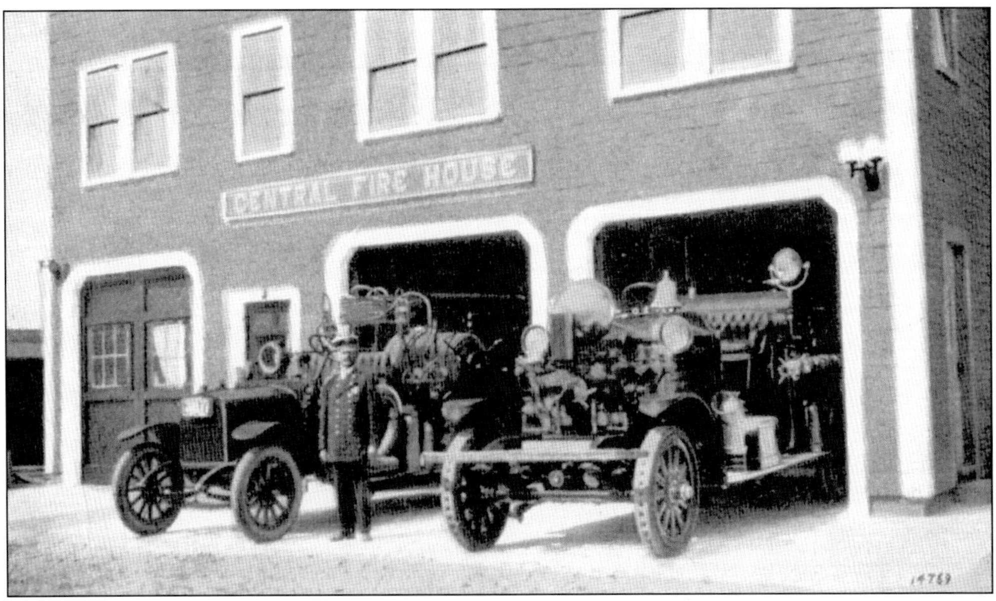

Another of the Beach Precinct's concerns was fire protection. The rapid development of the beach and the lack of good water resources left the beach community vulnerable to destructive fires, which swept through the area a number of times in the early 20th century. One of the precinct's early aims was to establish a fire department for the beach. This mid-1920s card shows the fire station, which was built in 1923 on Ashworth Avenue behind the Casino. The two engines in front are the first motorized fire trucks: the 1916 Kissel hose and chemical truck and the 1923 Ahrens-Fox pumper. This station is still the headquarters of the Hampton Fire Department.

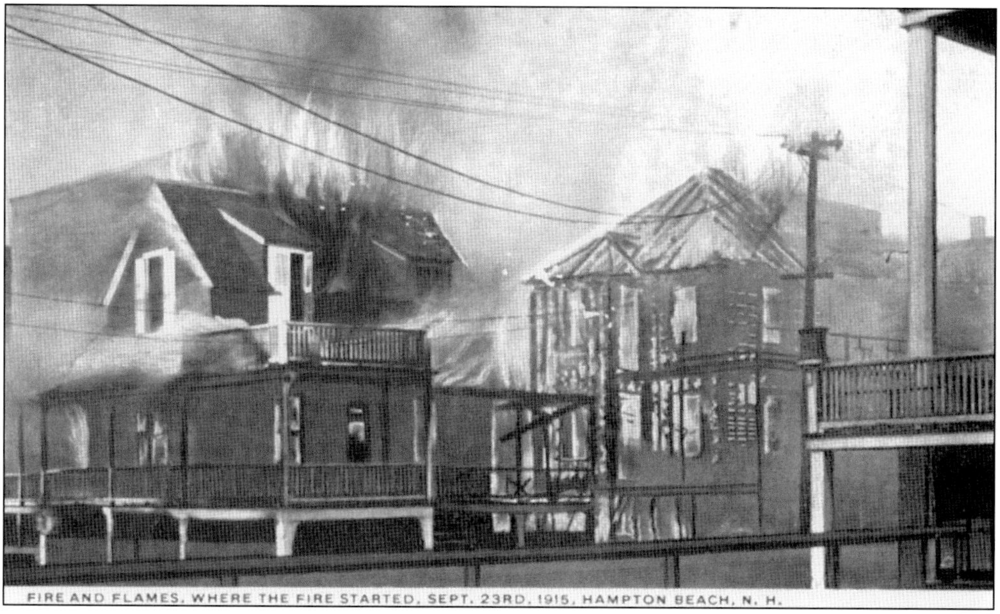

The devastating fire of September 1915 destroyed a large area north of the Casino, which was spared because the wind blew the fire away from it. The fire spread so quickly that people were unable to save their possessions. One man noted that he and some others pushed a piano balanced on a wheelbarrow out of the Ferncroft on A Street, up Ocean Boulevard, and finally across the street onto the sandy beach, where, despite all their efforts, it caught fire and was destroyed. The spread of the fire was finally halted by dynamiting buildings in its path.

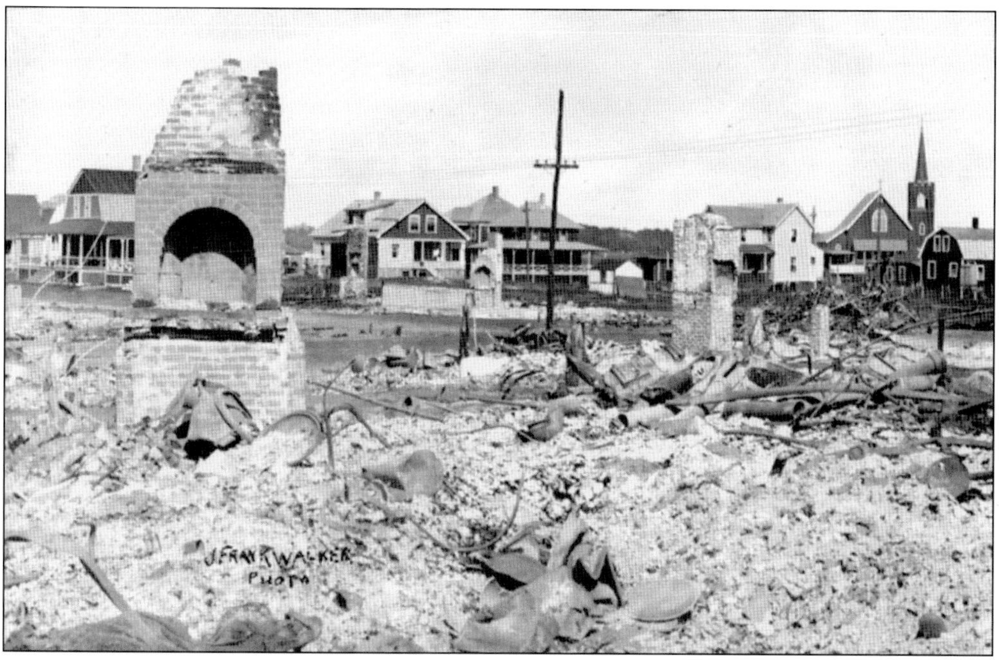

The popularity of images of disasters led to local photographers publishing their photographs as postcards. Frank Walker published a number of such cards of Hampton events. This scene is the aftermath of the 1915 fire. In the background can be seen St. Patrick's Church on Church Street.

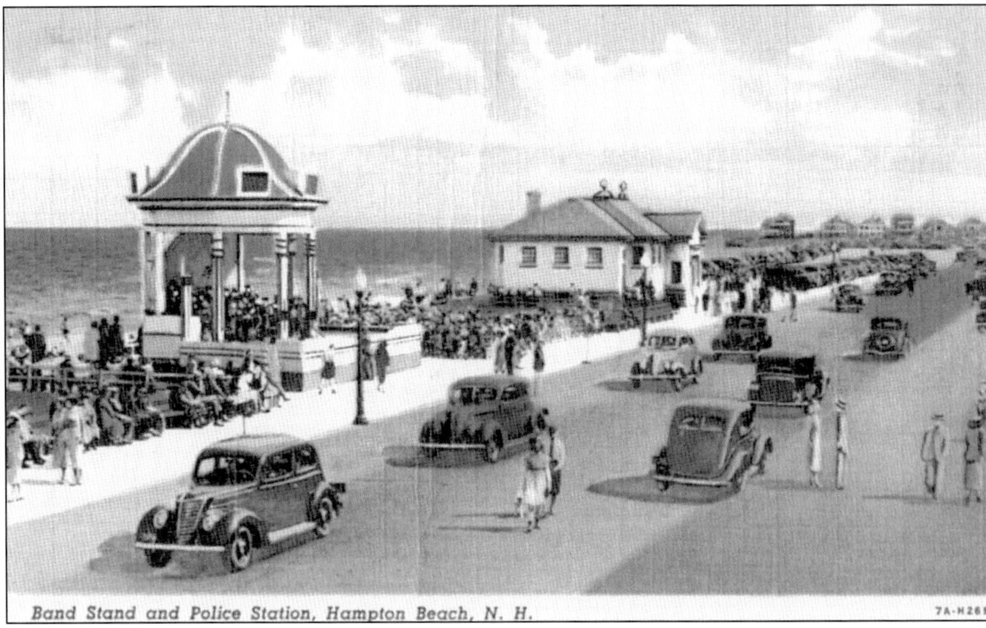

Development at the beach raised the question of police patrols to deal with traffic and with occasional lawless behavior. After using some makeshift facilities for a number of years, in 1921 the town finally built a combined police and comfort station next to the bandstand at the main beach. This building served the entire town for over 40 years; it was replaced in 1963. The headquarters of the police is still at the beach.

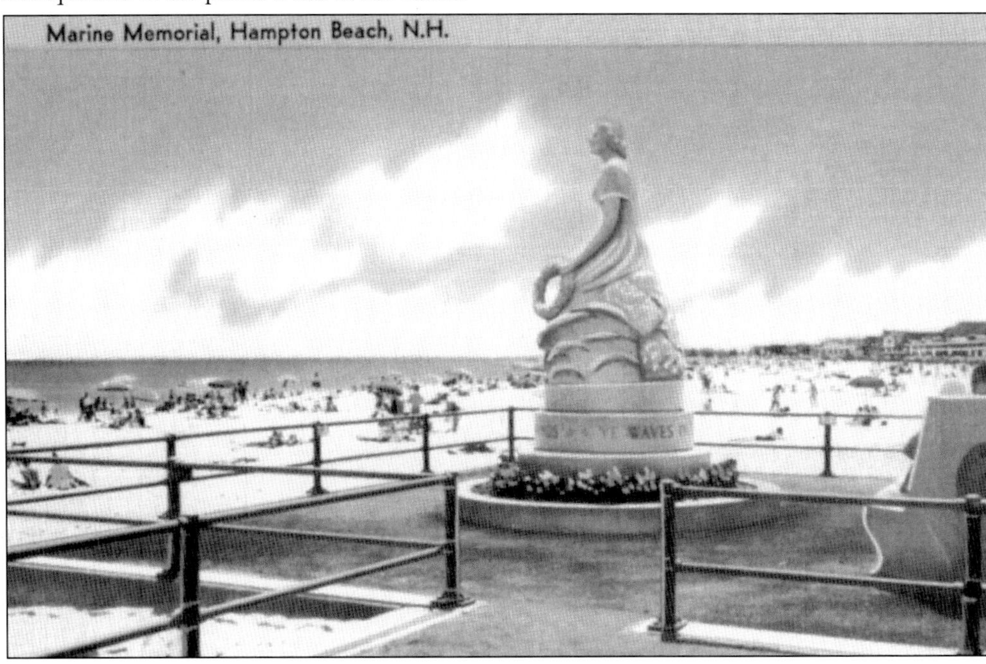

The New Hampshire Marine Memorial stands on the sand across from the Ashworth Hotel. The memorial is the result of efforts to honor those who lost their lives at sea during wartime. A commission formed in 1955 chose Alice Cosgrove to design the memorial, which is the site of Veterans Day and Memorial Day ceremonies at the beach.

Four

The Beach Experience

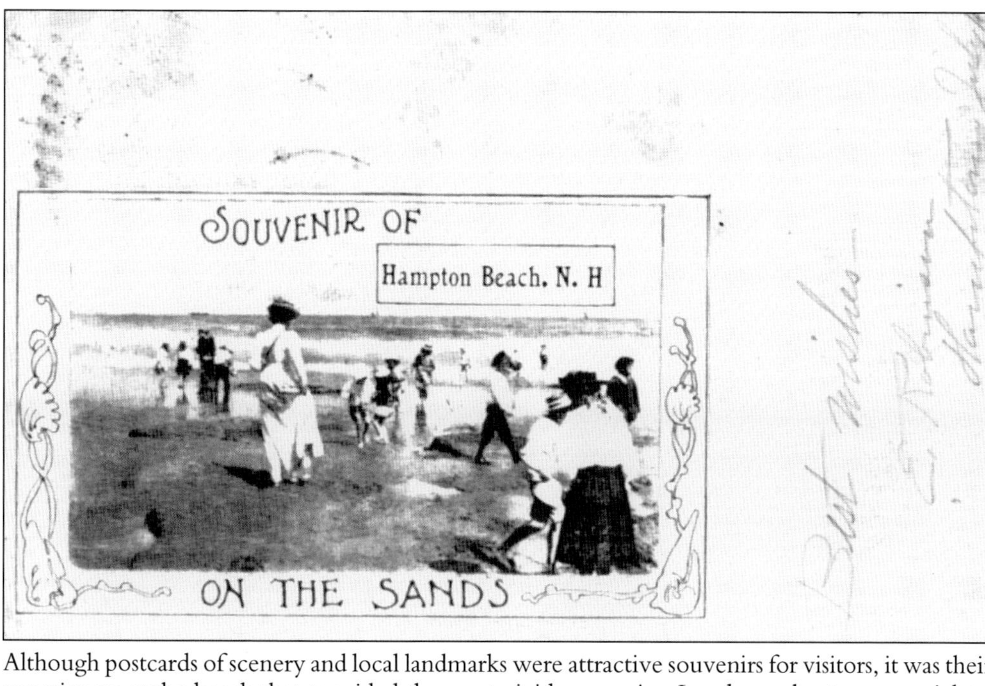

Although postcards of scenery and local landmarks were attractive souvenirs for visitors, it was their experiences at the beach that provided the most vivid memories. Local merchants were quick to publish postcards of events or of tourists just enjoying the beach. In this 1905 card, visitors dressed in street clothes pick their way across the sands as they enjoy a stroll on the beach.

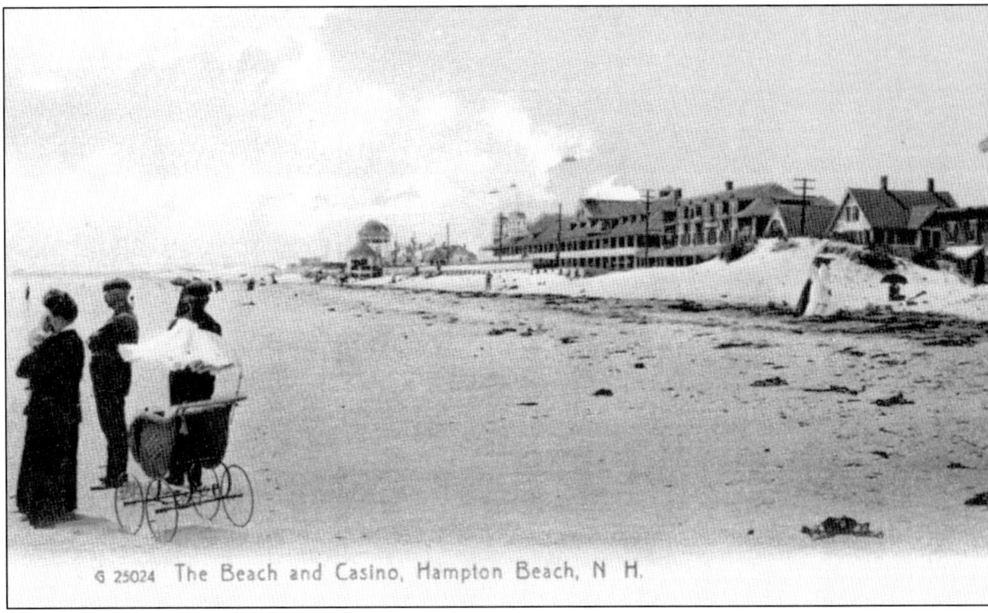

This postcard from the early 1900s shows the main beach at low tide, when the hard-packed sand allowed baby carriages to be pushed along easily as the adults savored the salt air. The Casino and the bandstand may be seen in the distance beyond the sand dune.

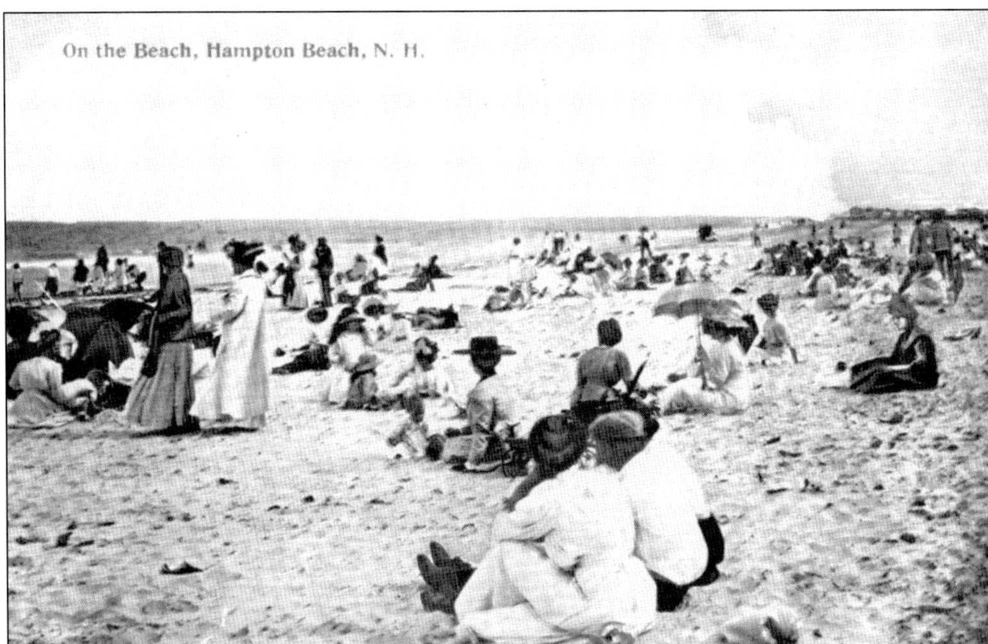

Early-20th-century beachgoers were careful to keep themselves well covered with large hats, coats, and long skirts. Note the lack of any beach equipment, such as chairs, large beach umbrellas, or even blankets. Regular rain umbrellas are being used to ward off the sun.

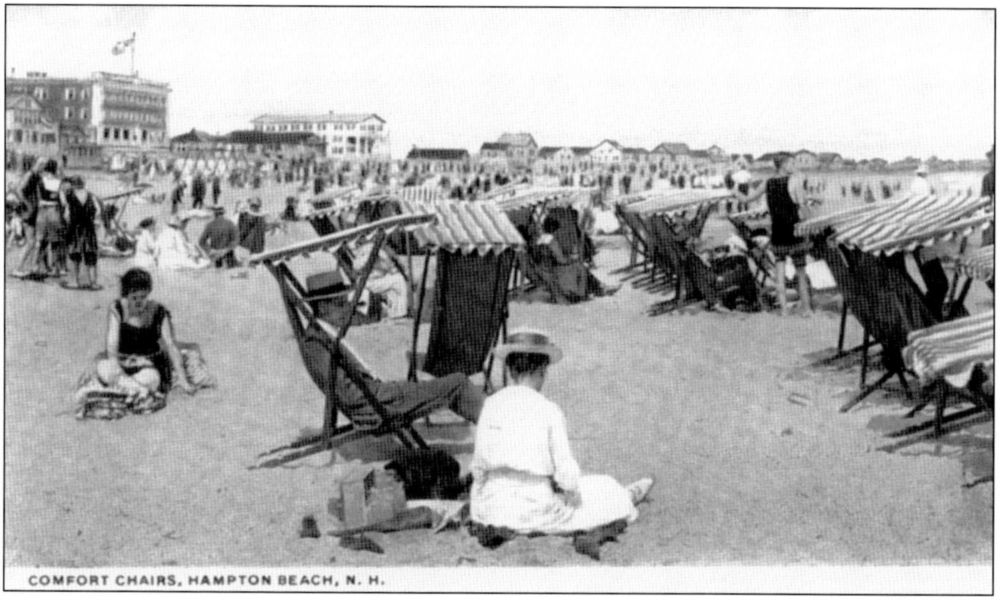

Local businessmen realized that the rental of beach chairs could be good business, and the chairs were immediately popular, as this *c.* 1920 card illustrates. The awning over the top of the chair kept the sun off, and, properly situated, served as a windbreak. Robert Ring, who owned a popcorn stand on the beach, rented chairs like these. The large hotel in the background is the Janvrin, and the Ashworth is on the right.

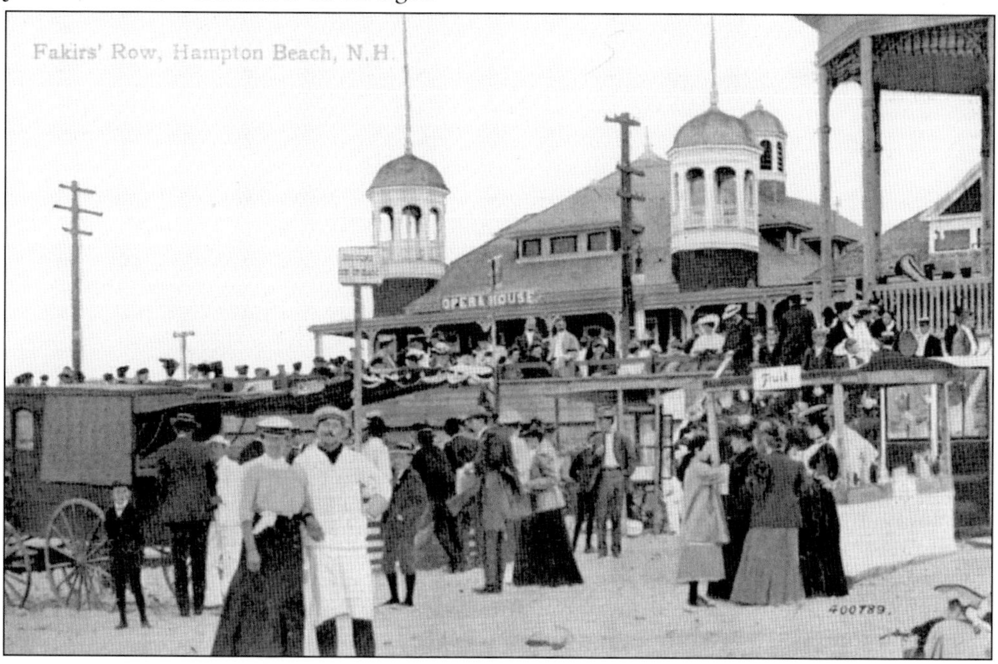

It was not only the resident businessmen who sought to make a profit from beach visitors. Peddlers obtained licenses from the town to set up stands right on the sands to sell food and souvenirs. The beach across from the Casino was particularly popular with these merchants. Fakir's Row, as the area came to be called, was a lucrative place of business for nearly 30 years. When the state assumed ownership of the beach in the 1930s, the practice was ended.

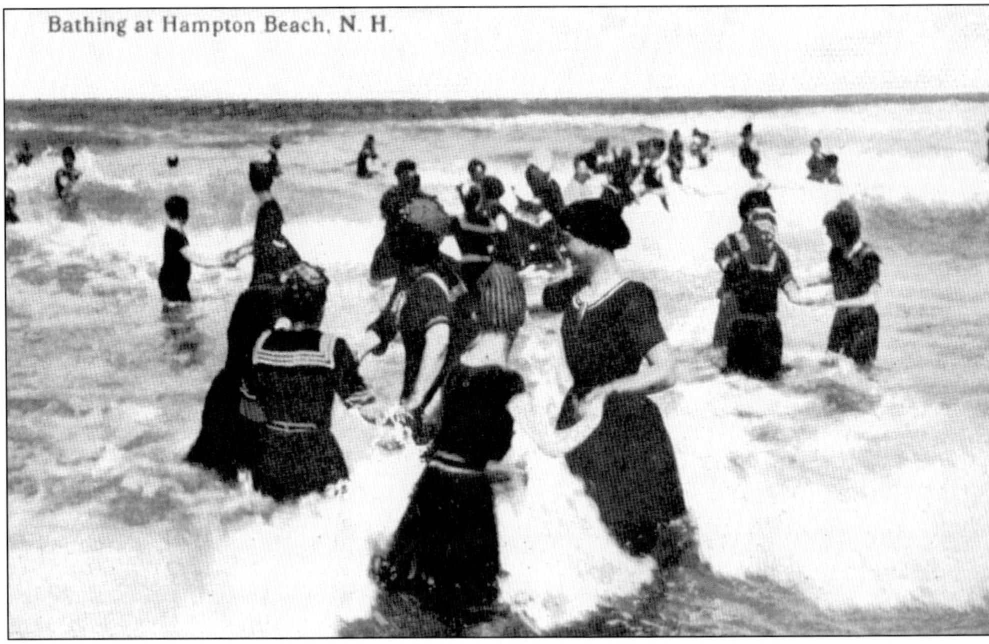

As swimming became a fashionable summer pastime, the question of women's bathing costumes caused lively debates among the town fathers. The idea of appointing someone to monitor the suits being worn on the beach was raised several times, but, other than stern warnings in the newspapers, nothing was ever done. Here, girls dressed in the latest style try out the surf in 1920.

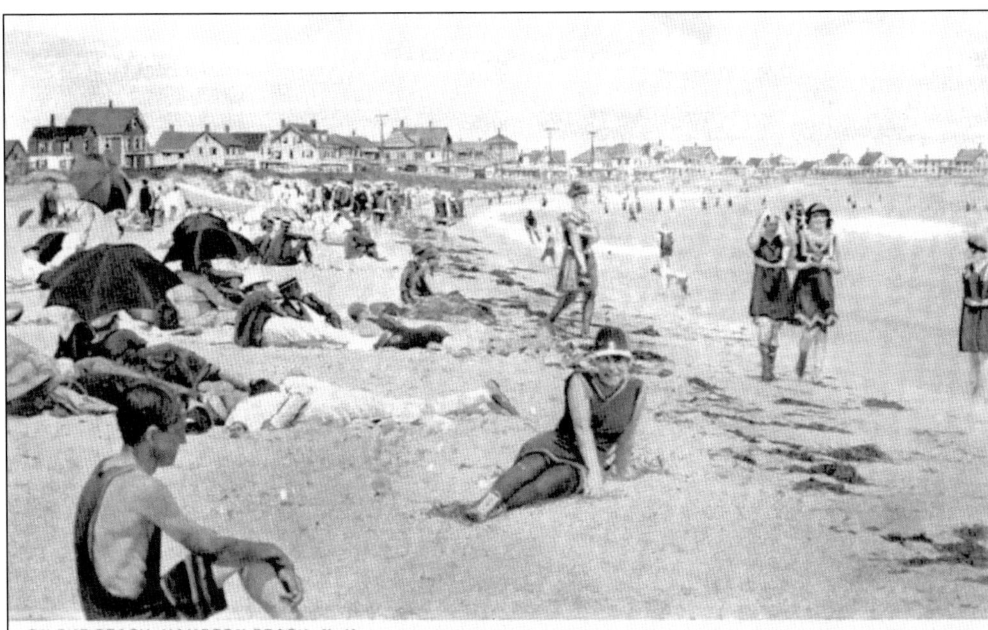

This view of the crowded beach near Church Street shows bathers in the 1920s. Note that the seated girl facing the camera is wearing the requisite dark stockings, while the girls at right have daringly shed their stockings and are bare-legged.

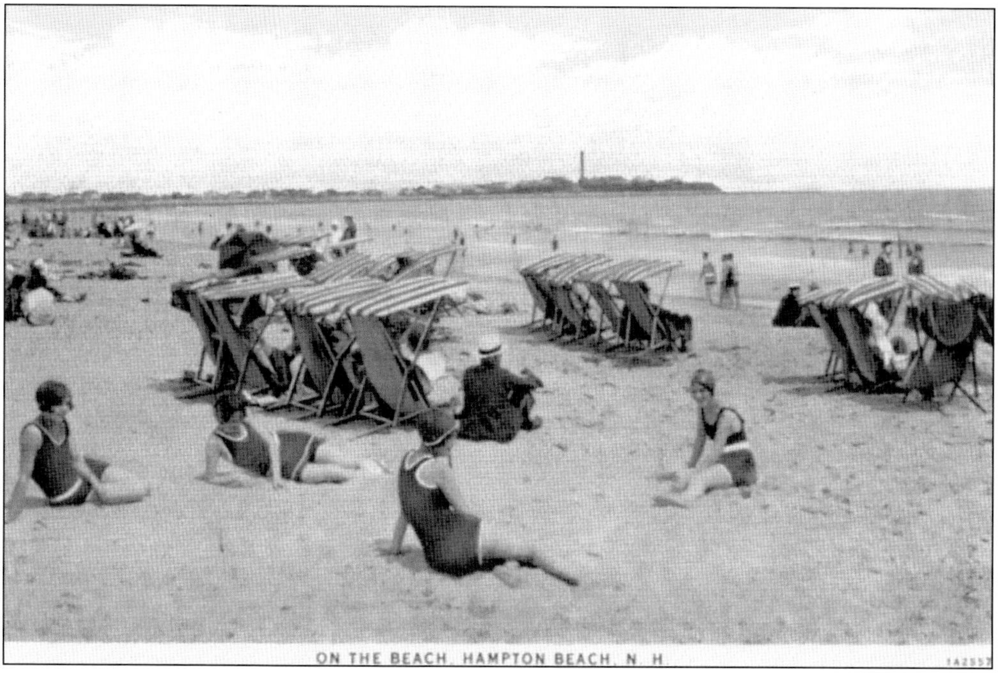

By the 1930s, women's bathing suits had become briefer and more revealing, as is illustrated by the four young women posing in the foreground. In the background is Great Boar's Head.

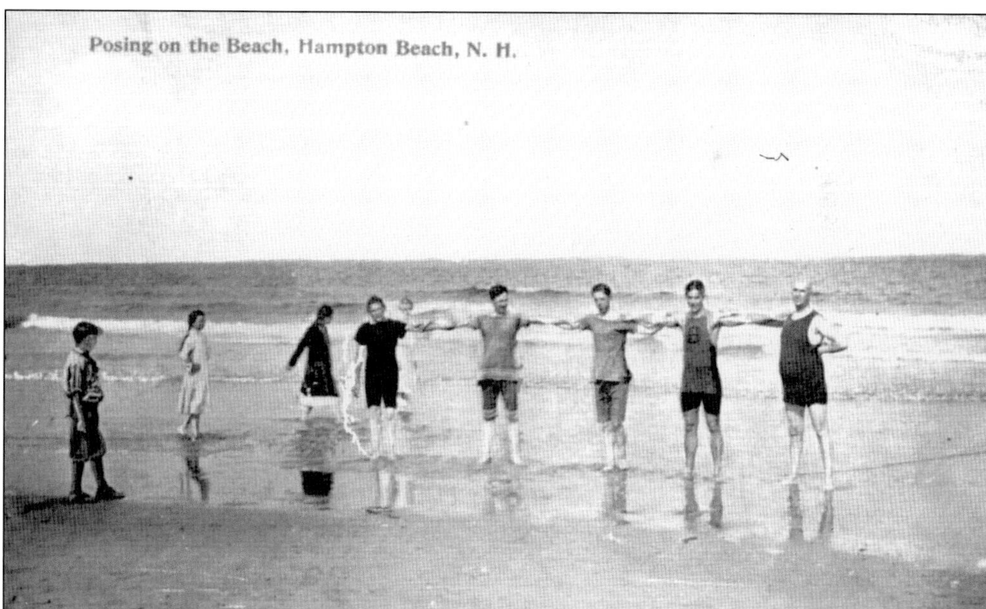

Women were not the only ones to show off at the beach. On this *c.* 1930 card, five men pose for the photographer. Note the boy in the cap and plus-fours at the left watching their antics.

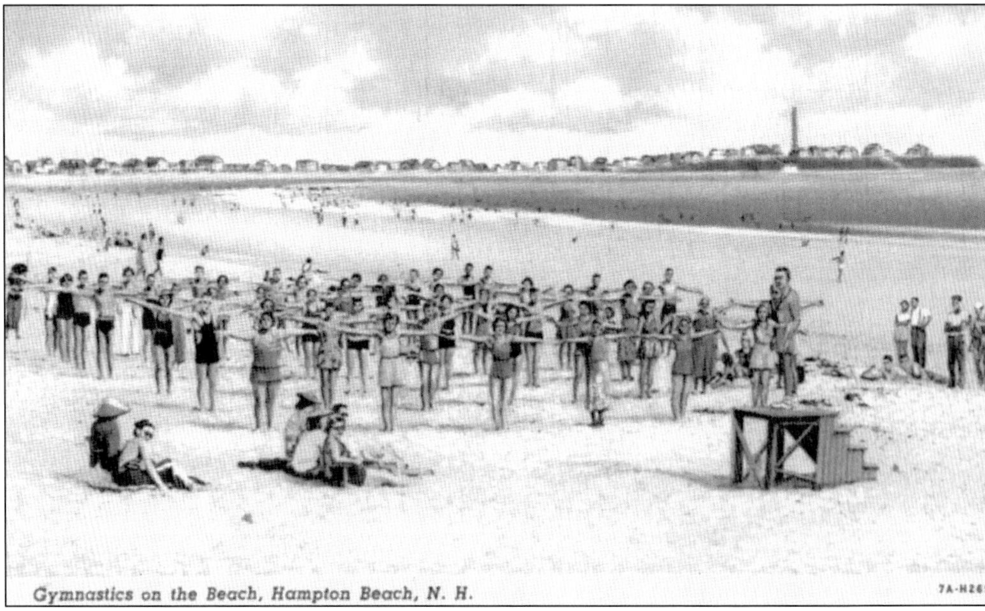

Dr. Earl Lorenz, an osteopath, conducted daily sessions of calisthenics on the beach. Attendance at his sessions averaged 200, with some classes having over 400 participants. He also ran classes of "reducing exercises" for those "careless about their calories." In 1936, he sponsored a posture contest in which the competitors were to wear masks to prevent the judges being influenced by a pretty face.

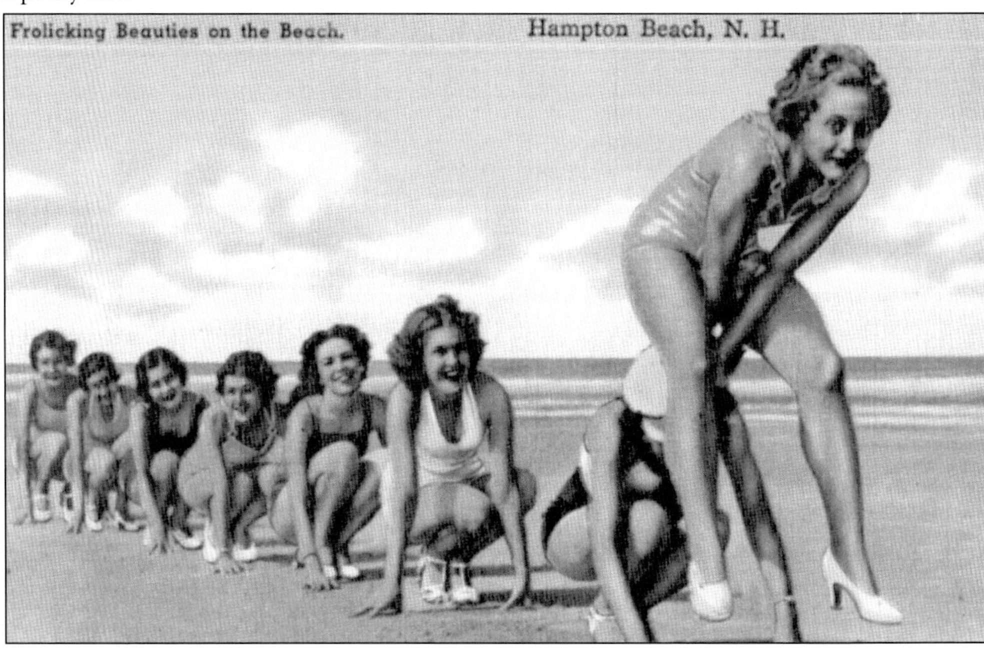

"Beauties on the Beach" remained an enduring theme, as this postcard from the mid-1940s illustrates. In 1946, John Dineen, owner of the Casino, capitalized on this interest by persuading the chamber of commerce to start the Miss Hampton Beach competition, based on the successful Miss America pageant of Atlantic City. With some changes, the contest has been held nearly every year since then.

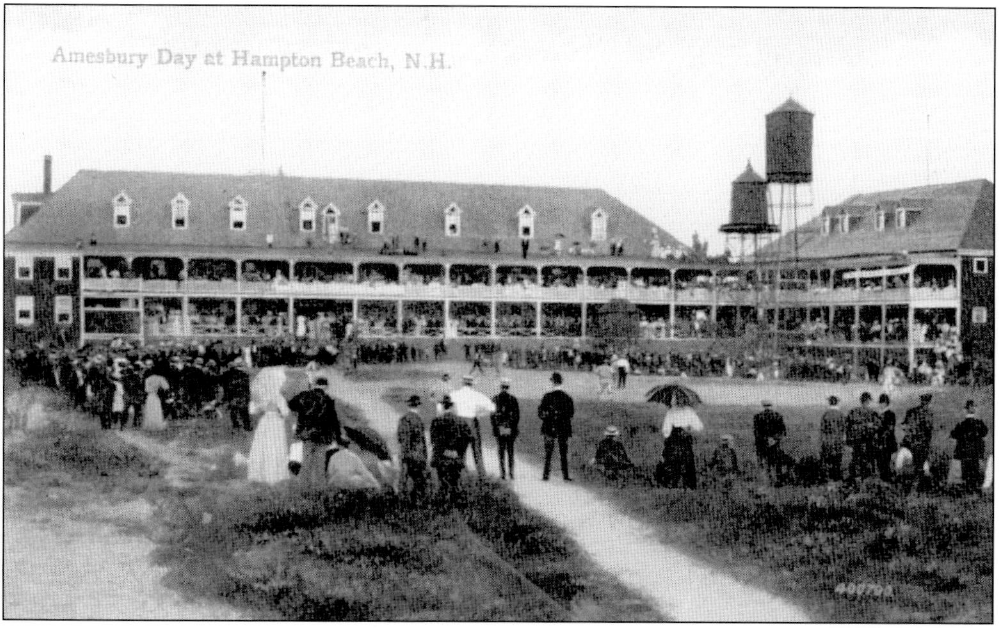

The Exeter, Hampton, and Amesbury Street Railway sponsored special days at Hampton Beach in order to encourage riders to spend the day. "Amesbury Day" was intended to draw visitors from that city in Massachusetts. On this *c.* 1905 postcard, a baseball game, probably between summer beach residents and Amesbury men, is being played on the sports field behind the Casino. Note the piazzas crowded with spectators.

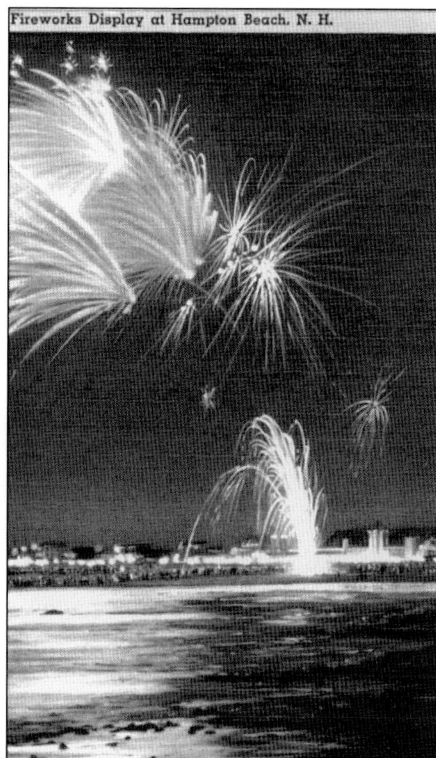

Fireworks have been part of the beach's summer season for nearly 90 years. The idea of providing a regularly scheduled show originated with local merchants, who were trying to lure customers away from the attractions in the Casino. Joseph Dudley and John White helped to put on the first fireworks display, hoping to encourage people to come into their store afterwards. By the 1920s, shows were being held three times a week, but it later became customary to have a display once a week on Wednesday night. Today the Wednesday tradition continues.

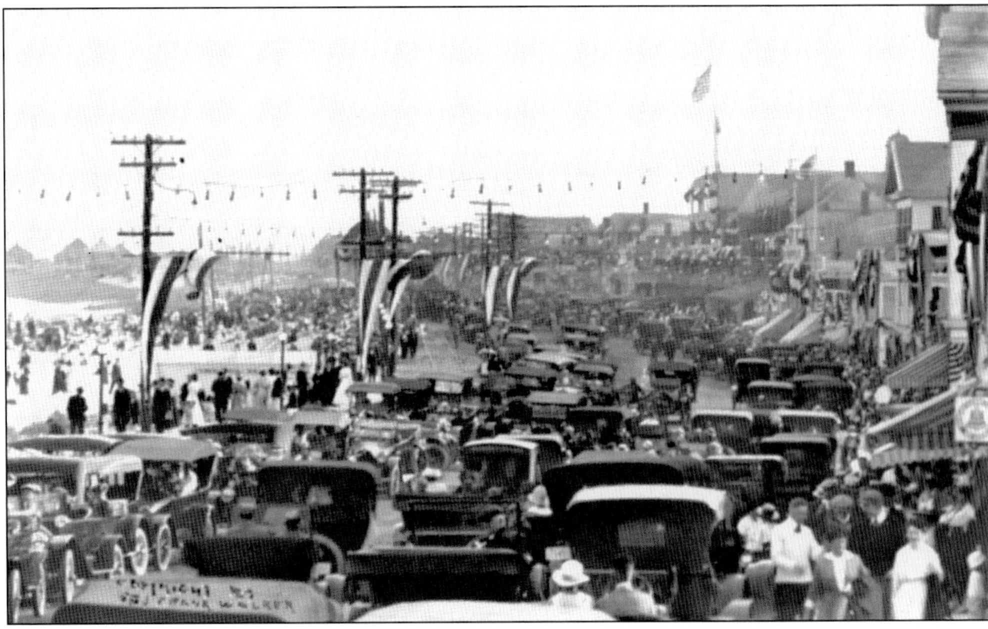

In 1915, in an attempt to extend the "beach season" past the end of August, a group of businessmen proposed a Carnival Week to be held in early September. During the week there were concerts, competitions, fireworks, and parades. All the buildings on the beachfront were gaily decorated with lights. The first carnival was a great success, and thousands flocked to the beach, creating huge traffic jams, as we can see on this card of the occasion produced by photographer Frank Walker.

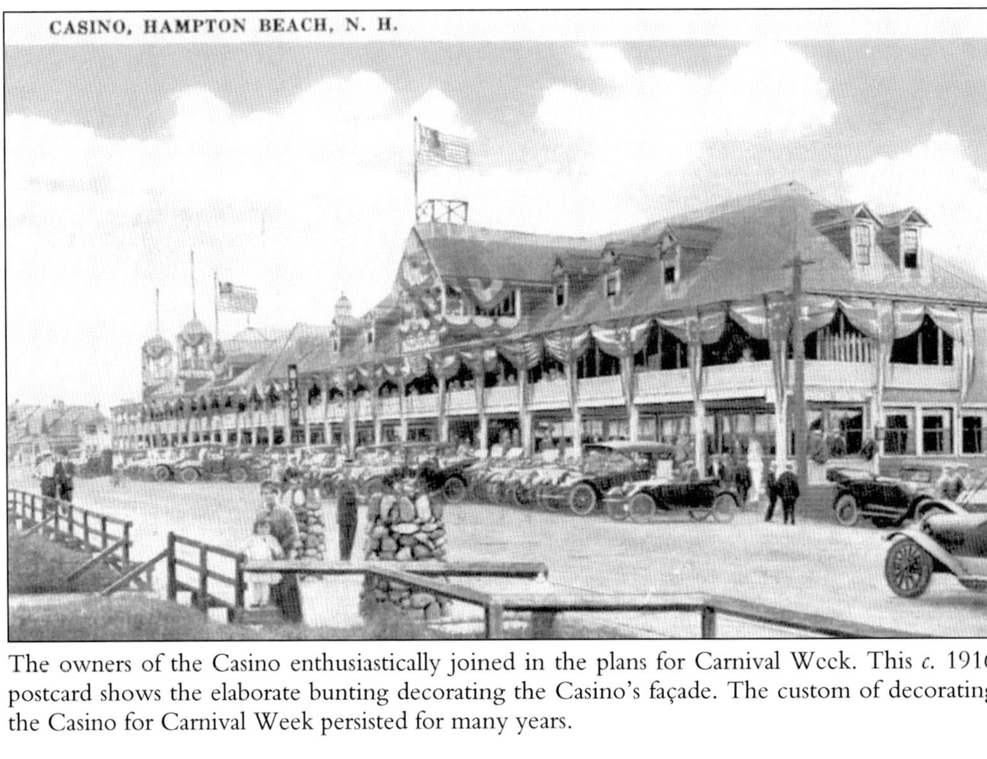

The owners of the Casino enthusiastically joined in the plans for Carnival Week. This *c.* 1916 postcard shows the elaborate bunting decorating the Casino's façade. The custom of decorating the Casino for Carnival Week persisted for many years.

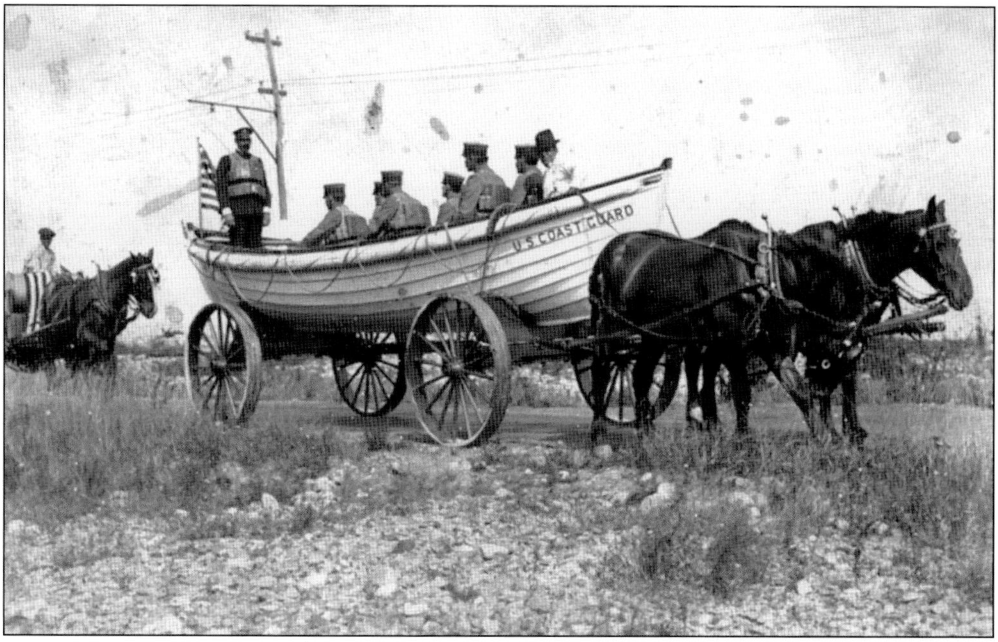

Parades were an essential feature of Carnival Week, and many institutions in town joined in. The lifesaving station, by now a part of the Coast Guard, participated in the 1916 parade by turning its lifeboat into a float.

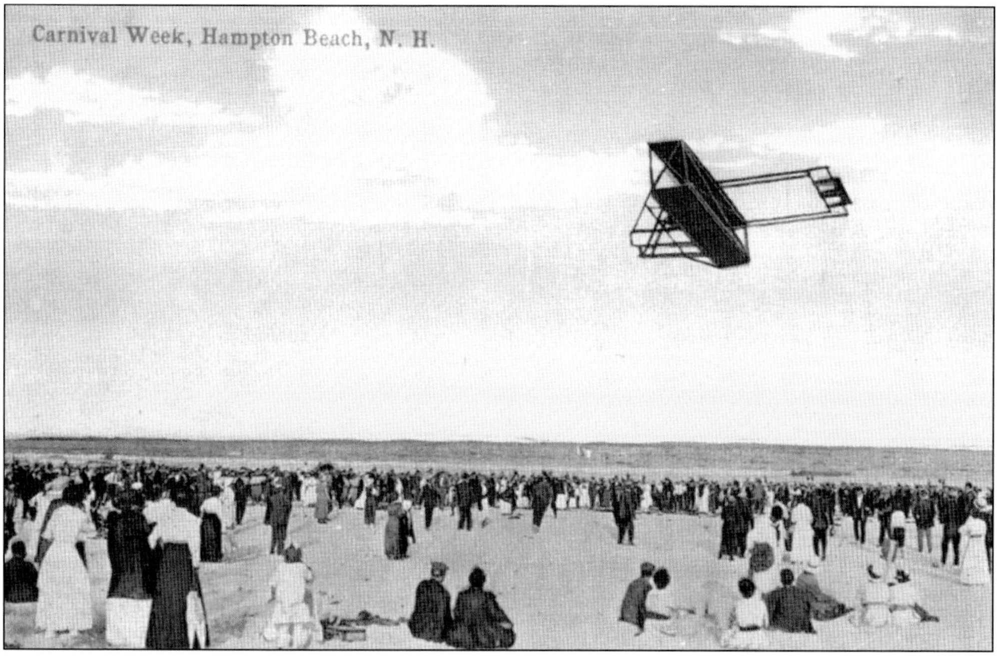

Airplane rides and aerial stunts were also part of early Carnival Week festivities. Here a biplane flies low over crowds of spectators standing on the beach. The planes landed on the firm sand at low tide and picked up passengers for short rides.

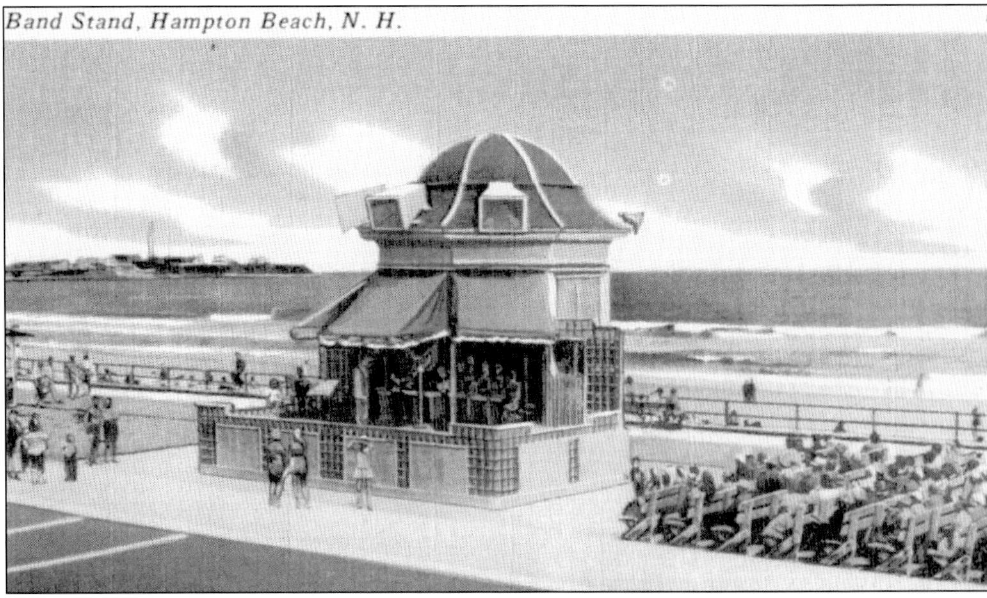

The bandstand remained a center of entertainment at the beach for decades. In the 1930s, awnings were added to shade the musicians, and in the 1940s an amplification system was installed. Many bands played there, but a regular performer was Hal McDonnell and his band. Often appearing with this band was Hampton police officer Bill Elliott, who became well known as a singer. He was called the "singing cop," since he frequently appeared on the bandstand in uniform. Note that the bandstand is now enclosed on the beach side in an attempt to improve the sound projection.

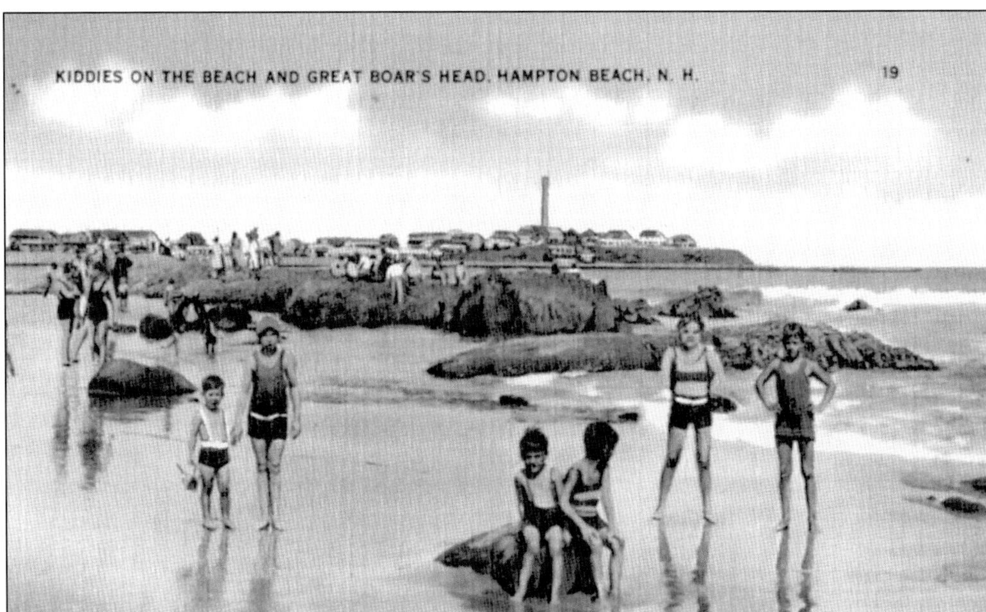

Hampton Beach has always advertised itself as vacation spot for families. To illustrate the fun available for families at the beach, postcards were published showing children playing on the sand. Here "kiddies" of the 1930s are shown on the rocks south of Great Boar's Head.

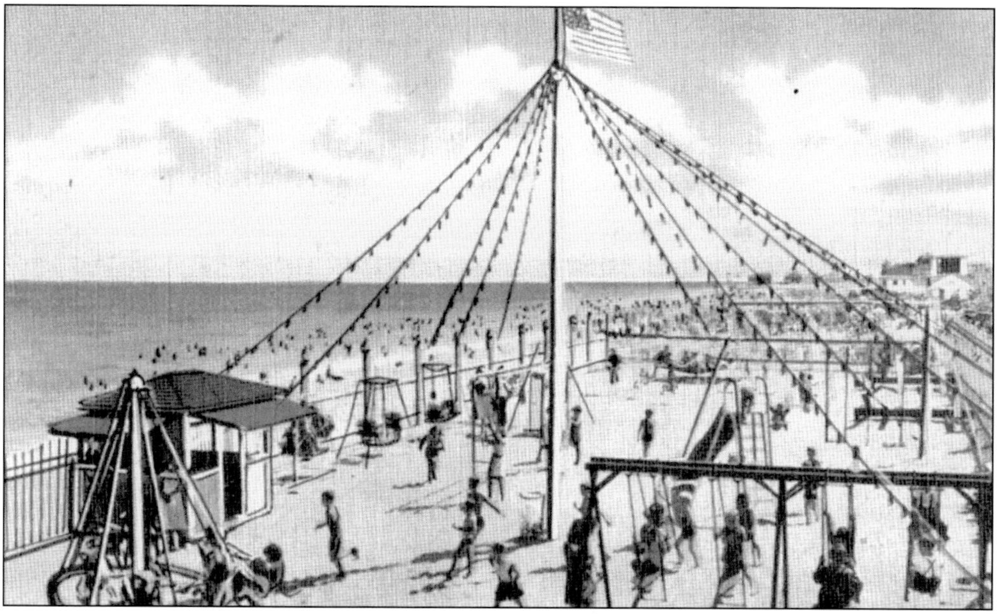

As early as 1917, a small playground had been built on the sand at the head of B Street. Its founder was John C. White, a partner in Dudley and White and a beach commissioner. After his death in 1927, the Beach Precinct voted to build a larger playground and name it in his honor. Despite damage from winter storms, the playground remained on that spot until 1954, when the construction of the sea wall prompted its relocation to its present site just south of the Casino.

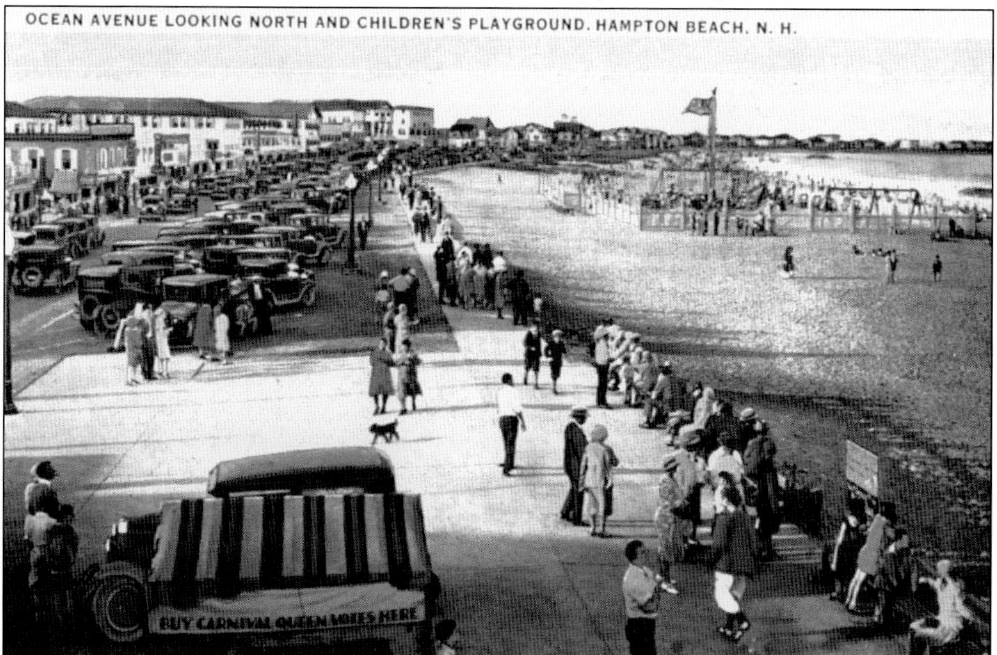

This *c.* 1930 postcard shows the playground at the right. In the foreground is a booth advertising the sale of votes for the queen of Carnival Week. Early carnival queens were chosen in various ways; at one point, the candidate who could sell the most raffle tickets would be named the winner. The contest for queen evolved into the Miss Hampton Beach competition that is familiar today.

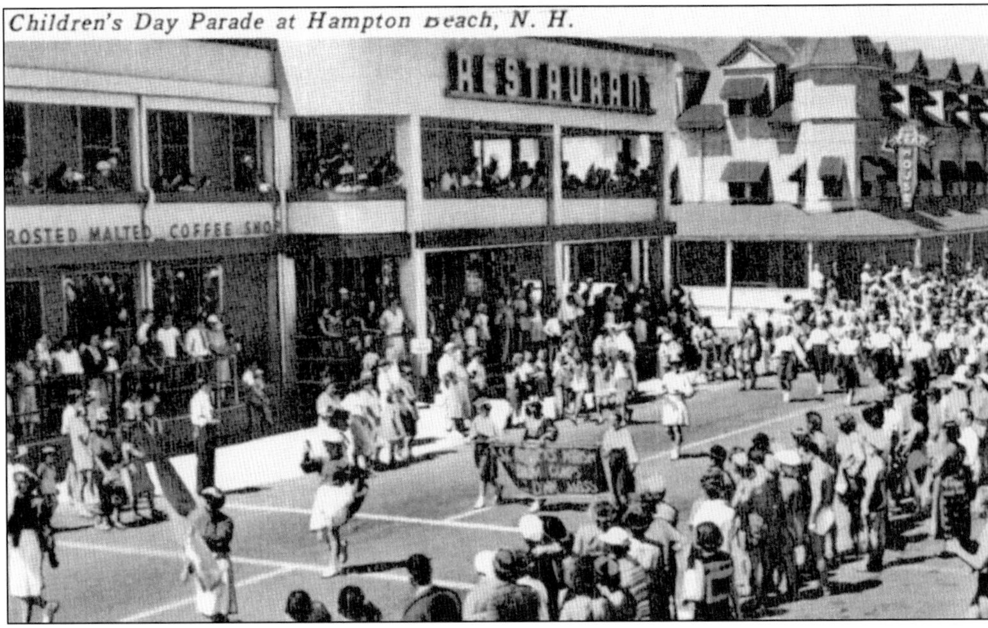

Children's Day has been an institution at Hampton Beach since at least the 1920s, when George Ashworth, owner of the Ashworth Hotel and a precinct commissioner, established the event. A great supporter of children's activities, Ashworth oversaw Children's Day, the playground, and the Boy Scout camporees held yearly at the beach. This postcard shows a Children's Day parade passing the Casino in the late 1940s.

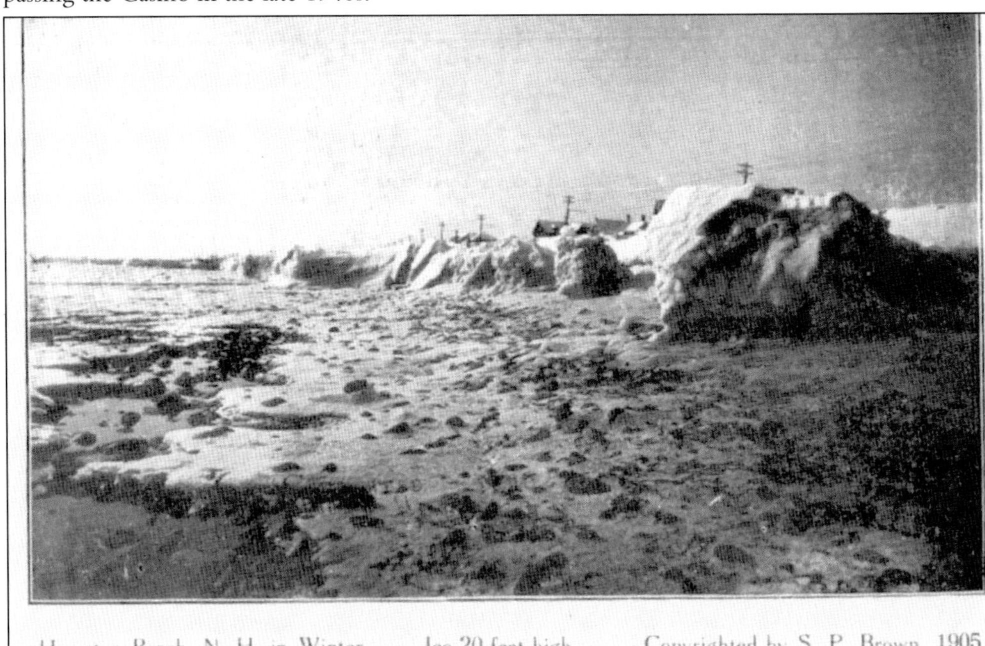

Hampton Beach has always been considered a summer resort, but a few hotels stayed open in the winter. Despite the small number of winter visitors, there was some interest in wintry beach scenes. The winter of 1905 was particularly severe, and several postcards were produced to show the ice and snow on the beach. This card shows the 20-foot drifts on the beach south of Boar's Head.

Five

Hampton Harbor and River

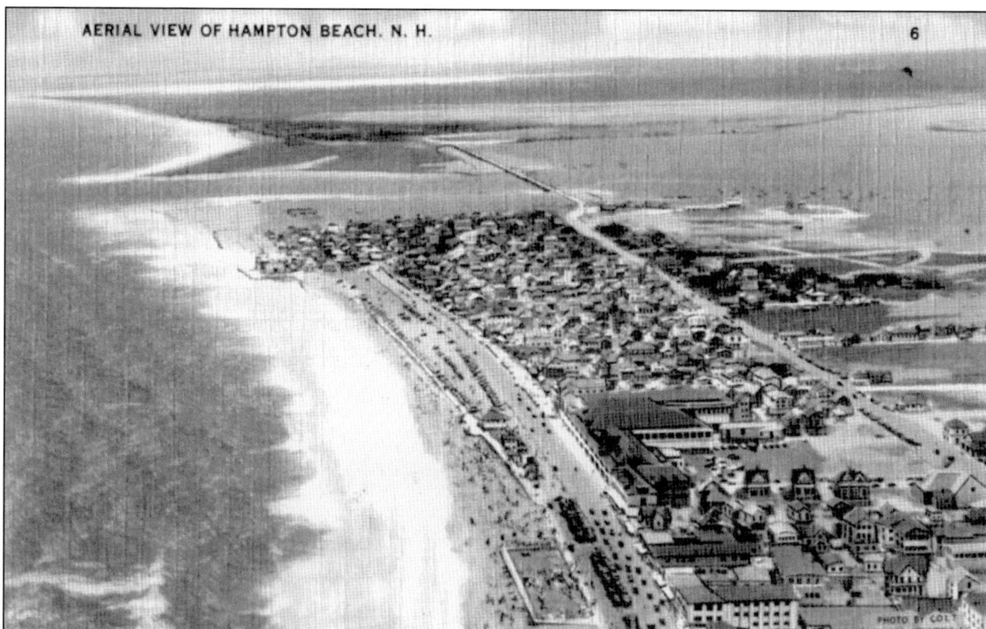

This *c.* 1940 postcard shows the south end of the beach at the mouth of the Hampton River. The large sandy area at the river's edge is filled land behind a granite jetty. This new land, on which is now located the Hampton Beach State Park, was created by the state in 1935 in an attempt to stabilize the constantly shifting channel in the harbor. At the top right is the wooden bridge that linked the north and south sides of the harbor. The photograph was taken by Hampton resident David Colt, who specialized in aerial photography.

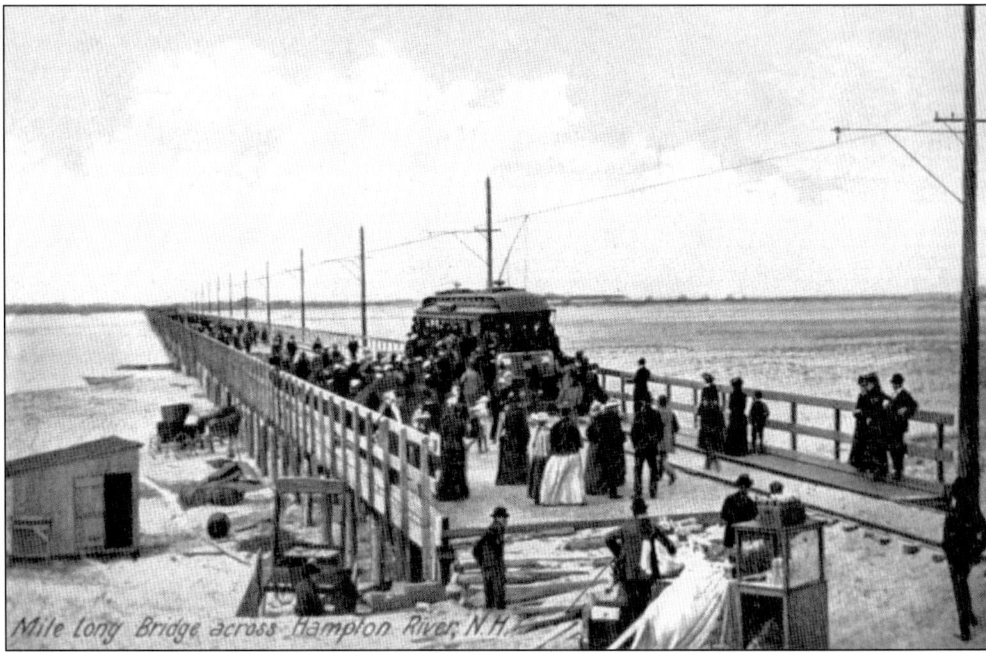

In 1901, the Exeter, Hampton, and Amesbury Street Railway began the construction of a bridge across the mouth of the Hampton River to Seabrook in order to expand its trolley network. Stretching nearly a mile, it was the longest wooden bridge in the world. In this image, the road approaching the bridge is still unfinished, but trolleys and pedestrians have already started to use the bridge.

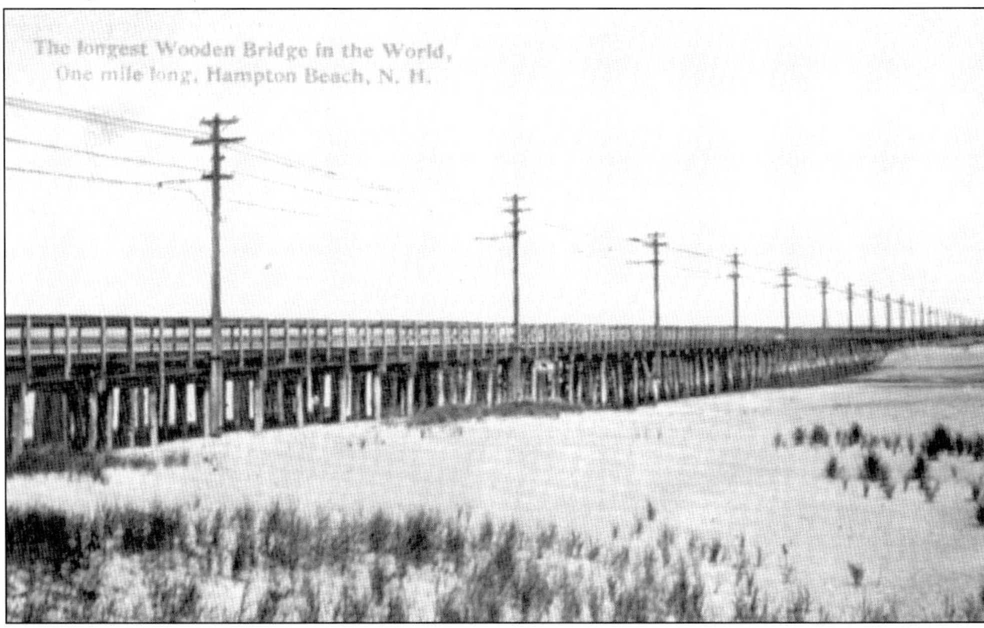

The bridge, known popularly as the "mile-long bridge" although it had no official name, was considered to be an amazing feat of engineering. The 5,270 oak pilings were shipped by rail to Portsmouth and then sent by raft to Hampton. Three of these rafts were destroyed in a fierce storm, and debris from them washed up on beaches from Hampton to Portland, Maine.

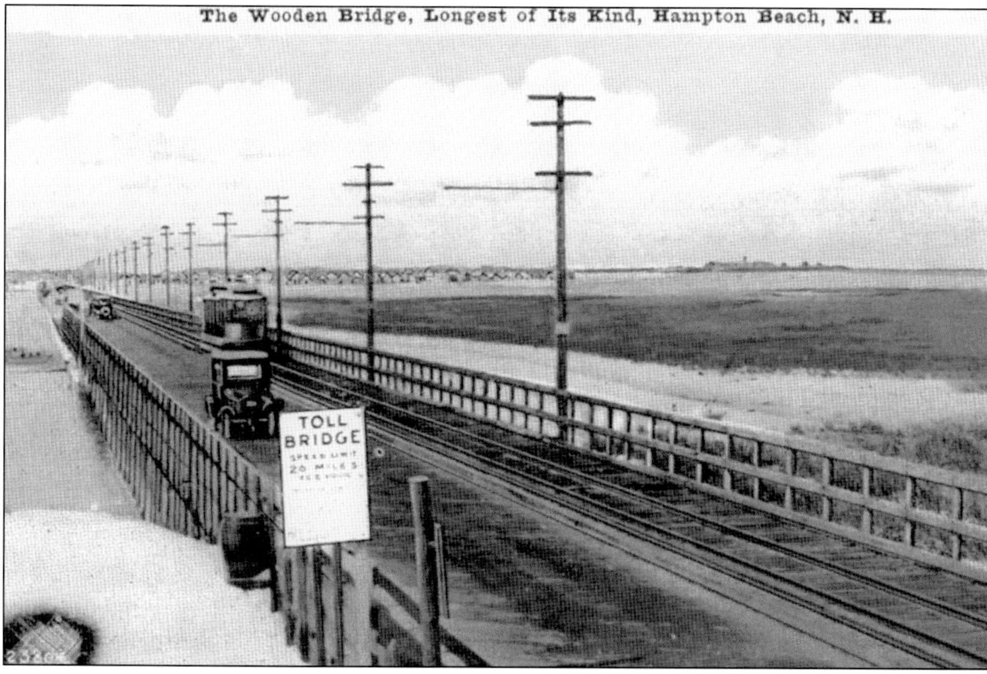

Trolley tracks ran on the western side of the bridge, while cars and pedestrians took to the other side. As the sign indicates, this was a toll bridge, with fees ranging from 1¢ to 10¢. In 1902, automobiles were charged 5¢, while sheep and swine cost 1¢ each.

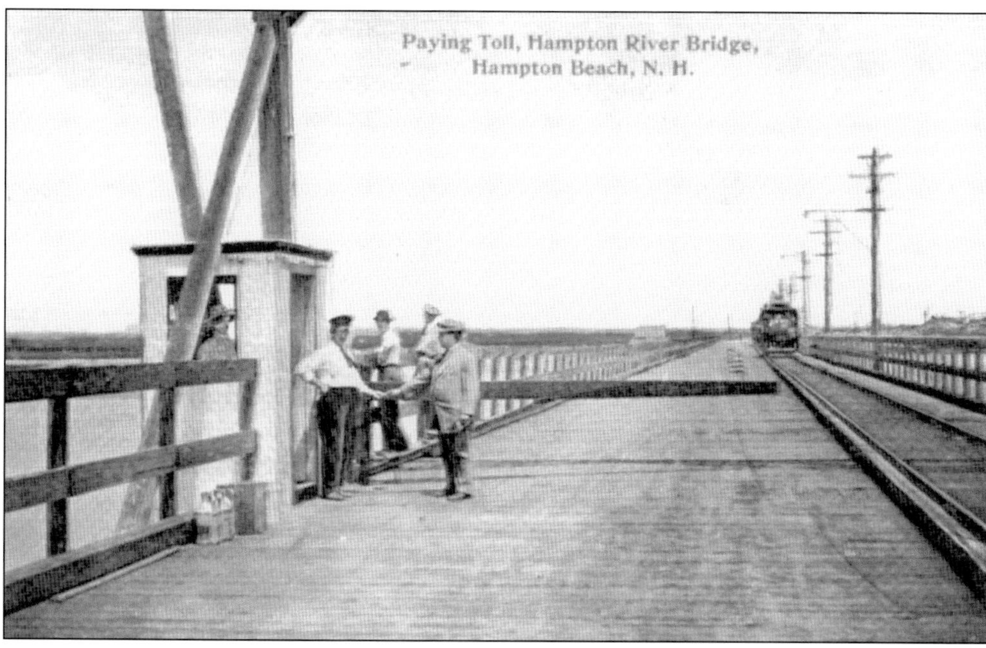

Even pedestrians paid a toll to walk across the bridge. The tollbooth was in the center of the span, where the bridge crew could also operate the drawbridge. The superstructure for the draw can be seen next to the tollbooth.

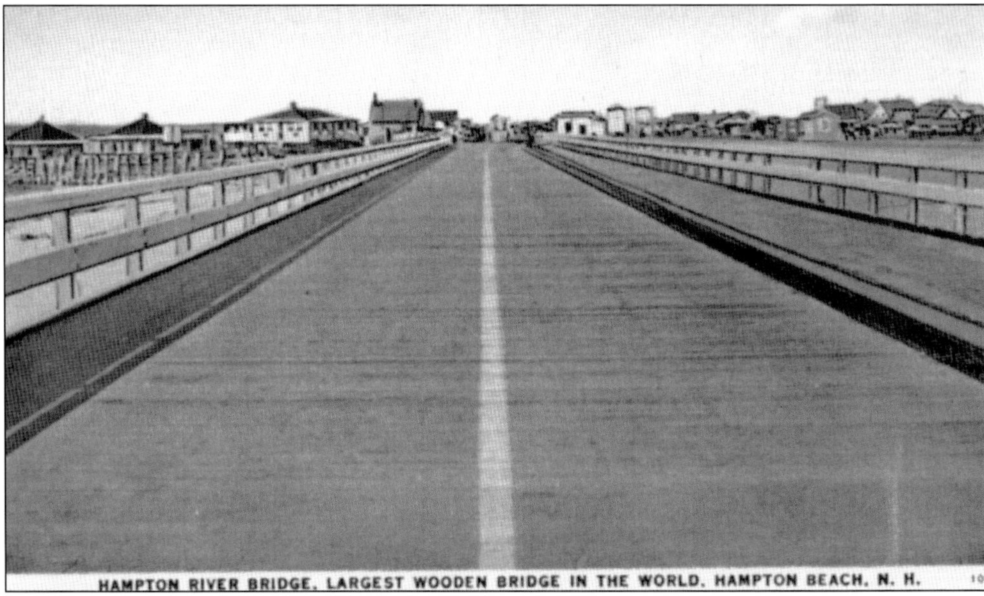

By the 1930s, when this card was published, the bridge, still privately owned, was showing unmistakable signs of deterioration. The shifting sands of the riverbed threatened its stability, and the wooden deck was prone to catching fire. The state finally acquired the bridge in 1933, but it was 16 years before a new bridge was built. This photograph was taken from the center of the bridge, looking back at Hampton Beach.

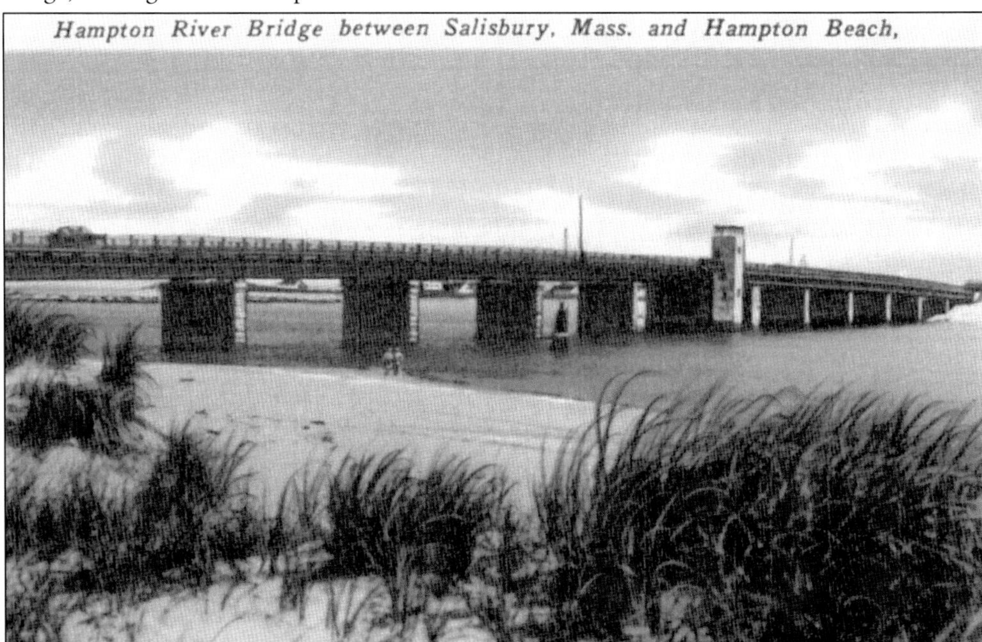

This *c.* 1950 postcard erroneously claims that the bridge connects Salisbury and Hampton. In fact, both ends of the bridge are within the town limits of Hampton, and Seabrook is the next town to the south. This crossing, built just east of the old bridge, opened in 1949. It was dedicated in honor of a Hampton man, Neil Underwood, who lost his life in World War II. Like the old bridge, it charged a toll, but this practice ended in 1964.

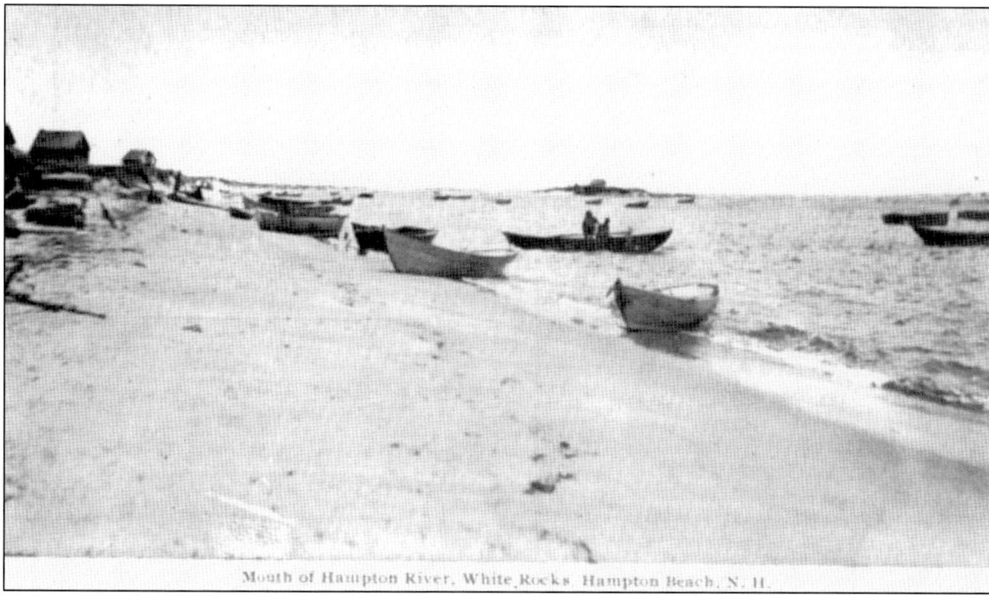

The mouth of the Hampton River was notorious for its constantly shifting channel, so few ships of any size attempted to navigate it. A late-18th-century order for a ship to be built in Hampton specified that it was to be delivered "outside the sand bar." White Rocks Island, seen here around 1910, was swallowed up by the Hampton River and no longer exists.

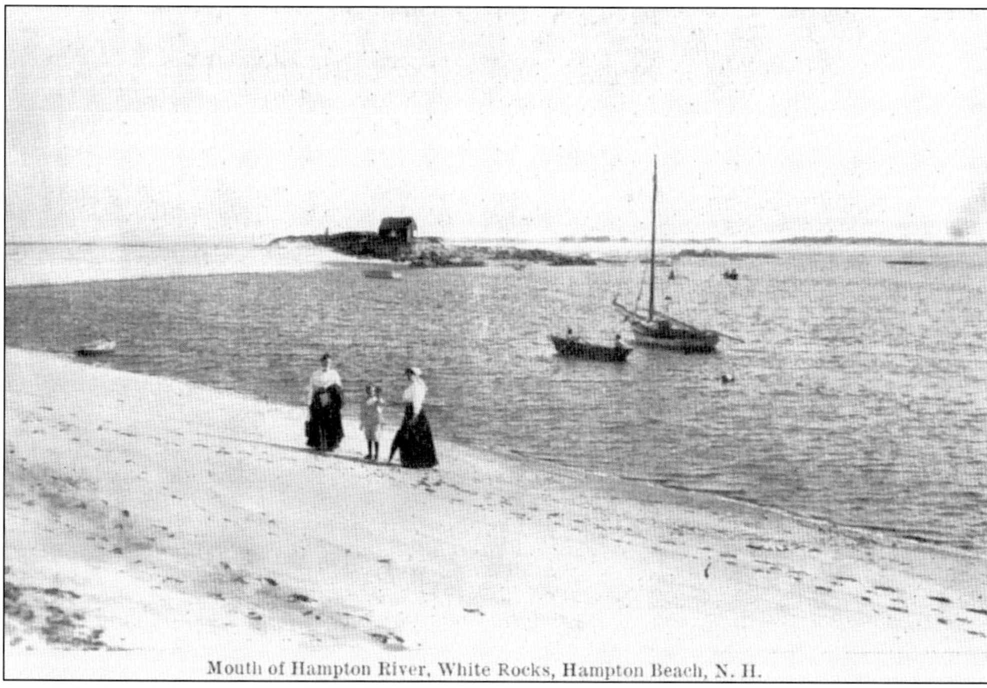

Until the beach began to be developed as a resort late in the 19th century, no one lived near the river's banks. Here in the distance is the first cottage at White Rocks, built by Frank Beckman at what was later called Beckman's Point. This *c.* 1900 image clearly shows that the channel ran south of the cottage, and a strip of beach attached White Rocks to the northern shore. Today, however, the strip of beach is gone, and Beckman's Point is on the south side of the river.

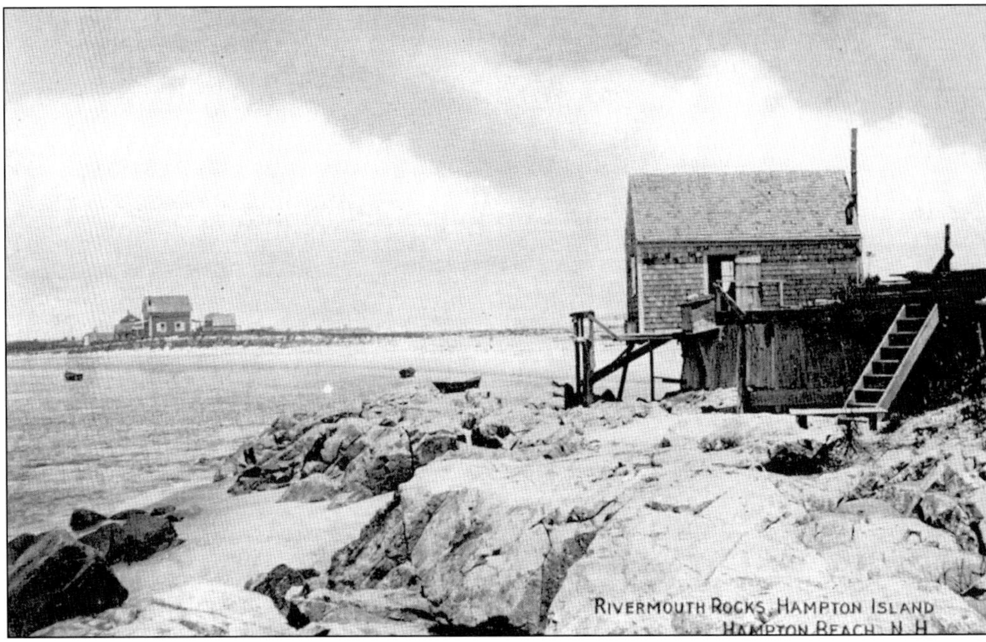

This view of Beckman's cottage, with White Rocks Island in the background, became a favorite subject for postcards. The first house in the area, it was also the last, clinging to the rocky ledge until it finally burned in 1935.

Fishermen used the sandy beach of White Rocks as a landing for their dories. Here a group of men proudly show their catch on the shore near the mile-long bridge. The writer of this card, perhaps inspired by the photograph, compliments the "comfortable place to stay" and the "fine eats" but complains that "it seems a long time between meals!"

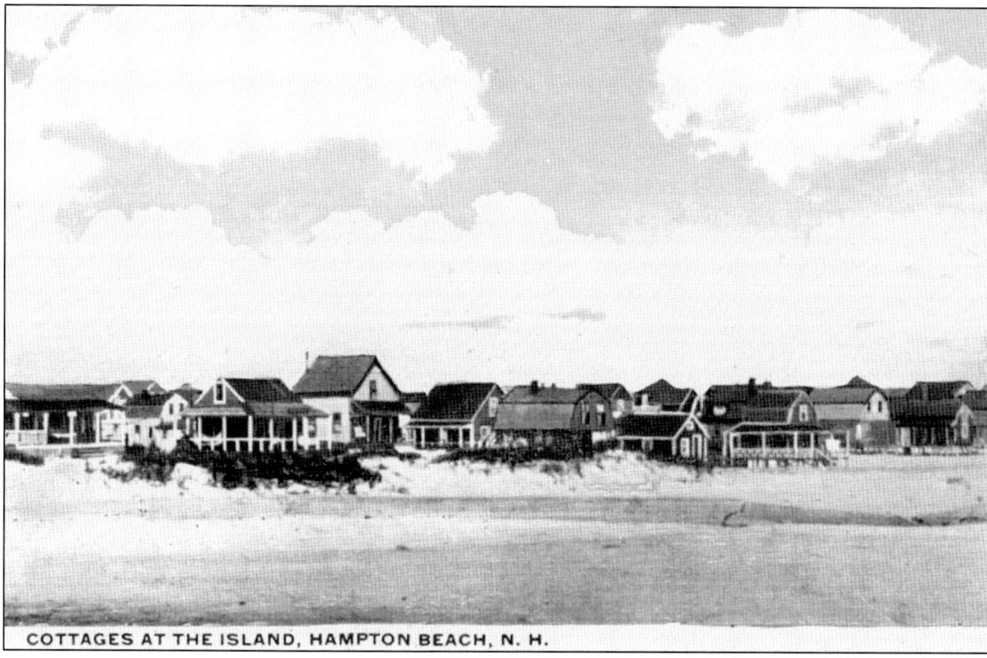

COTTAGES AT THE ISLAND, HAMPTON BEACH, N. H.

At one time there were more cottages on White Rocks Island than on any other section of the beach. The first house lots were leased by the town in 1908, and by 1910 taxes were being paid on 70 lots. Only a few years later, however, erosion from storms and the shifting of the river channel caused several lots to disappear under the water.

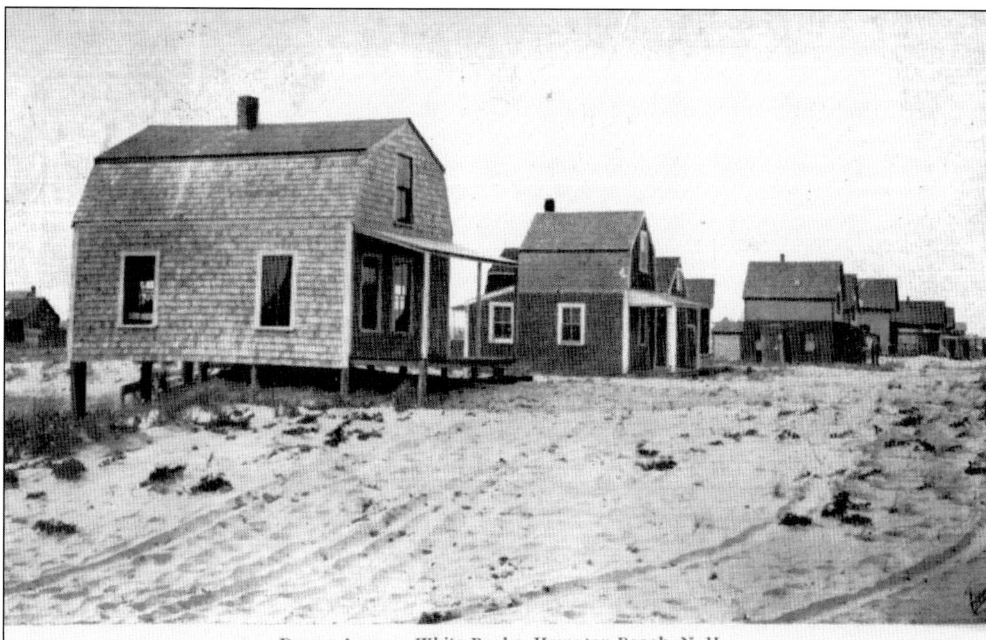

Dewey Avenue, White Rocks, Hampton Beach, N. H.

This *c.* 1915 view of White Rocks shows cottages on Dewey Avenue, a street that no longer exists. Homeowners either watched their houses wash away in fierce winter storms or moved them farther up the beach to more secure lots. Dewey Avenue and the streets around it were eventually washed out.

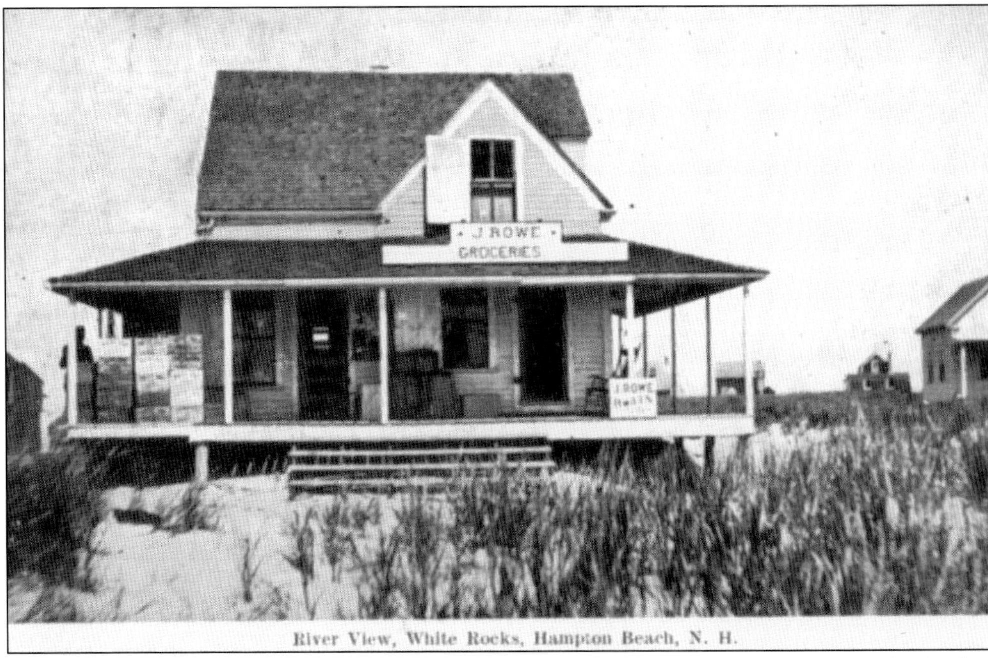

Jere Rowe was one businessman who saw the potential for a store on White Rocks Island when there were dozens of cottages there. However, he also fell victim to storm damage and erosion, and he moved his business to Dover Avenue. By 1928, only the ledge where Beckman's Cottage stood was still above water, and the rest of White Rocks Island had vanished under the river.

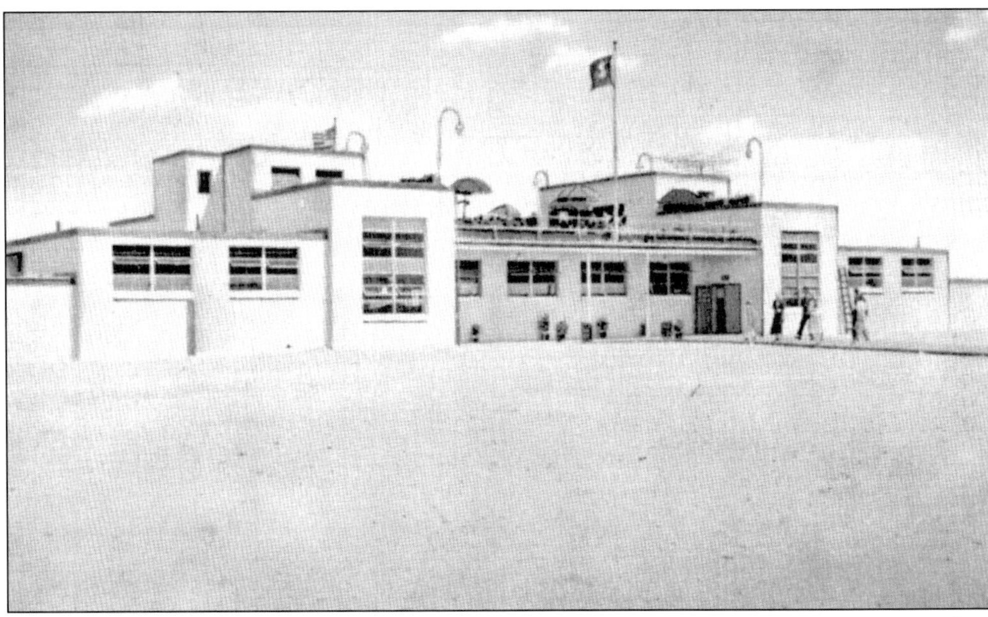

The ultramodern bathhouse of the Hampton Beach State Park was built in 1937 on new land created by pumping sand from the river bottom. Jetties of granite blocks were placed along the shore to prevent erosion. During the 1934 excavations for the north jetty, a workman found several gold and silver coins, prompting a mini gold rush and fueling rumors of a pirate shipwreck and buried treasure.

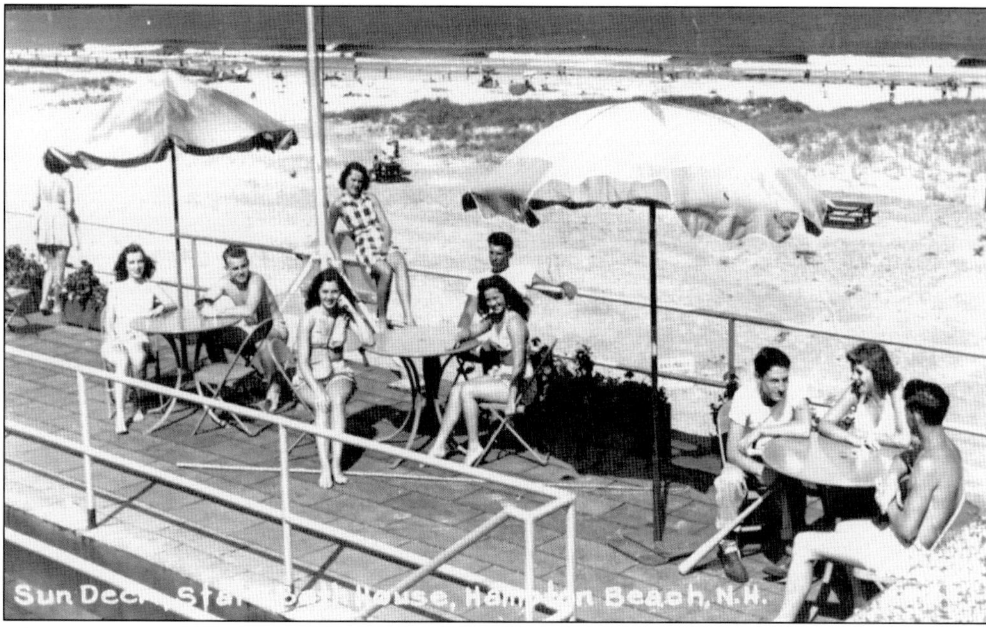
The sun deck of the state bathhouse was an observation platform and an open-air dining room for the snack bar. The bathhouse, with its 178 cubicles for changing, was considered outmoded by the late 1980s and was replaced by a smaller building in 1988.

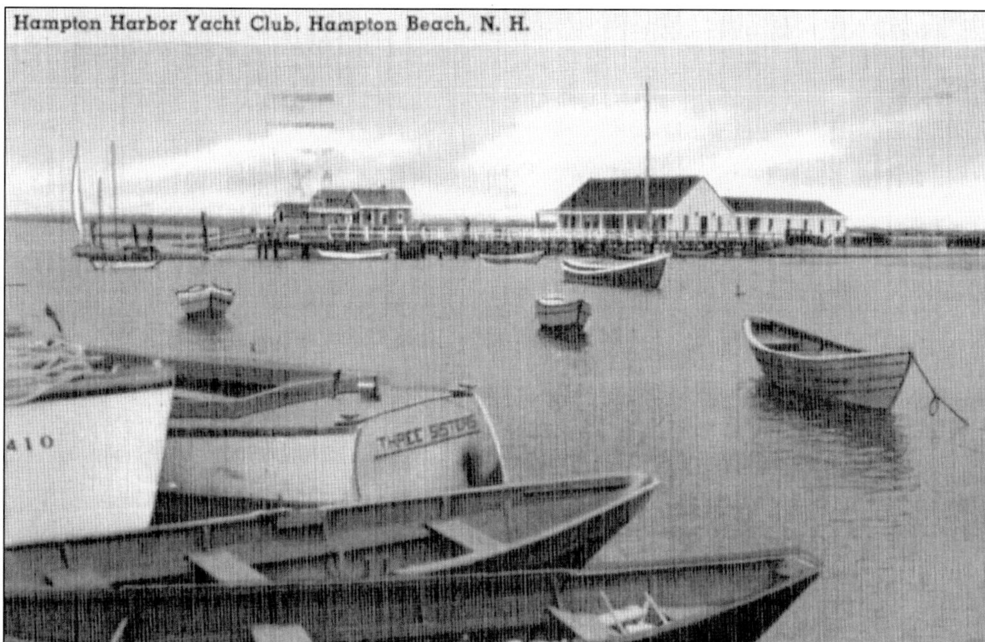

After the harbor was dredged in the 1930s, more space for recreational boat moorings became available. In 1935, the Hampton Harbor Yacht Club was founded, and the next year its clubhouse and pier opened just upriver from the mile-long bridge. The club moved farther upstream to a site off Landing Road when the increasing summer traffic at the beach became troublesome for the boat owners.

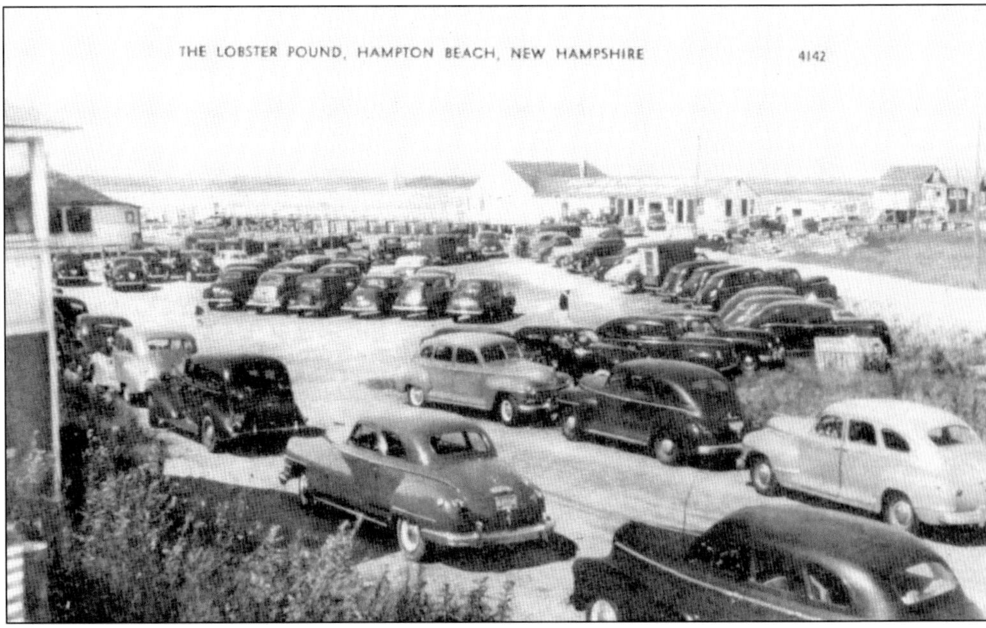

In 1949, the yacht club building and pier were sold to Smith and Gilmore, operators of fishing-party boats. The lobster pound at the rear of the building was rented to the New Hampshire Lobster Company, which not only sold lobsters here but also served as a shipping station for lobsters from both Maine and New Hampshire. Before refrigerated trucks were available, lobsters were held overnight in large underwater pens beneath the floor of the pound.

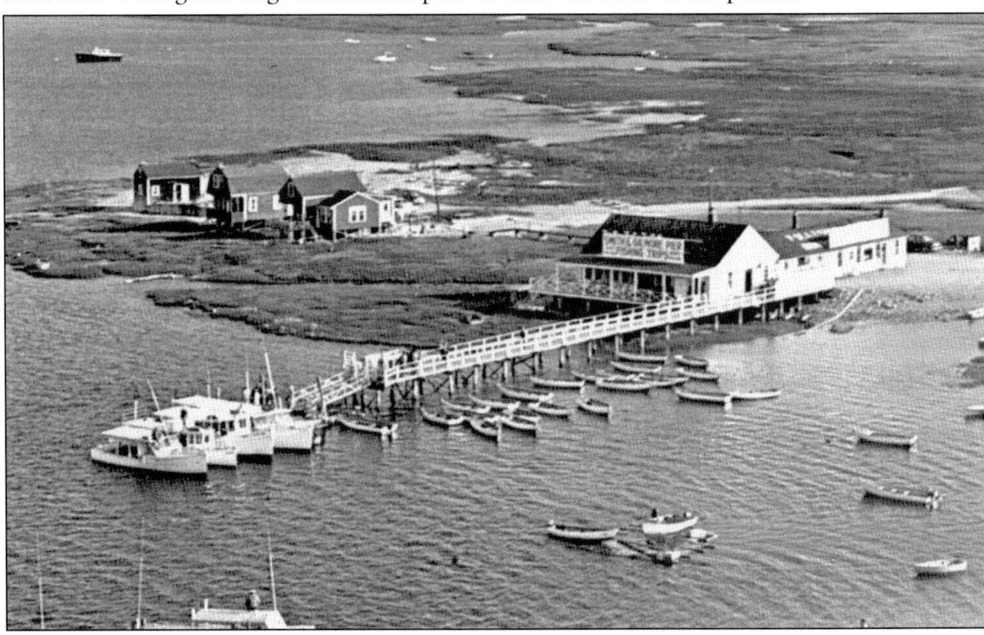

Claude and Helen Gilmore started their business in 1924 with one party boat. After Claude Gilmore's death in 1941, Helen Gilmore's father, Roy Smith, joined her in business. During World War II, a shortage of fuel forced the party boats to stay in the harbor, but the business rented rowboats instead. This *c.* 1950 image shows the party boats lined up at the pier, with the rowboats tied at the side.

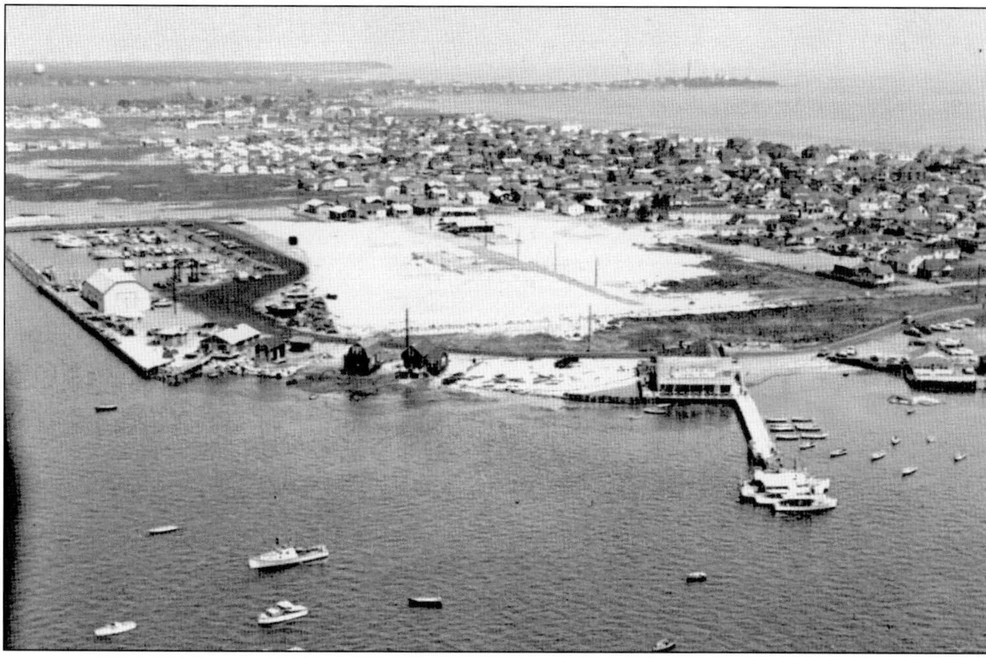

A postcard from the mid-1950s shows a panoramic view of Hampton Beach from the harbor. At the right, on the edge of the river, is the Smith and Gilmore pier, and at the left is the new Hampton Beach Marina established by Smith and Gilmore. The large sandy area in the center is filled land, a part of a marsh-reclamation project, and today houses and cottages cover the area. The reclamation of the marshes is no longer possible under current wetlands laws.

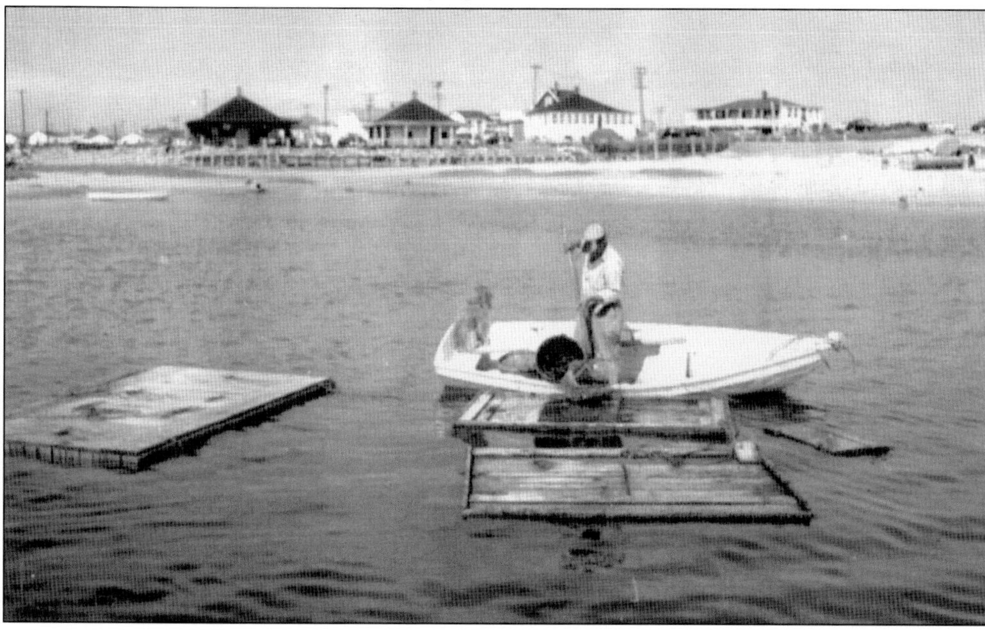

Lobstering has been an important fishing occupation in Hampton for over a century. Although some lobstermen used larger boats and set their traps offshore, in this *c.* 1955 view a man works from his skiff near the Underwood Bridge. He is loading his catch of lobsters into floating storage pens called lobster cars.

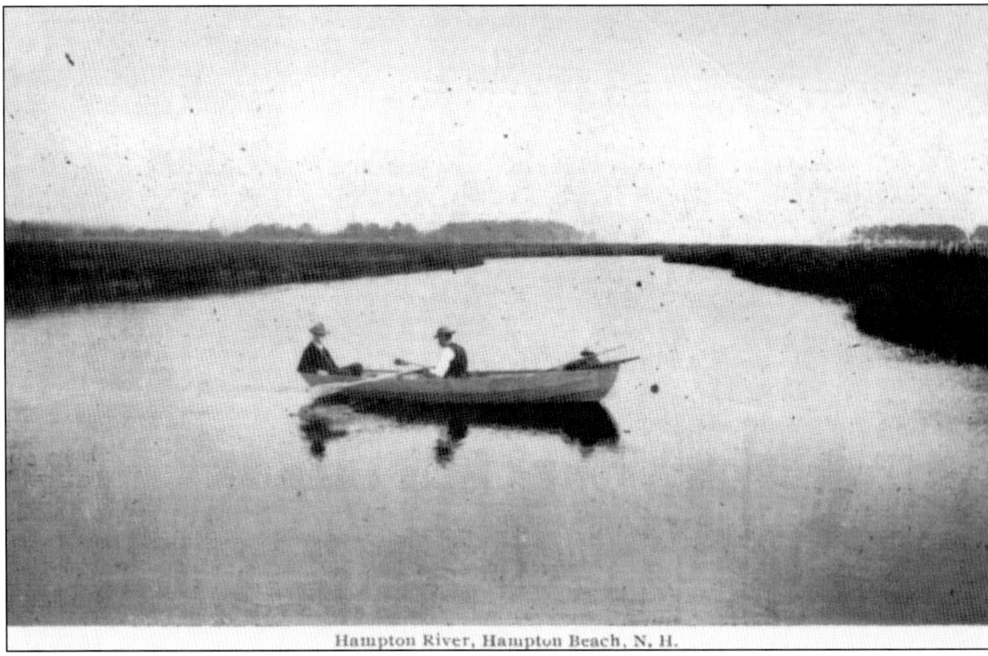

In the early 19th century, David Nudd maintained his office and warehouse up the river near Landing Road. Because the river turns and twists on its course through the marshes, in 1823 he and some other businessmen built a canal that cut across from one loop to another, eliminating some distance on the trip downriver to the harbor. On this card, two men are rowing across the canal. Hampton village is in the background.

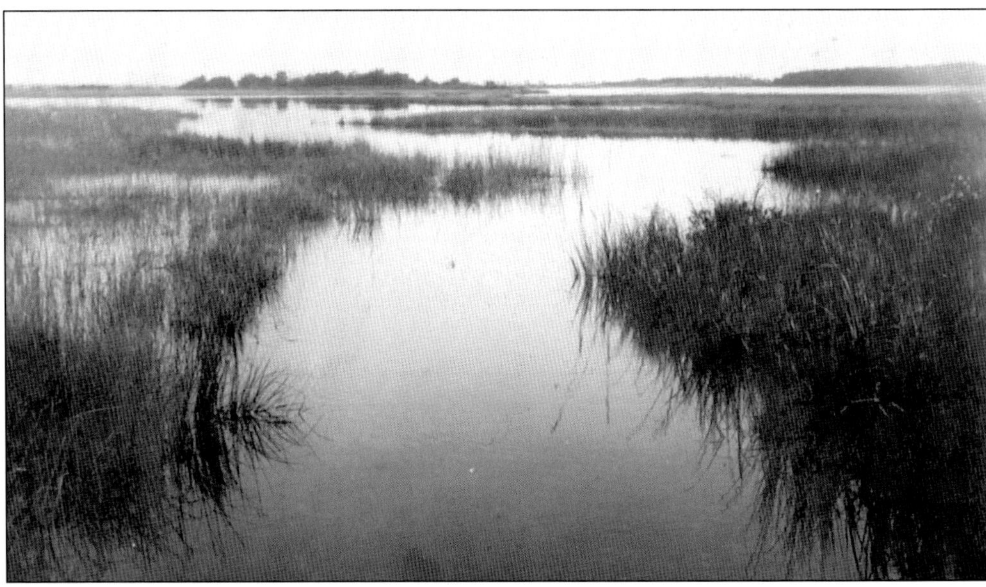

An old postcard of the marshes shows a scene that, thanks to conservation efforts in the last 50 years, has changed relatively little. Despite development on land all around the marshes, strict wetlands restrictions and marsh restoration work ensure that the river will continue to wind peacefully through the salt marshes on its way to the sea.

Six

Hampton Beach Hotels, Guesthouses, and Cottages

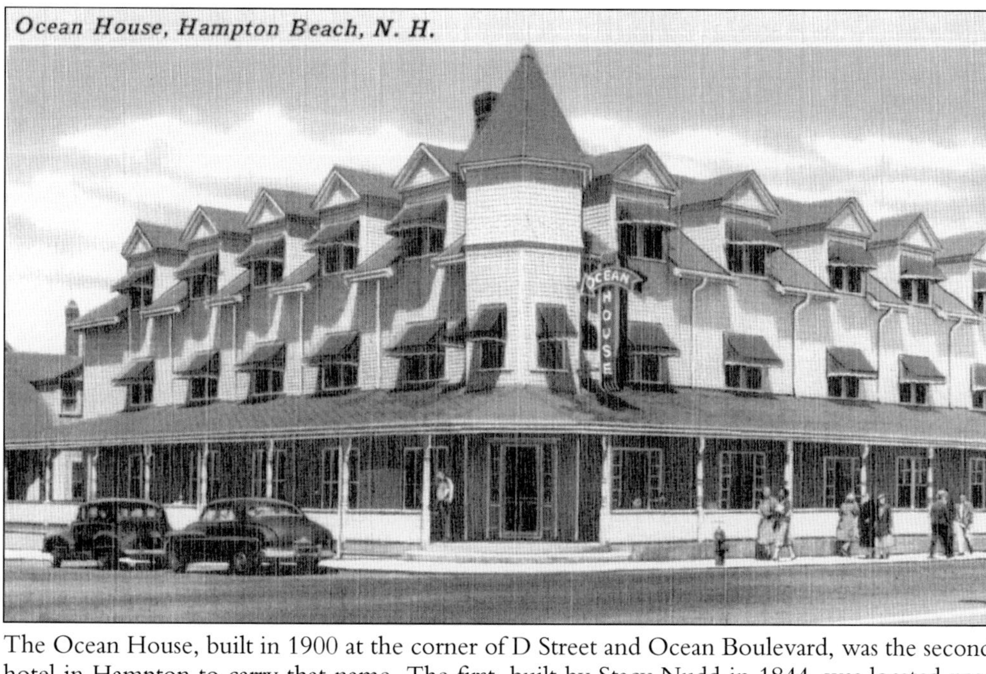

The Ocean House, built in 1900 at the corner of D Street and Ocean Boulevard, was the second hotel in Hampton to carry that name. The first, built by Stacy Nudd in 1844, was located near Church Street. It burned in 1885 and was not rebuilt. The new Ocean House, owned by the street railway, was intended as a complement to the Casino.

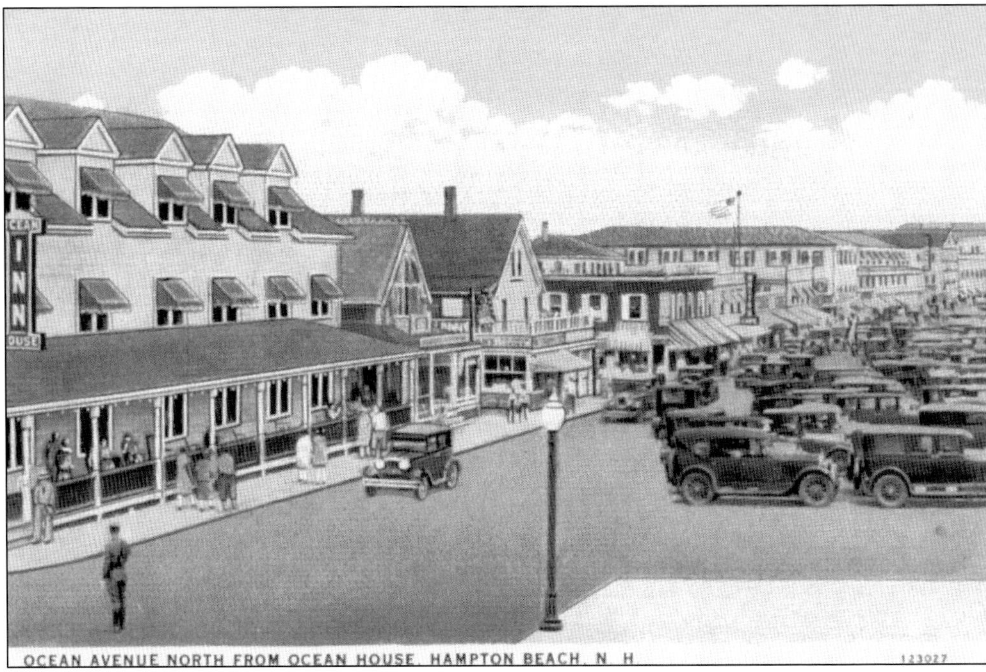

The Ocean House escaped damage in several fires that devastated other areas of the beach, but it finally fell victim to the wrecking ball in 1976. A McDonald's restaurant now stands on the site.

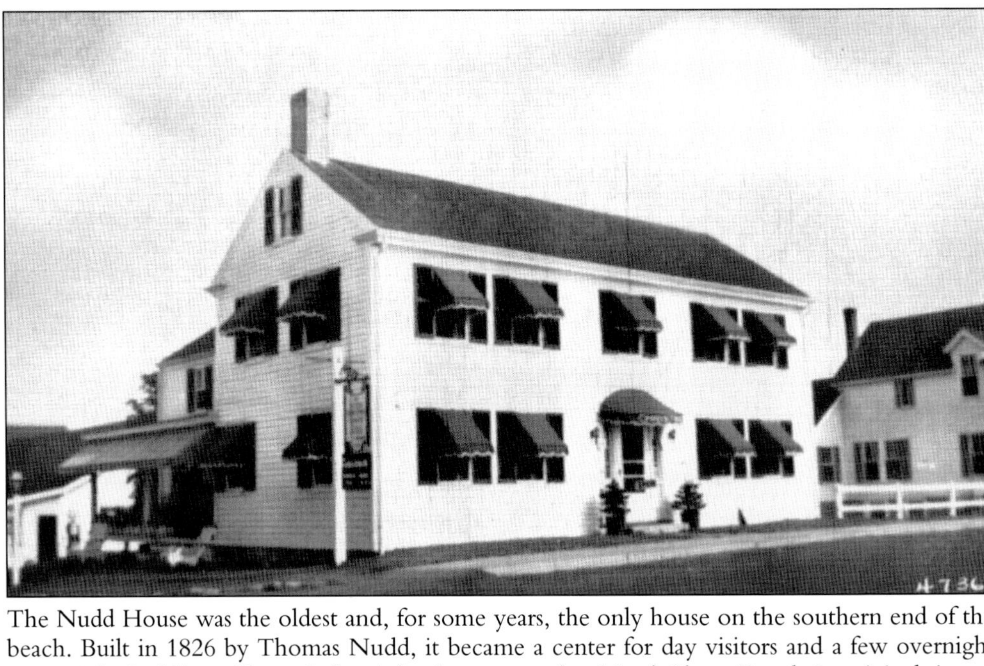

The Nudd House was the oldest and, for some years, the only house on the southern end of the beach. Built in 1826 by Thomas Nudd, it became a center for day visitors and a few overnight guests. The building still stands, but it has been moved to North Shore Road. Its original site on Ocean Boulevard is now a parking lot.

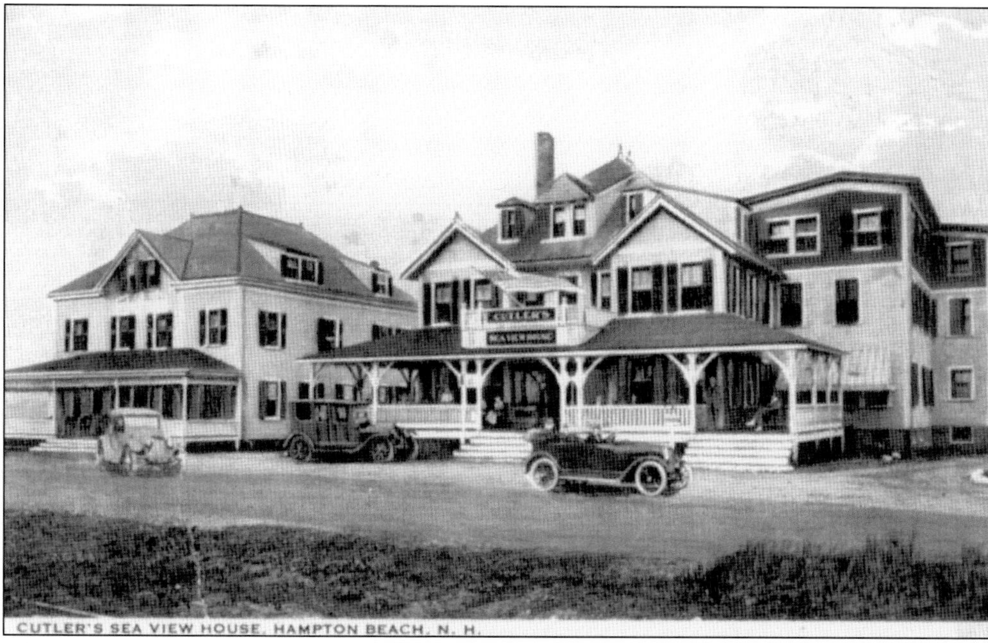

John G. Cutler's Sea View House stood on Ocean Boulevard north of Church Street. This hotel was built in 1885, after an earlier building was consumed in the same fire that destroyed the first Ocean House. Unlike others at the beach, Cutler kept his hotel open year-round. At left is Cutler's Café, which opened in 1898. While the hotel itself is gone now, the café survives as a restaurant at 379 Ocean Boulevard.

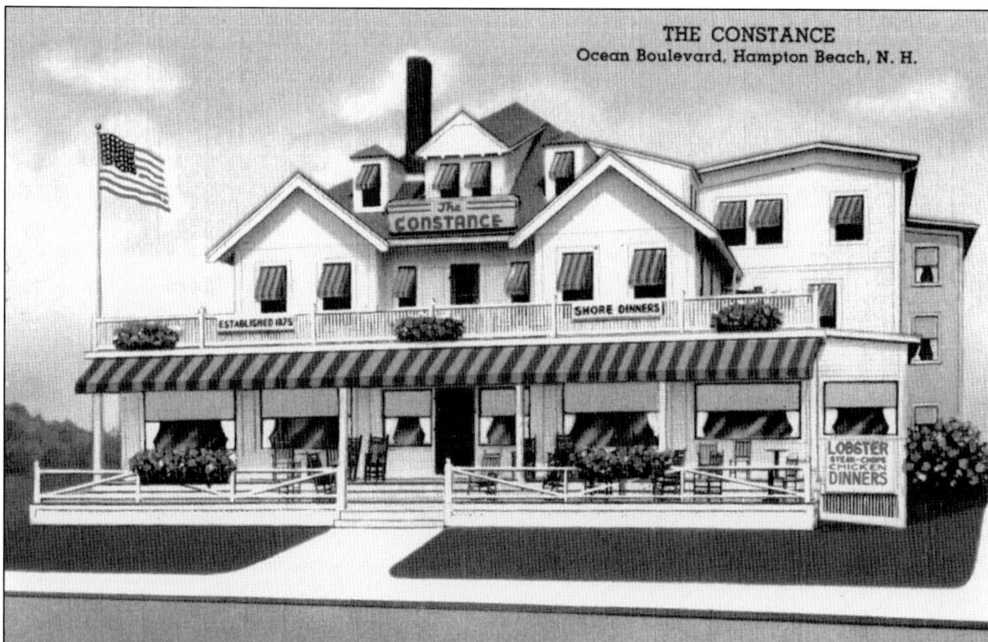

Cutler's Sea View House was later owned by Edgar P. Lessard, who called it the Constance Hotel. The hotel remained in business, although renamed by other proprietors, until 1985, when it was destroyed by fire.

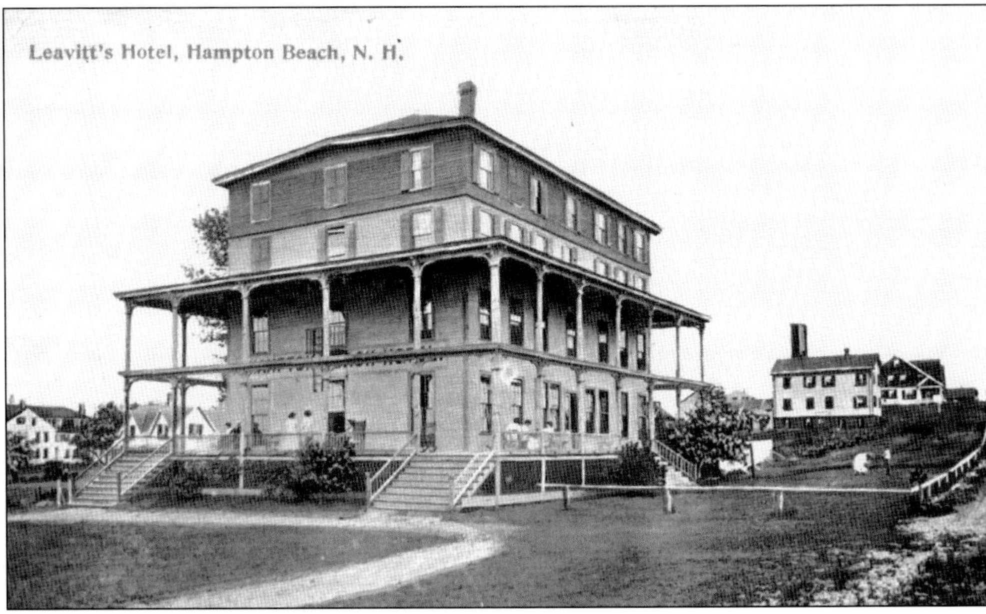

The Hampton Beach Hotel, seen here around 1908, was usually called Leavitt's after its owners Thomas and Joseph Leavitt, who opened the hotel in 1872 at the base of Boar's Head. Four stories tall with a wide veranda on all four sides, it was a prominent landmark on the beach until its final demolition in 1921.

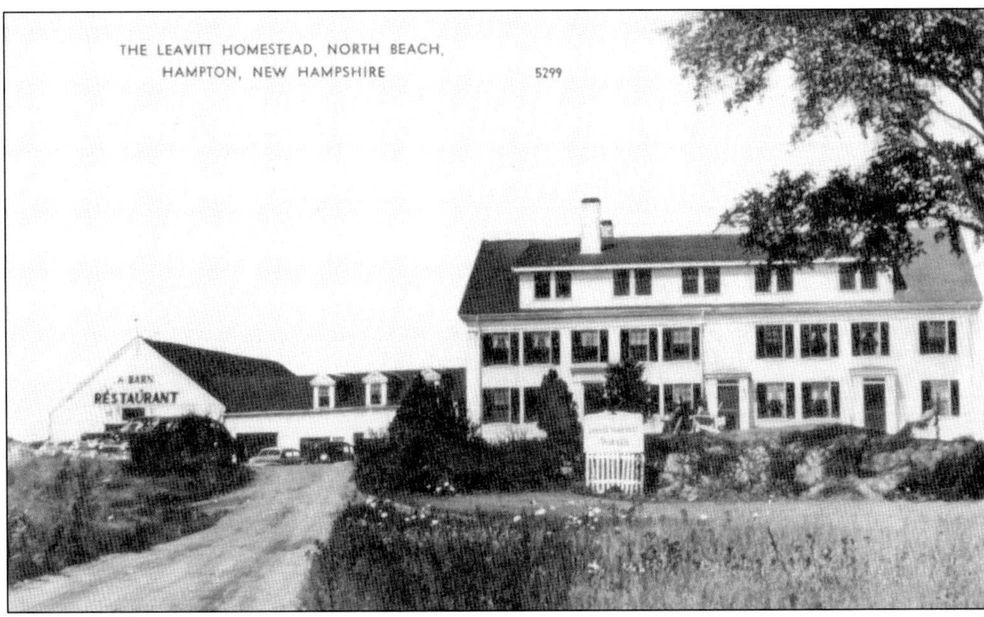

Members of the Leavitt family were major innkeepers and hoteliers at Hampton Beach for nearly a century. The Hampton Beach Hotel was in business for nearly 50 years, while Leavitt's Homestead at the North Beach has served tourists for over a century. It survives today as the Windjammer Motel.

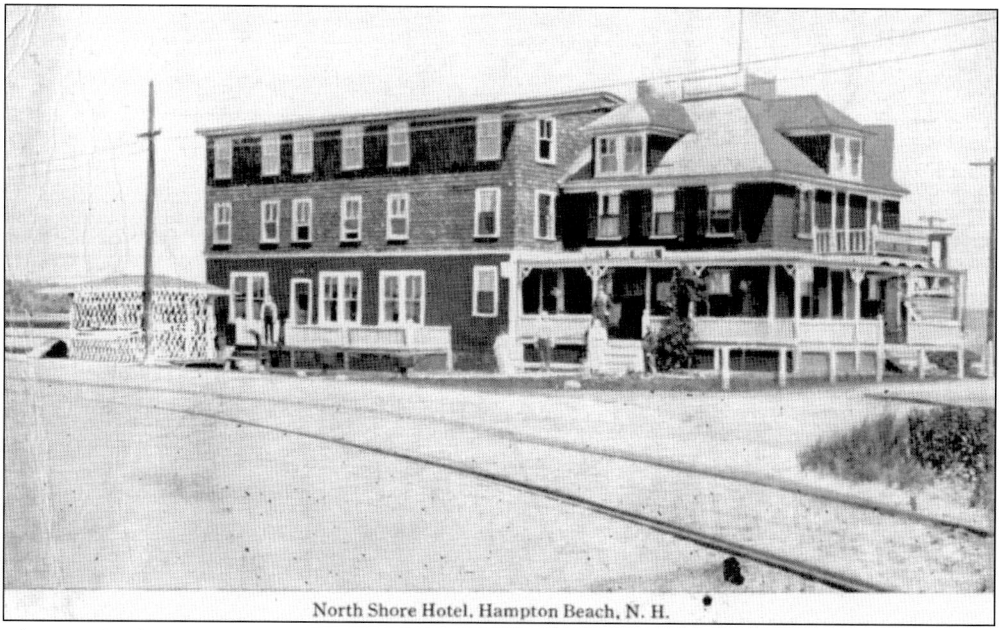

The North Shore Hotel stood on the north corner of Ocean Boulevard and Winnacunnet Road. It was owned by Arthur Dumas and was originally known as the Dumas House. However, the cottage hotel was enlarged more than once, as this postcard shows.

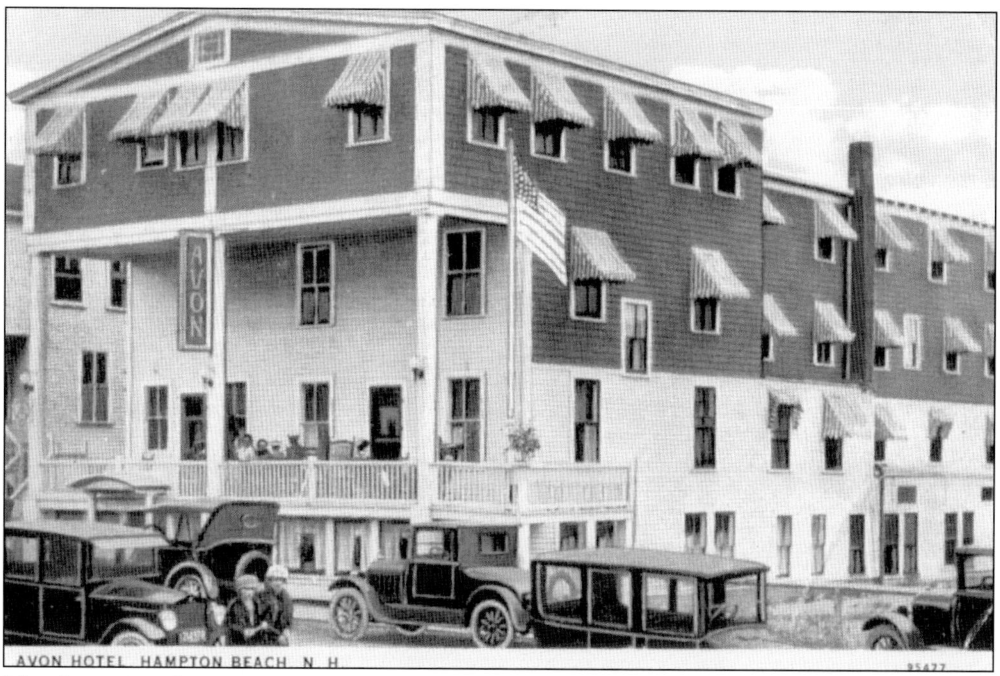

The Avon Hotel, on B Street, was originally built in 1900 for George Ashworth, who sold it when his new larger hotel, the Ashworth, opened in 1912. Ethel Powers managed the Avon for 25 years, even running the business from her sickroom during her last illness in 1939. She was an important figure in the chamber of commerce, working with George Ashworth on the Children's Day Parade and running the coronation pageants during Carnival Week.

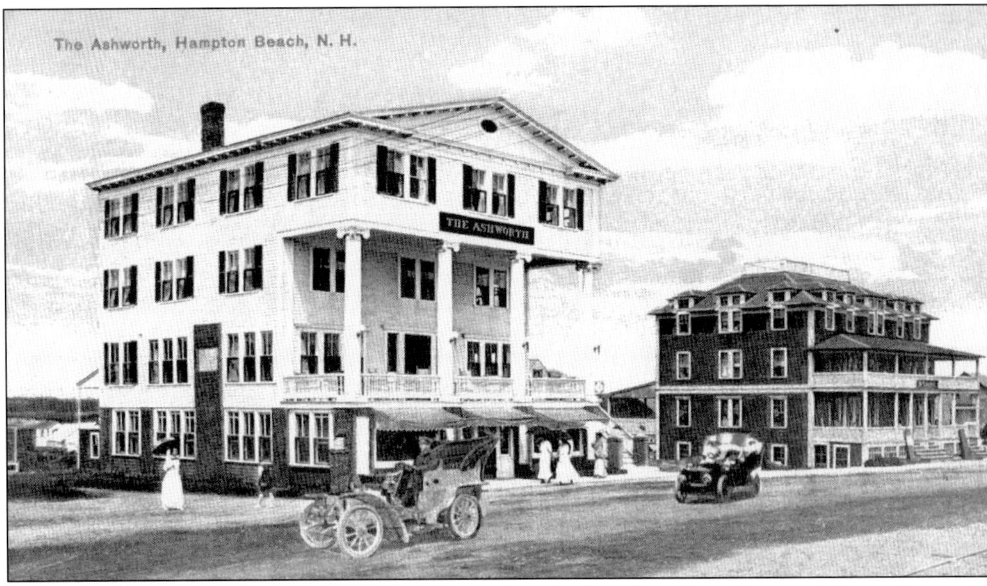

The Ashworth is probably the best-known hotel at the beach today. George Ashworth saw his hotel burn twice, and he rebuilt both times. This postcard illustrates the first Ashworth, built in 1912 by Lemuel C. Ring. The distinctive façade, with its Greek columns, has been a hallmark of the Ashworth since the beginning. In a fairly common technique used on early postcards, the cars have been added to the photograph to make the scene livelier, but they are out of scale with the building.

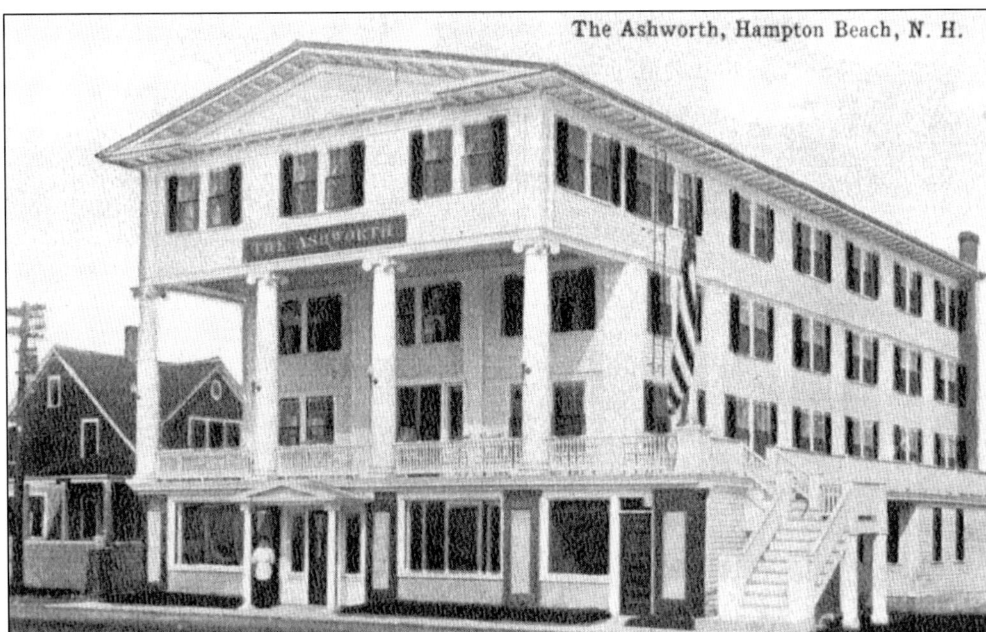

The first Ashworth burned in 1913, only a year after opening. It was promptly rebuilt in the same design as before. The second Ashworth met the same fate as the first in the great beach fire of September 1915.

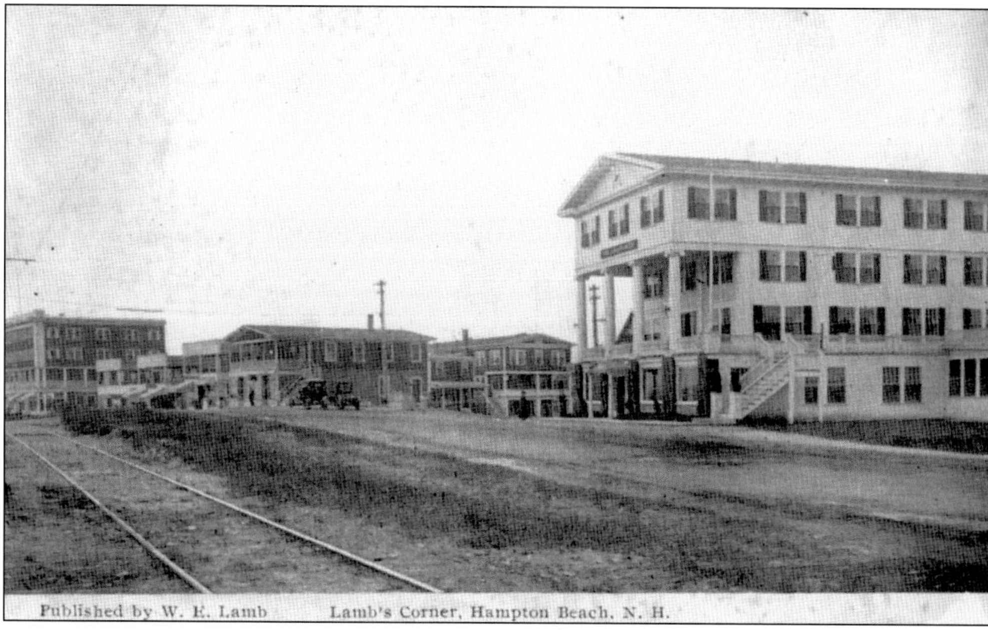

George Ashworth rebuilt once again in time for the 1916 season. This postcard, published that same year, shows the new, larger Ashworth at the right. In the middle is Lamb's store, which sold groceries and newspapers year-round. It was so well known that the corner of Ocean Boulevard and Marsh Avenue (now Ashworth Avenue) where the store stood was called Lamb's Corner. All the buildings to the left of the Ashworth in this image were destroyed in the 1921 fire.

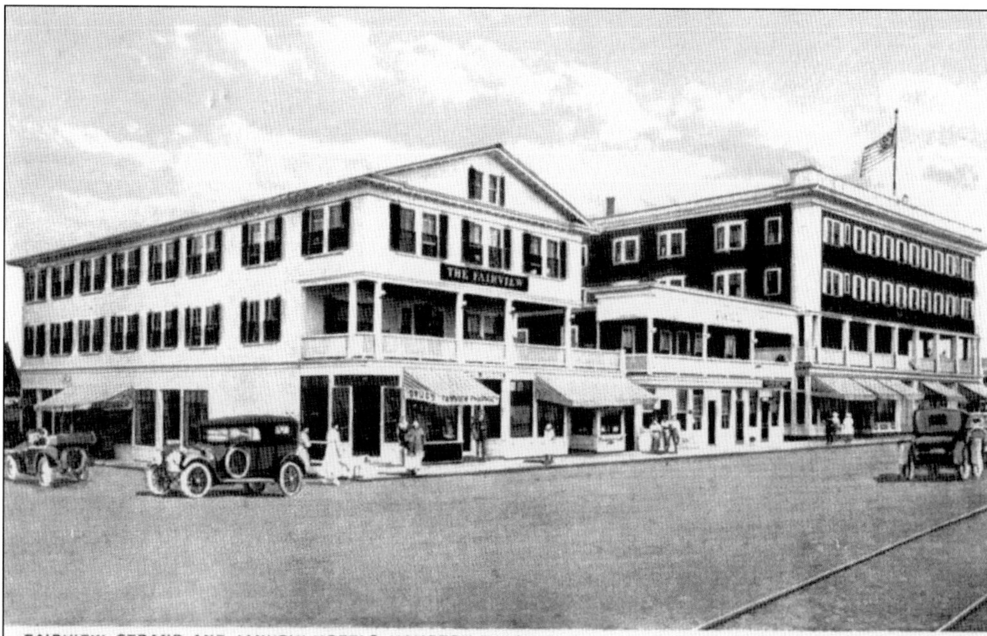

The Fairview, the Strand, and the Janvrin Hotels, between B and A Streets on Ocean Boulevard, are pictured here sometime between 1915 and 1921. All three hotels were destroyed in 1915, were rebuilt, and burned again in the 1921 fire.

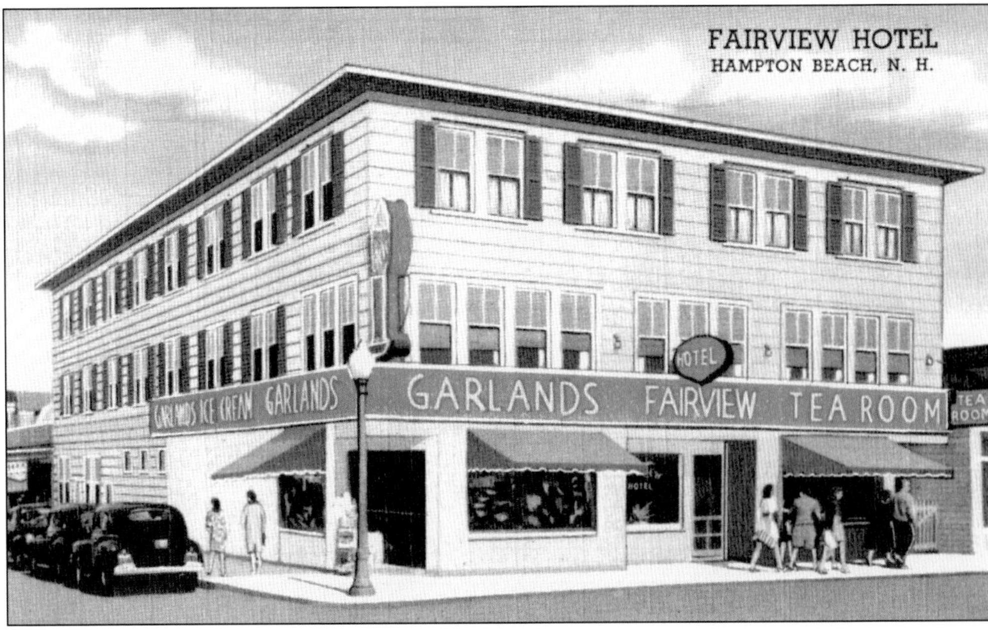

In the 1940s, the Fairview Hotel, rebuilt after the 1921 fire, was known as Garland's Fairview. Mabel Garland ran the tearoom on the first floor, and the ice cream served by the Garlands was sometimes called "the best on the beach."

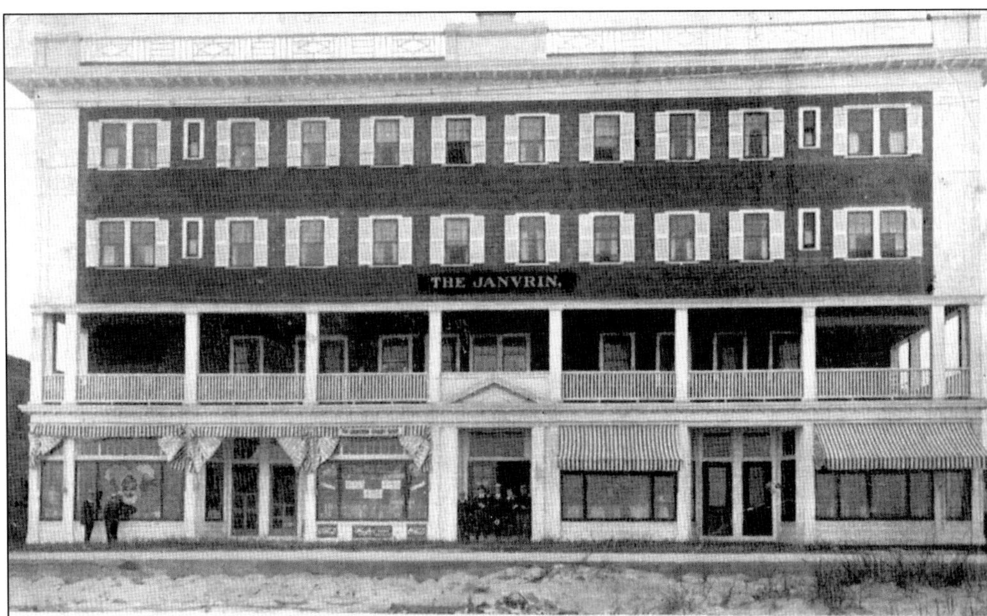

This is the third Janvrin Hotel to stand on Ocean Boulevard at A Street. Florence Munsey, a local businesswoman, bought the original building in 1911 and relocated it, constructing a new hotel on the site. After losing it to fire in 1915, she built this hotel, only to see it burn in 1921. A new Janvrin Hotel later occupied the site, but under different owners.

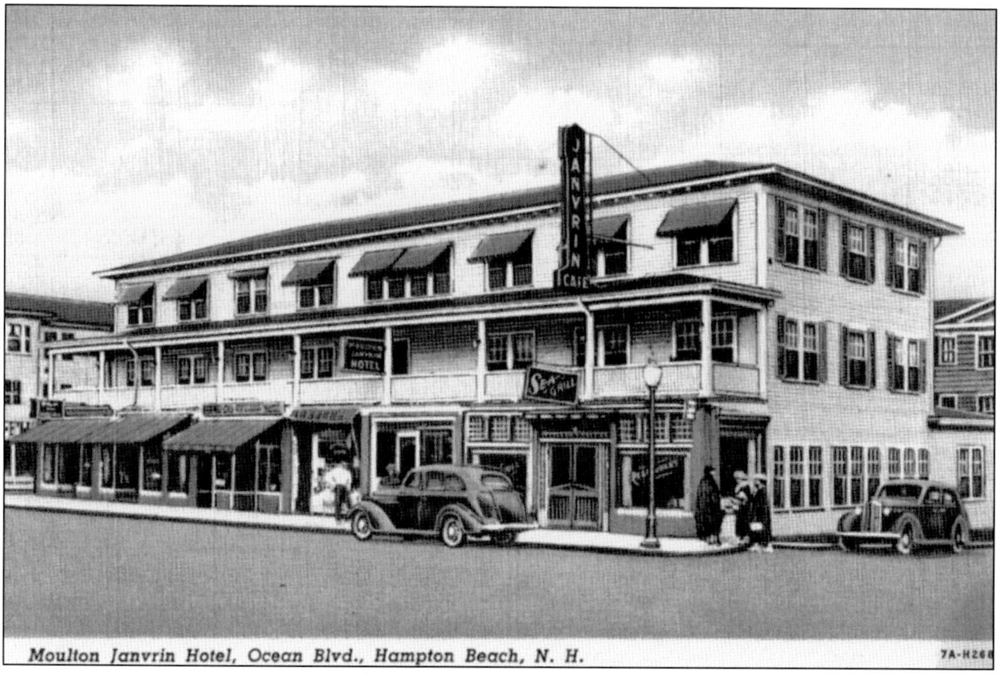

In 1937, Ralph Moulton bought the Janvrin and added his name to it. Later it became known simply as the Moulton Hotel. The Sea Grill seen in the right corner on the ground floor was managed by Florence Munsey.

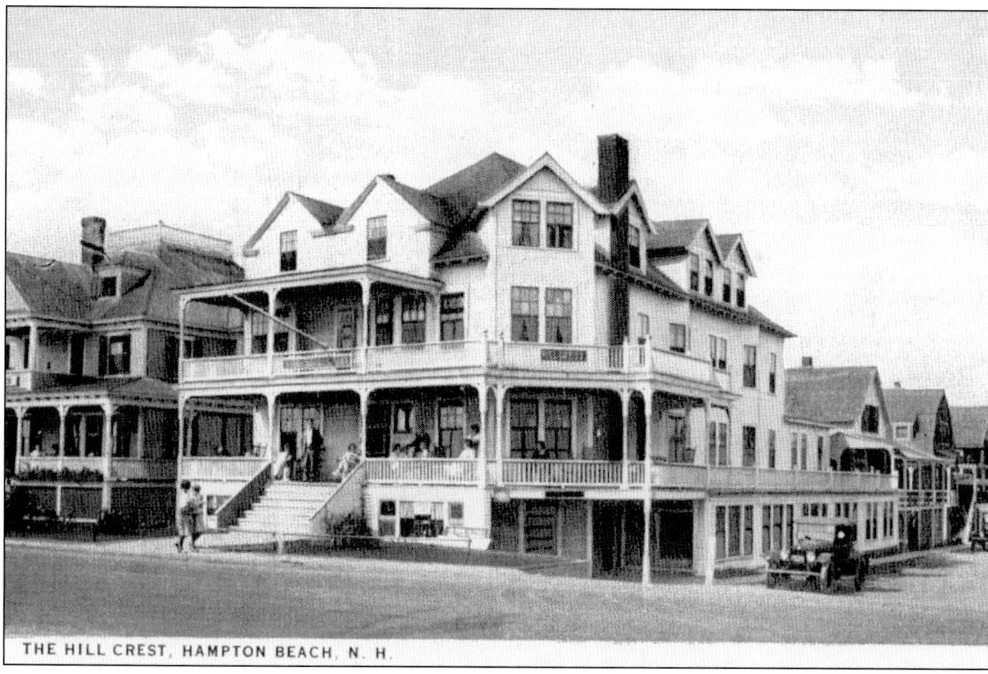

When the new Hampton River bridge opened for traffic in 1902, the beach south of the Casino began to be developed for summer residents and tourists. William Ham opened his fine new hotel, the Hill Crest, that same year on the corner of H Street. It is still in business today as the Hill Crest Motor Inn, and an Italian restaurant, Mama Leone's, occupies the ground floor.

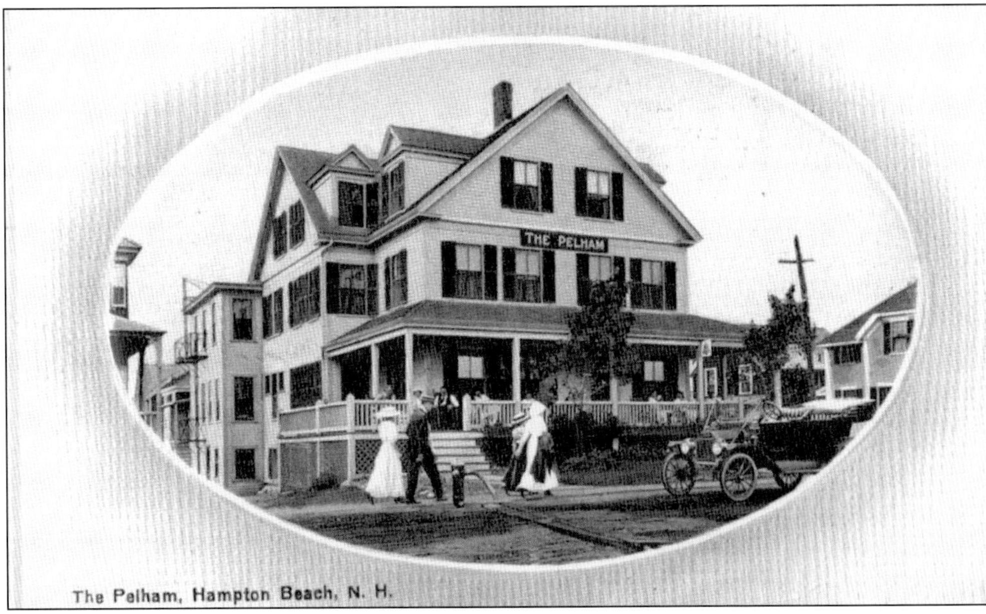

The Pelham, at 121 Ocean Boulevard, opened about the same time as the Hill Crest. Although it has had additions and a number of renovations in the last century, it still serves the public as a hotel. This view shows the hotel shortly after the section at the back was added in 1911.

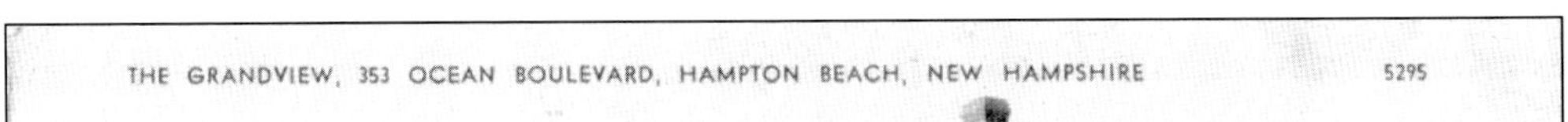

The Grand View, at 353 Ocean Boulevard, is the second hotel to carry the name. The original building burned in 1915 and was promptly rebuilt. This *c.* 1949 card shows the second Grand View. It is still in business today, but it has been much enlarged to suit the changing tastes of tourists, who now prefer private baths and air conditioning.

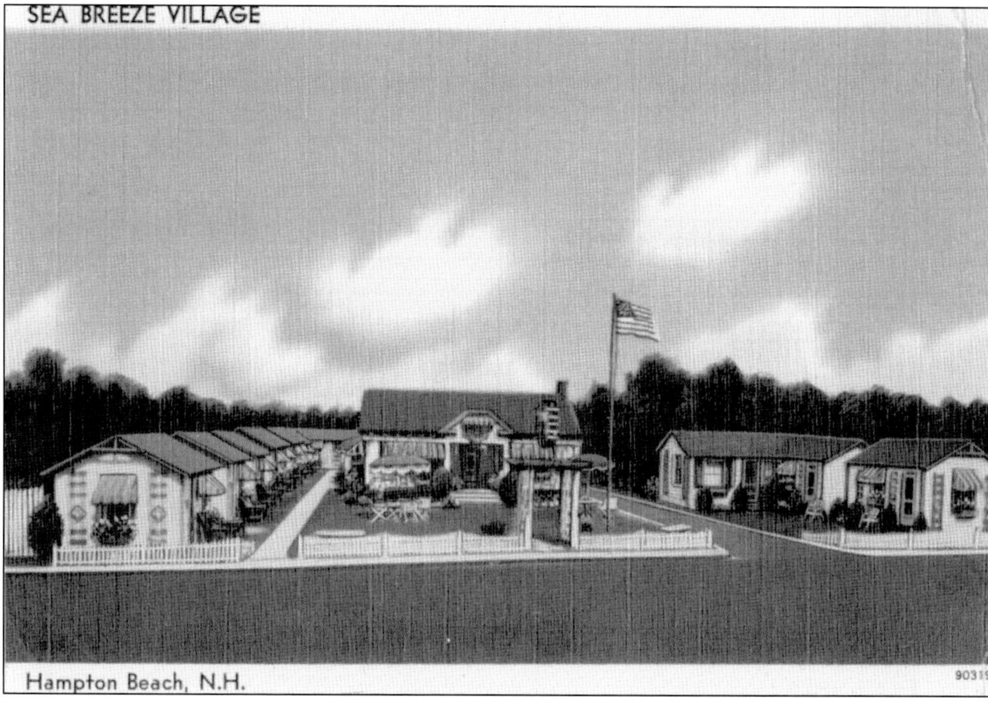

Sea Breeze Village, at 453 Ocean Boulevard, is a good example of a new type of hostelry that appeared in the 1920s and 1930s: the tourist cabin. Shown here around 1940, these small, separate units were popular with families who traveled to their vacation destinations by car. Cabins like these were once a common sight on highways and in resort areas, but most have now disappeared.

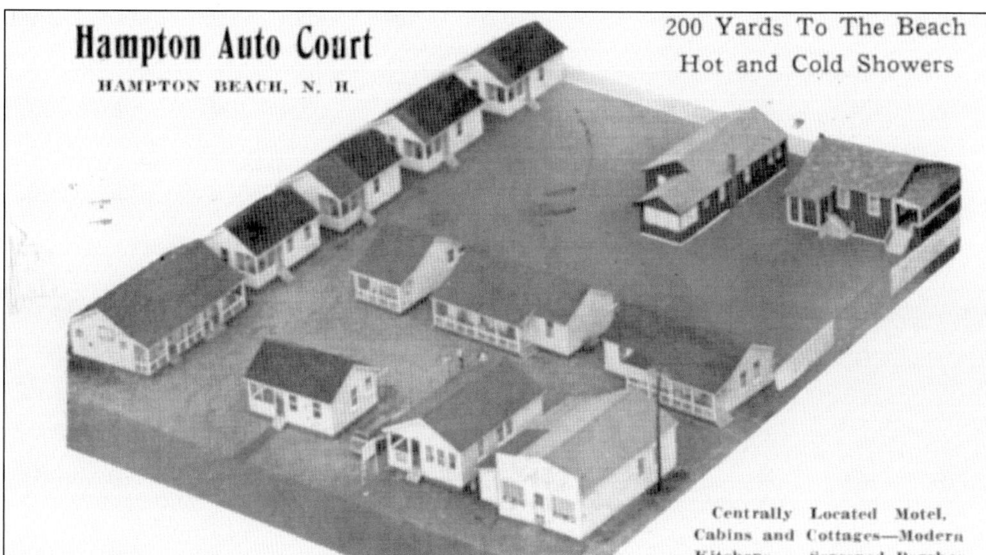

The Hampton Auto Court, at 128 Ashworth Avenue, offered cabins of different sizes equipped with kitchenettes. The cabins could house two to seven people and were advertised by the proprietors, Mr. and Mrs. Joseph Perras, as being "modern." This card dates from the late 1940s.

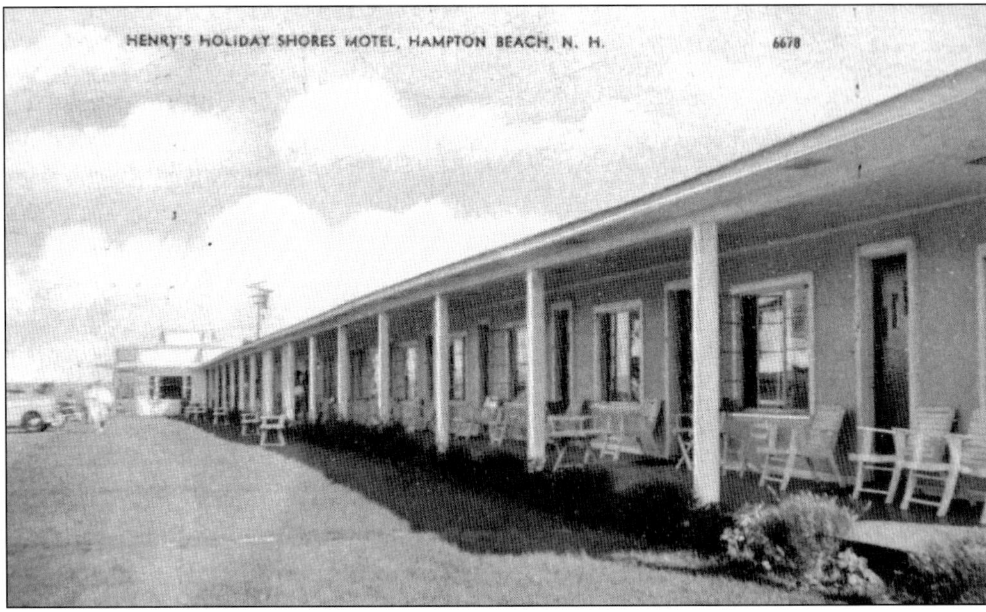

Henry's Holiday Shores Motel stood at the end of Winnacunnet Road and Ocean Boulevard. Henry Dupuis, a prominent beach businessman, was responsible for this, the first "motel" at the beach, and for the first shopping center, built just across Winnacunnet Road in 1950. He was also a partner in the Hampton Airfield, which opened in 1945 in North Hampton.

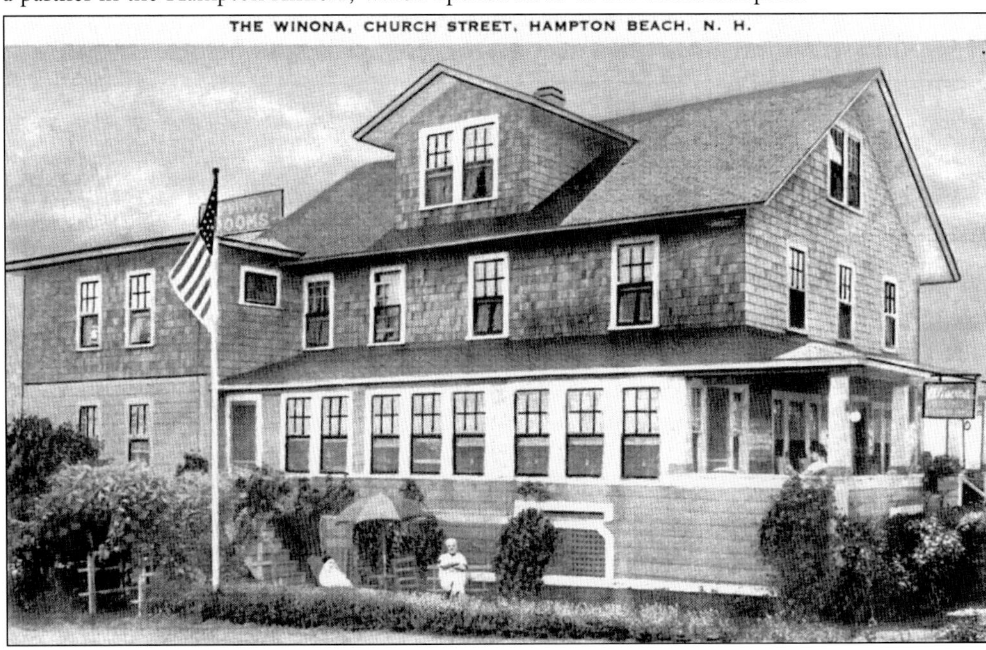

Small guesthouses and boardinghouses used to be more prevalent at Hampton Beach than they are today. The Winona, on Church Street, offered comfort but not luxury. Seen here around 1936, it was in business from the 1920s up to the 1970s. One longtime resident tells the story that when a later owner began renovations to turn the building into apartments, he found a wall packed with thousands of dollars in bills. Apparently, the two ladies who had formerly owned the house had not trusted banks.

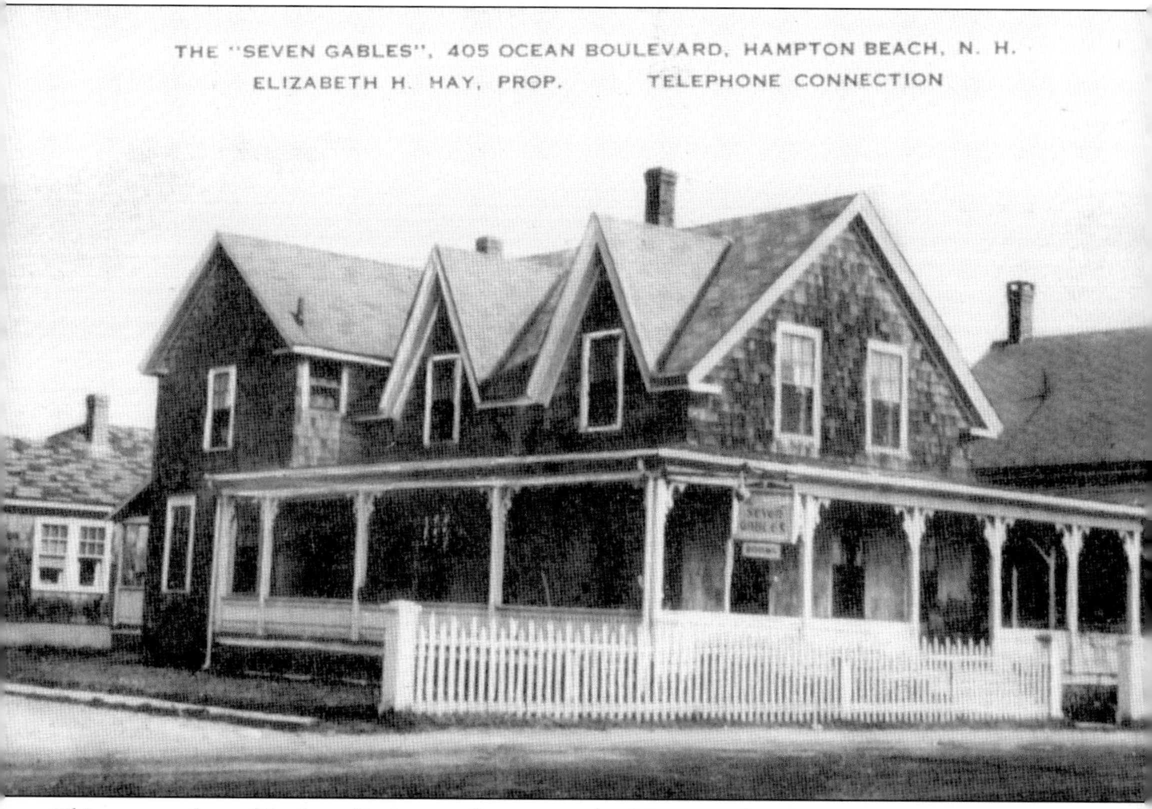

This was another of the boardinghouses that operated at Hampton Beach every summer, offering a more homelike atmosphere than the larger hotels. The Seven Gables was owned in the 1930s by Elizabeth Hills Hay, who was the well-known Hampton school nurse from 1929 to 1937. During World War II, she joined the Army Nurse Corps and served in Europe, earning the Bronze Star during the Normandy campaign. She also nursed Gen. George Patton after the automobile crash that led to his death. After the war, the property was sold to realtor J. Walter Hollis. The building is now the site of the Seven Gables Condominiums on Ocean Boulevard.

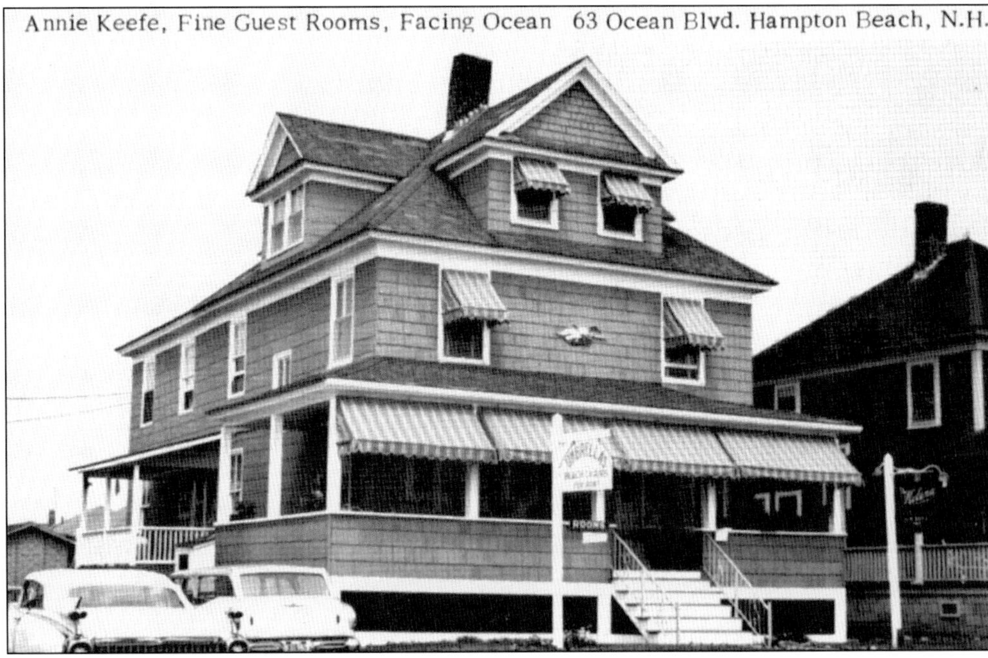

At the southern end of the beach was Annie Keefe's guesthouse, offering "fine guest rooms" as well as rentals of umbrellas and beach chairs, as the sign indicates. The building was bought by the Keefe family in 1903 and stood until 1980. The Keefes at one time owned all of L Street and also gave their name to Keefe Avenue. The present building on the site, Boardwalk South, is still in the family and houses a store, an office, and rental apartments.

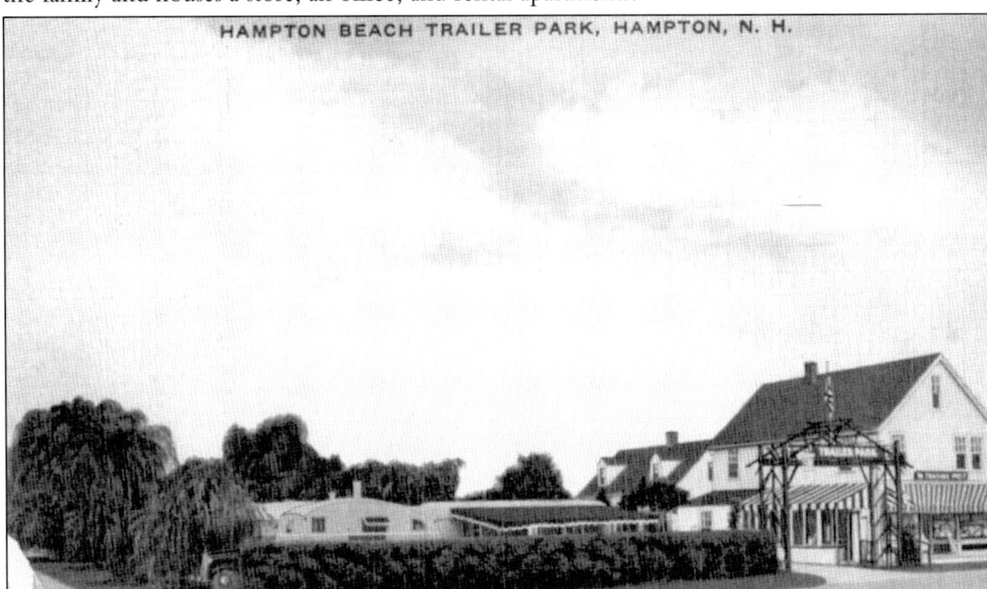

In the 1930s, the popularity of automobile travel spurred an interest in camping trailers, which could be taken along to provide a "home away from home." These were sizeable vehicles, and special parks to accommodate them began to appear in this area. Dan Mahoney established a trailer park at 79 King's Highway that is still in business today. This *c.* 1948 postcard boasts that there is "no cleaner camp on the coast."

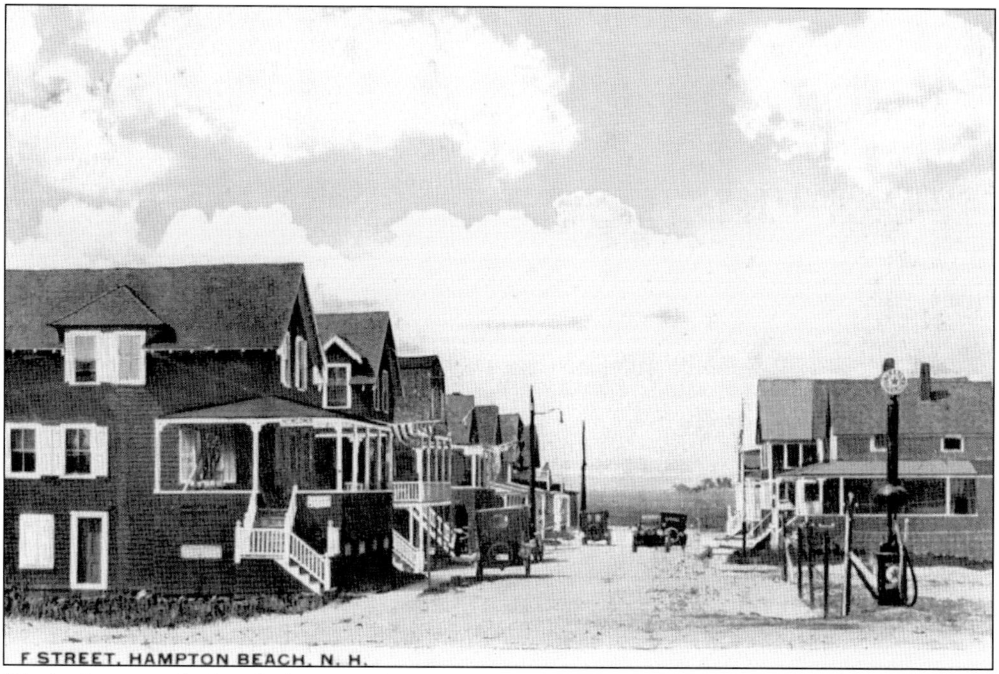

The businesses at the beach also catered to those who wanted to rent a house. In 1912, cottages could be rented for less than $300 for the whole season. This view of F Street around 1920 shows typical beach cottages lining both sides of the street. The marsh can be seen at the far end of the street.

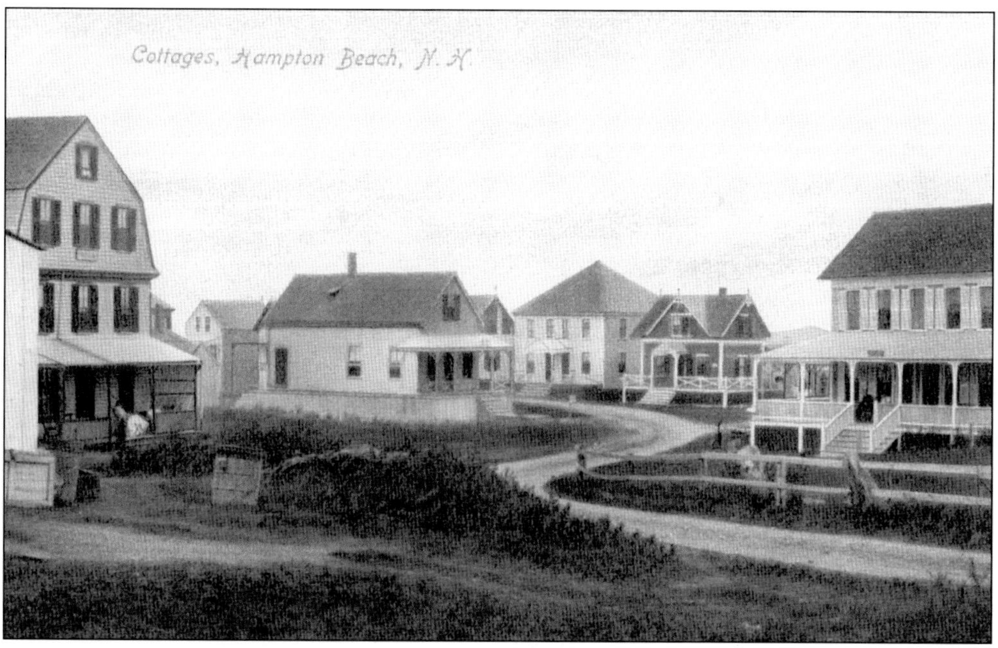

This card, postmarked 1907, depicts the corner of Marsh Avenue (now Ashworth Avenue) and Ocean Boulevard when the beach was less built up. The houses are fairly large and were clearly meant to accommodate families for an extended stay at the beach.

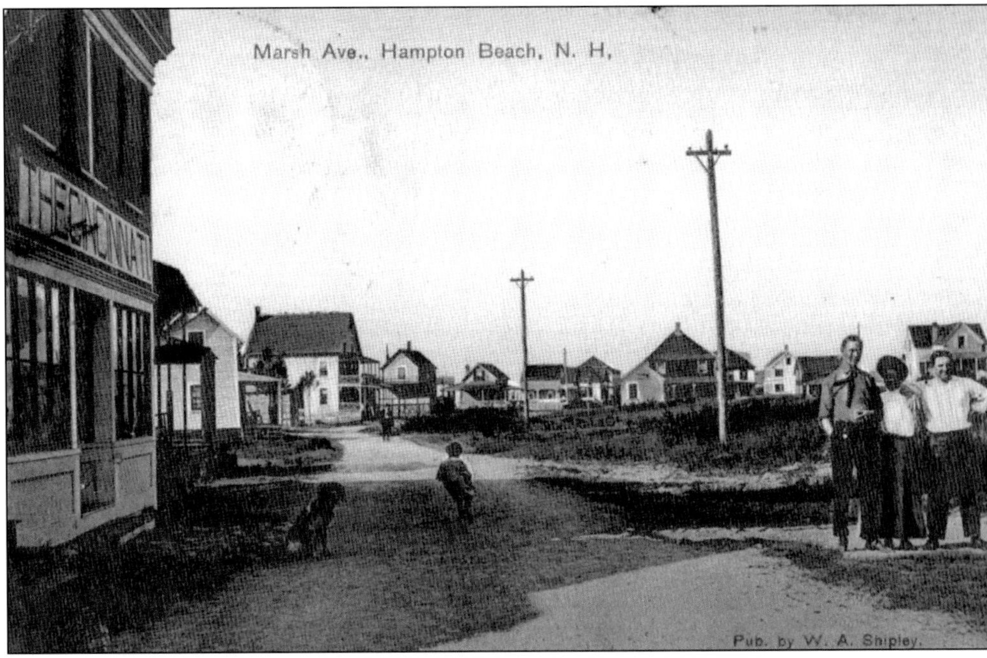

Marsh Avenue ran from the Ashworth Hotel behind the Casino to the river. This *c.* 1905 view shows the cottages that were quickly built to accommodate the growing number of summer residents. Marsh Avenue was renamed Ashworth Avenue in 1957. Note that the publishers of the card have added people to make the card more interesting, although they seem rather awkwardly placed.

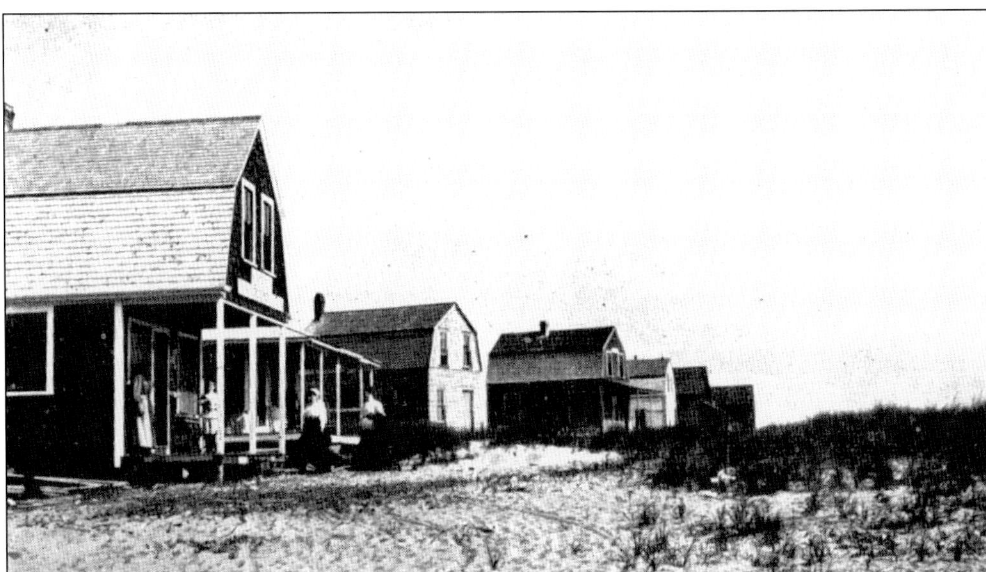

This card shows small cottages at White Rocks before erosion forced their removal. A gambrel roof allowed a far more spacious and airy second floor than a standard pitched roof. Such a feature, when seen today, is often a clue to the age of the cottage.

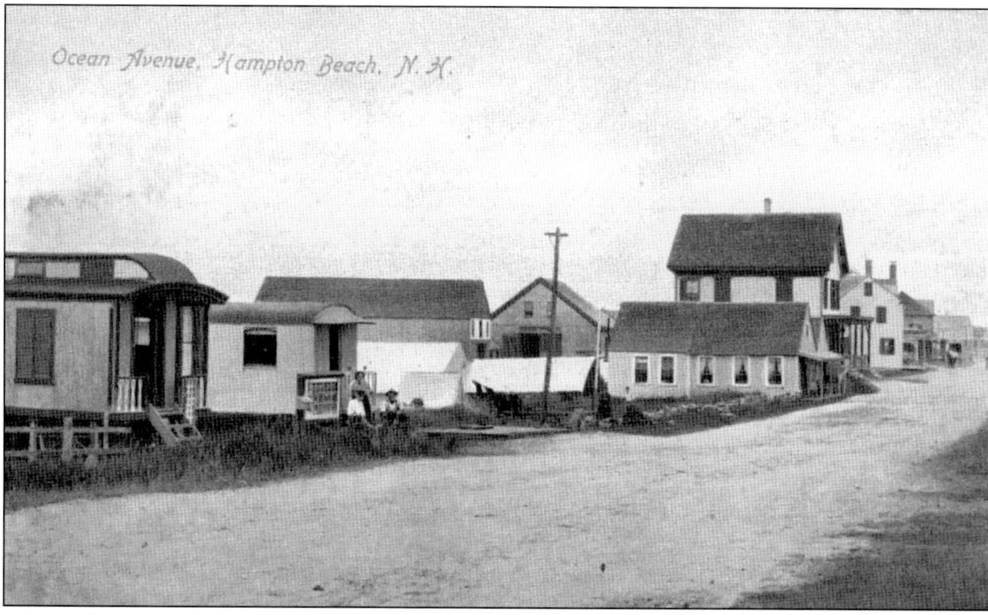

This early-20th-century postcard illustrates the wide range of housing at Hampton Beach. There is a substantial house with a barn behind it, small wood-framed cottages, and two small dwellings fashioned from old trolley cars. There are also tents pitched in the yard behind the cottages.

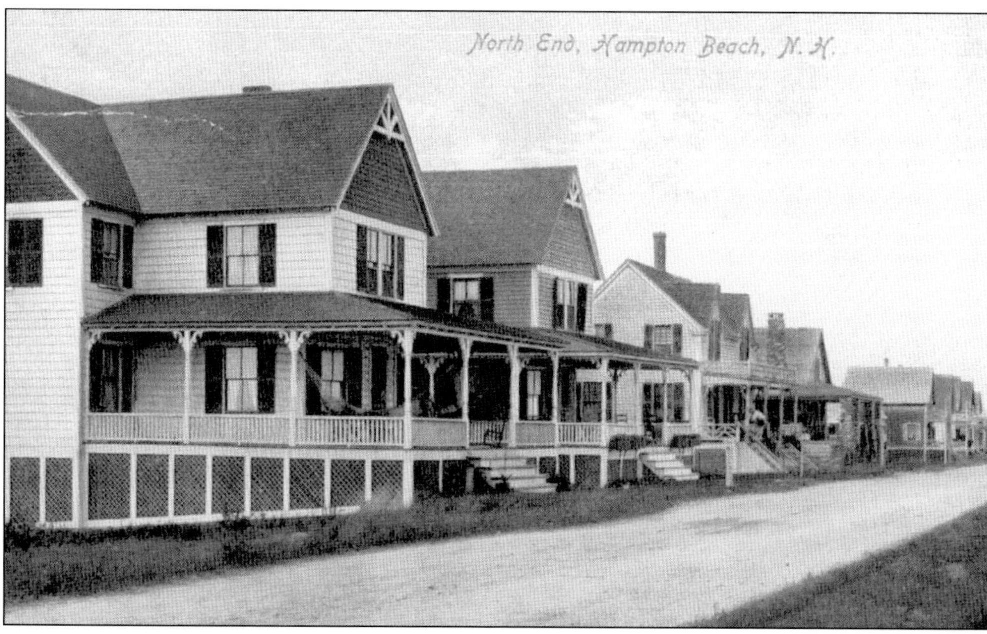

Larger cottages lined the boulevard north of Boar's Head. The decorative fretwork on the porches and gables mark these buildings as homes for the prosperous families of the 1890s. The fourth building from the left is the stone cottage at 550 Ocean Boulevard, which is also seen at the top of page 29.

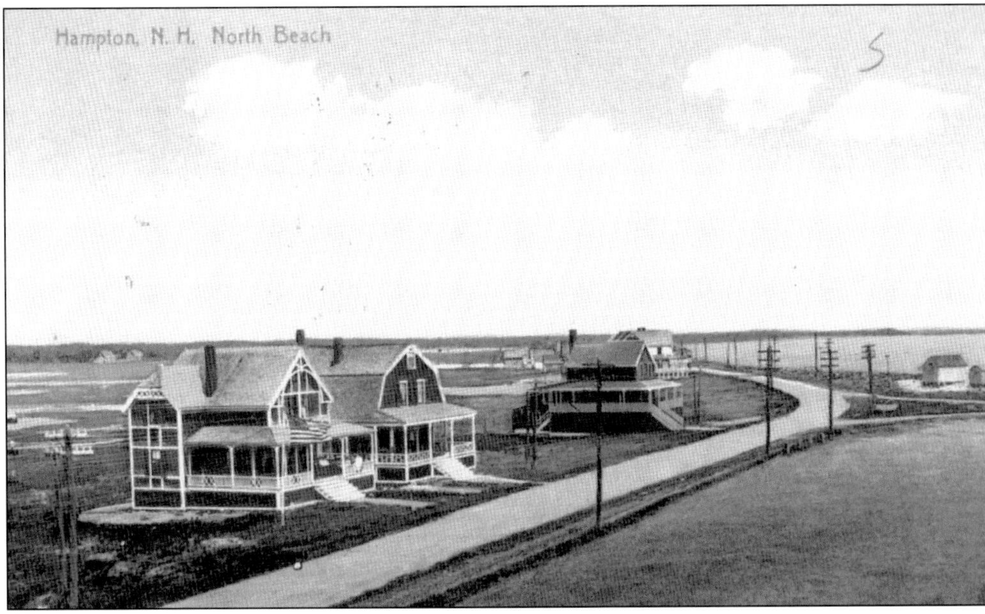

Large summer houses stand at the foot of Great Boar's Head in this *c.* 1900 view. This card was made before the great development filled in all this expanse of land with houses. Note the electric poles that provided power for the trolley and the beach in general.

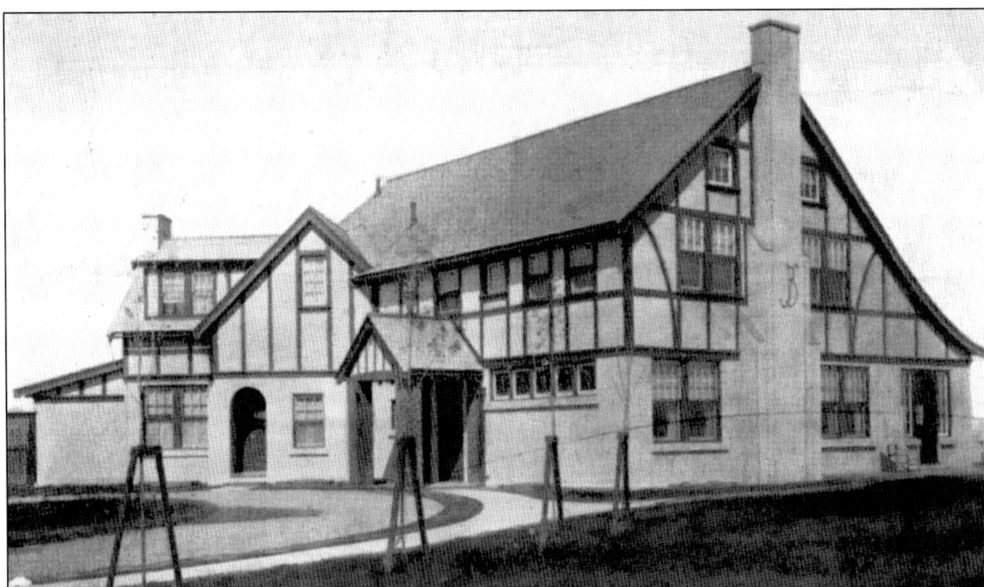
Samuel K. Bell's Summer Residence, Boar's Head, Hampton Beach, N. H.

Not all the houses at the beach were cottage architecture. Samuel Bell of Exeter bought the lot at the tip of Boar's Head in 1914 and hired an architect from Boston to design a large house in the Tudor Revival style. The house, which still stands, was later owned by Charles Greenman, who operated a shoe factory in the center of town.

Seven

UPTOWN

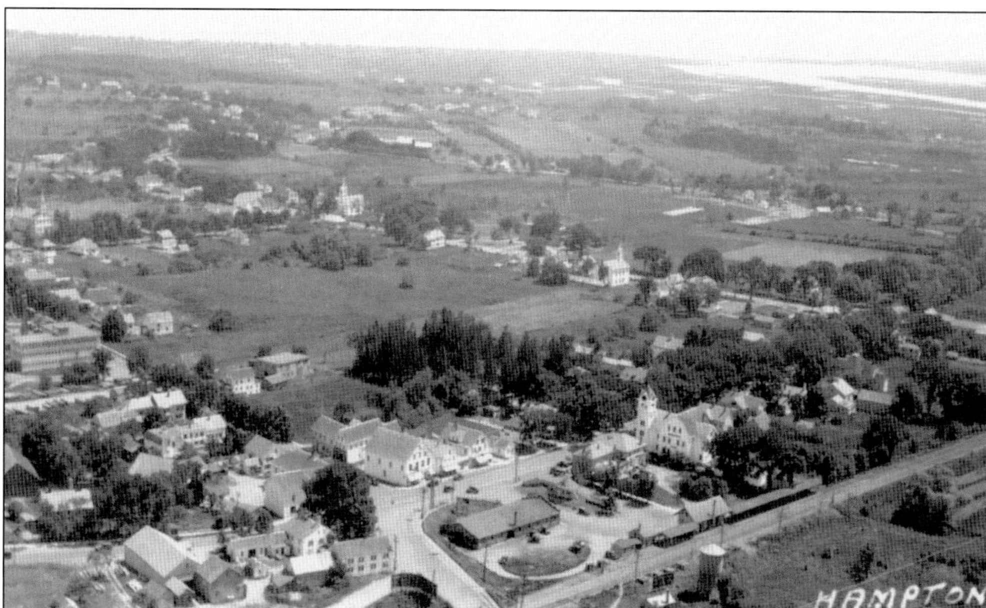

This card, featuring an aerial view of Hampton center, was printed around 1926. David Colt, who owned Colt's Photo Service, took the photograph. The road in the foreground is Exeter Road where it meets Lafayette Road, and in the far distance are the marshes and the Hampton River.

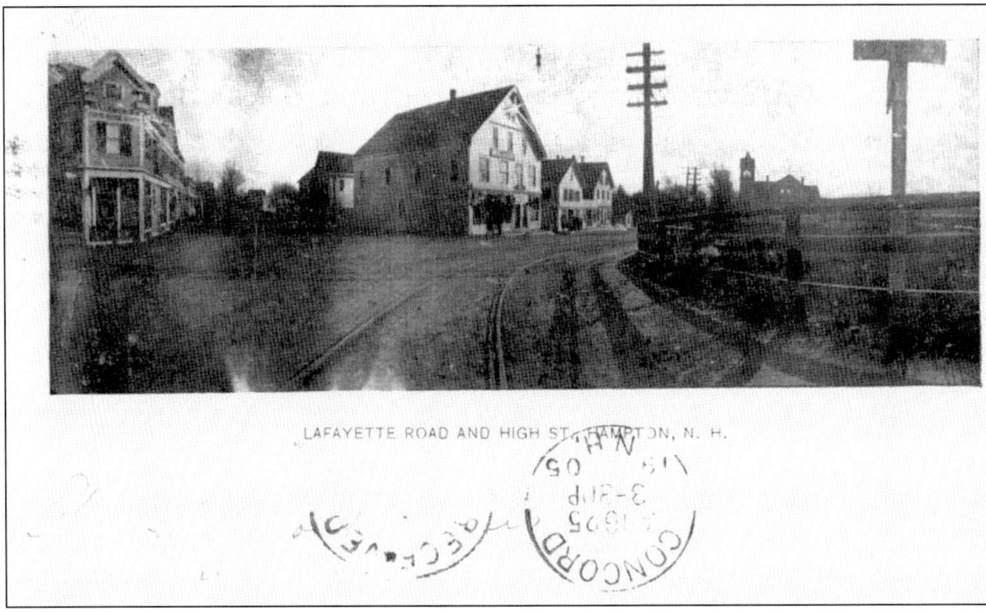

A card postmarked 1905 illustrates the view of the center of Hampton from the railroad bridge on Exeter Road. The building at the left is now Hampton Village Hardware. Note the trolley tracks in the foreground.

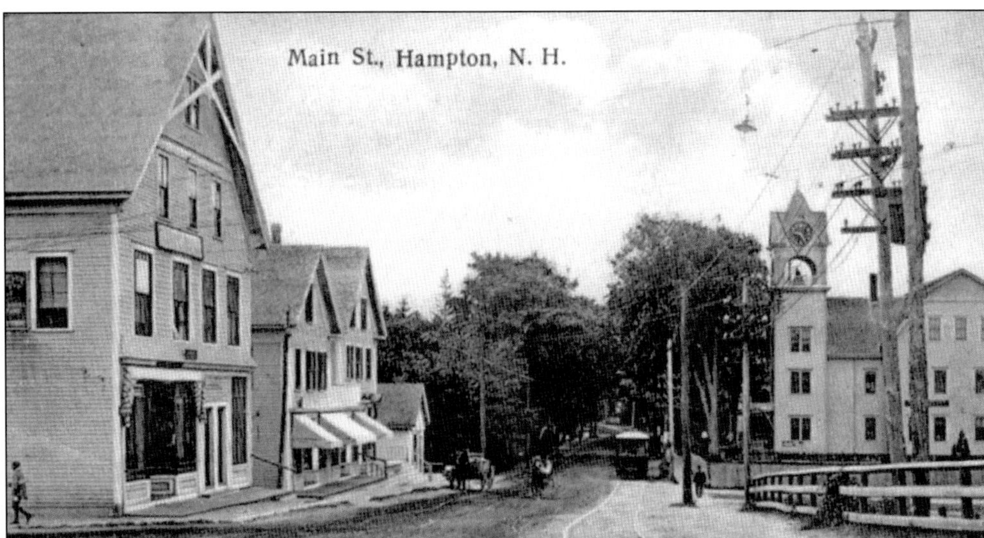

This is a view from the north, looking toward the part of Lafayette Road that was unofficially known as Main Street. The building at left, the Shaw Block, had been moved from Exeter Road when the railroad overpass was constructed in 1900. At right is the Odd Fellows hall.

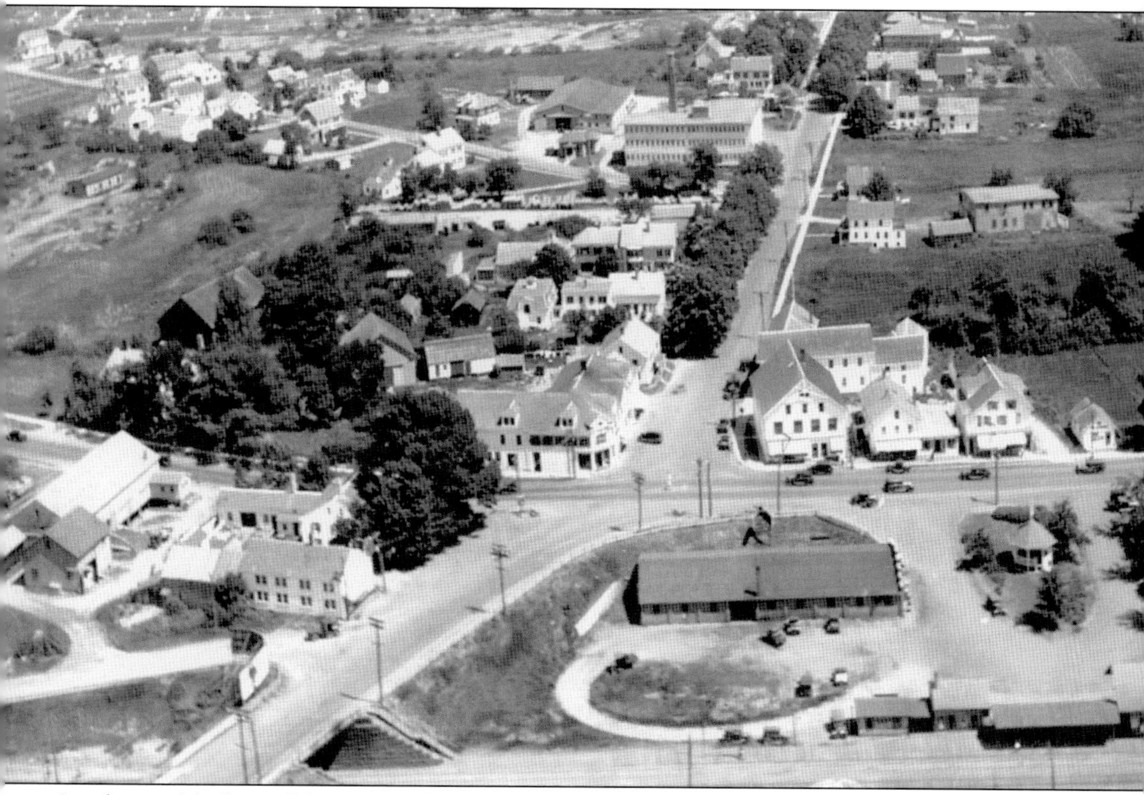

Another aerial view of the center clearly shows the intersection of Exeter and Lafayette Roads with High Street. In the right foreground is the railroad depot, and just behind it is Depot Square (now Marelli Square) with the bandstand erected in 1925. In the center distance is the Greenman shoe factory with its tall smokestack.

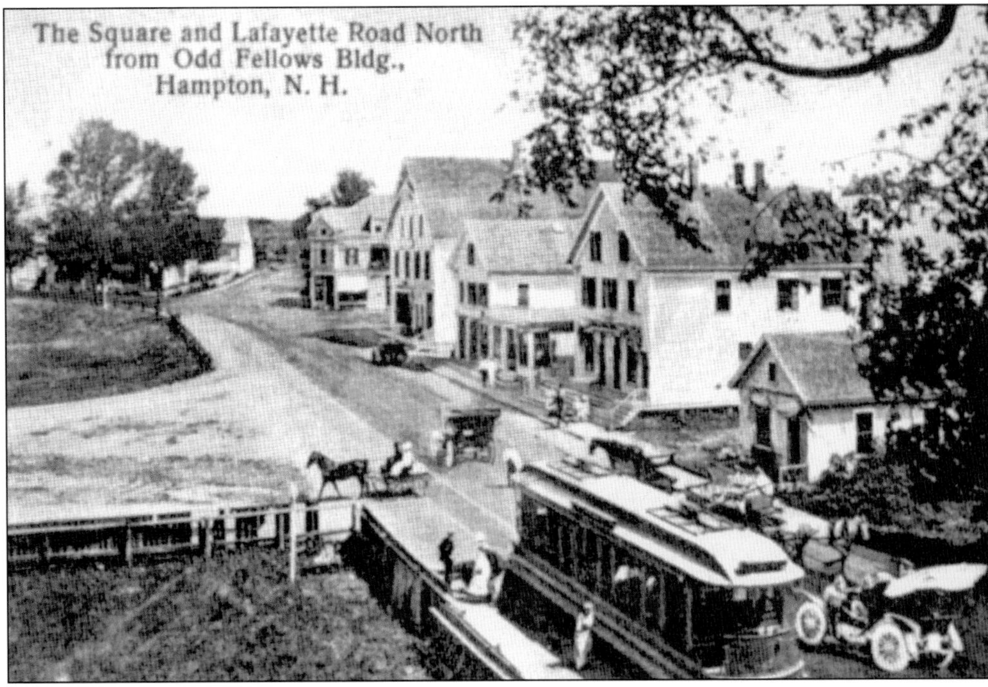

This postcard illustrates the three types of transportation available around 1910: the trolley, the automobile, and the horse and buggy. The trolley route from Exeter followed Exeter Road, turned south on Lafayette Road, and then went east on Winnacunnet Road.

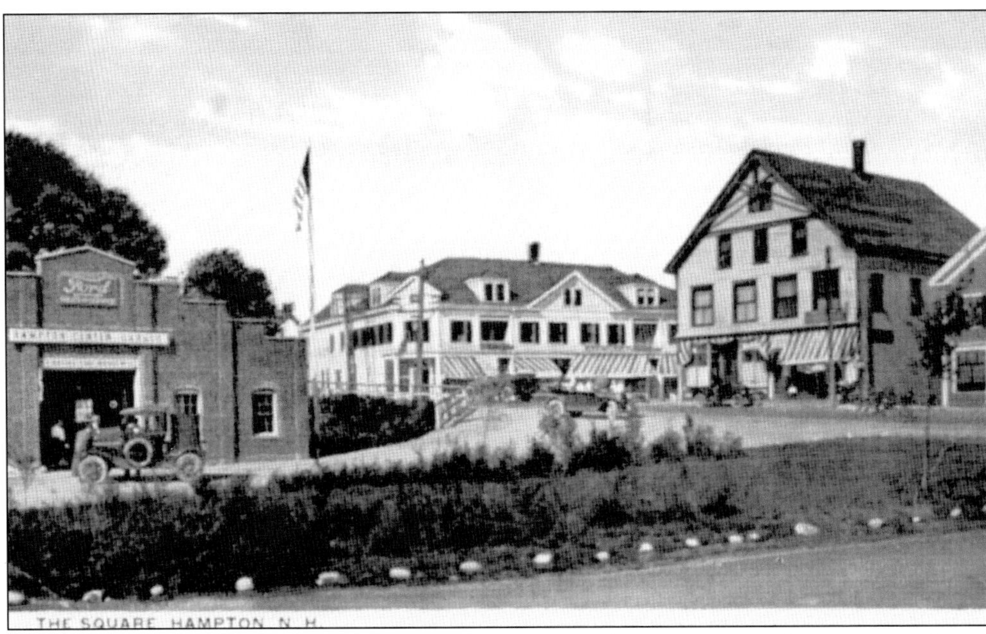

This postcard shows Depot Square and Lafayette Road in the early 1920s. The Hampton Center Garage, at left, was the first automobile dealership in Hampton. In the center is the Lane Block, built by Joshua Lane and his son Howard in 1900. It now houses a hardware store, a restaurant, and several other businesses.

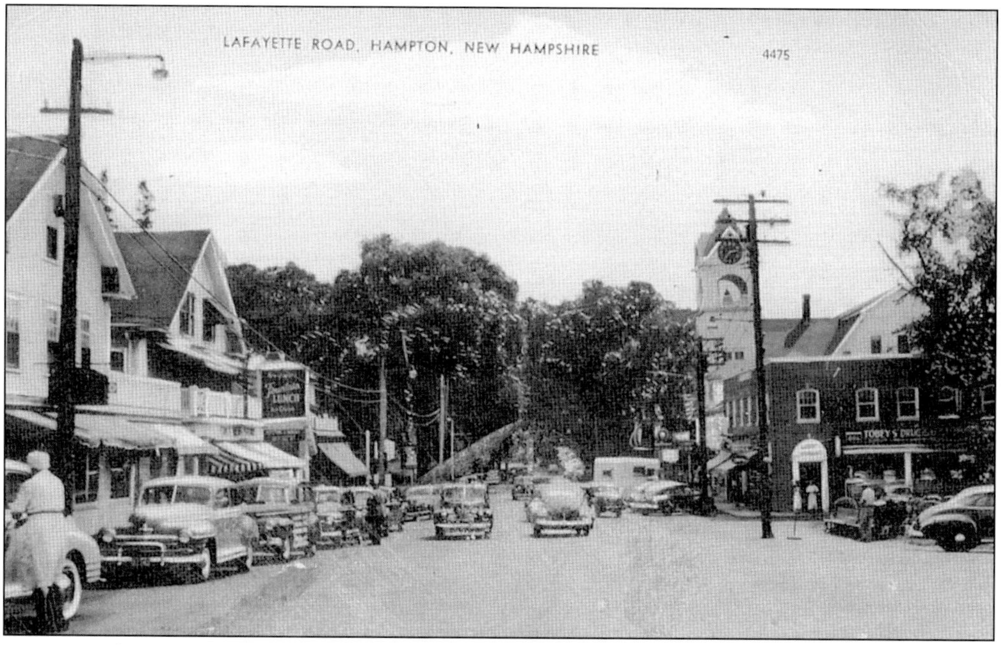

By 1948, the tranquil center of town had been transformed into a bustling shopping area on a main route of travel. Until the New Hampshire Turnpike opened in 1949, most people traveling between Boston and Portland drove through the center of Hampton on Route 1.

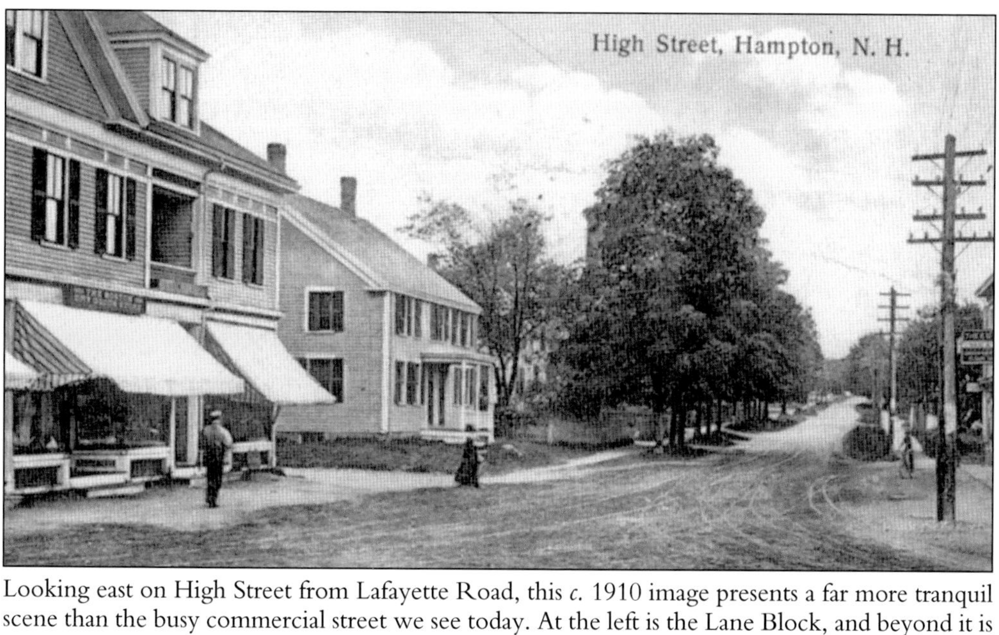

Looking east on High Street from Lafayette Road, this *c.* 1910 image presents a far more tranquil scene than the busy commercial street we see today. At the left is the Lane Block, and beyond it is the Cotton Brown house, which was moved from the corner to make way for the Lane building. Tobey and Merrill Insurance now occupies the Brown house.

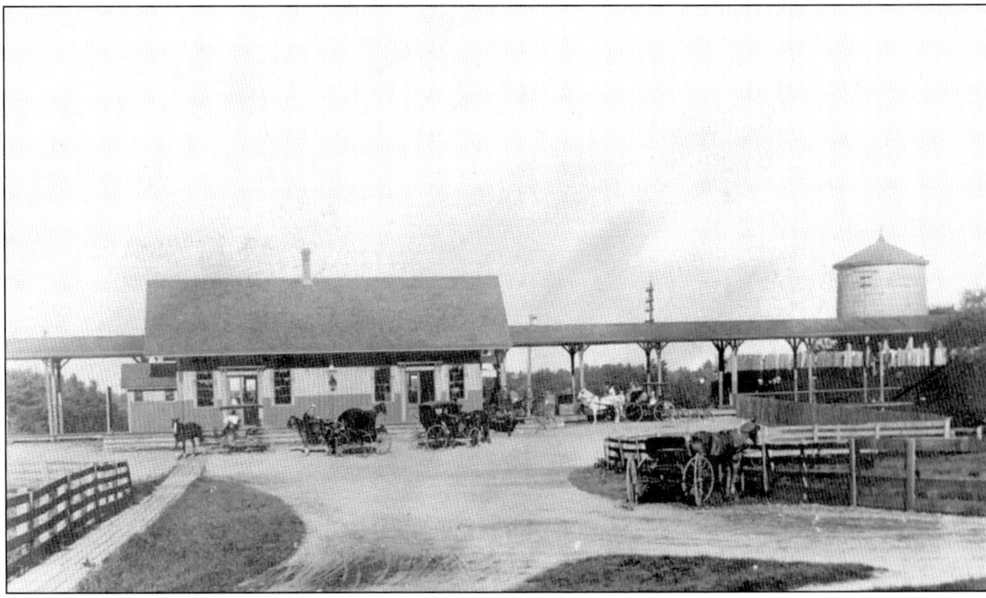

The depot was an important place in Hampton from the start of rail service in 1840 to the cessation of passenger rail travel in 1965. During the early days, wagons awaited the arrival of the trains to pick up passengers and goods bound for the hotels and businesses at the beach. Until the trolley line was built in 1897, there was only a stagecoach service to the beach.

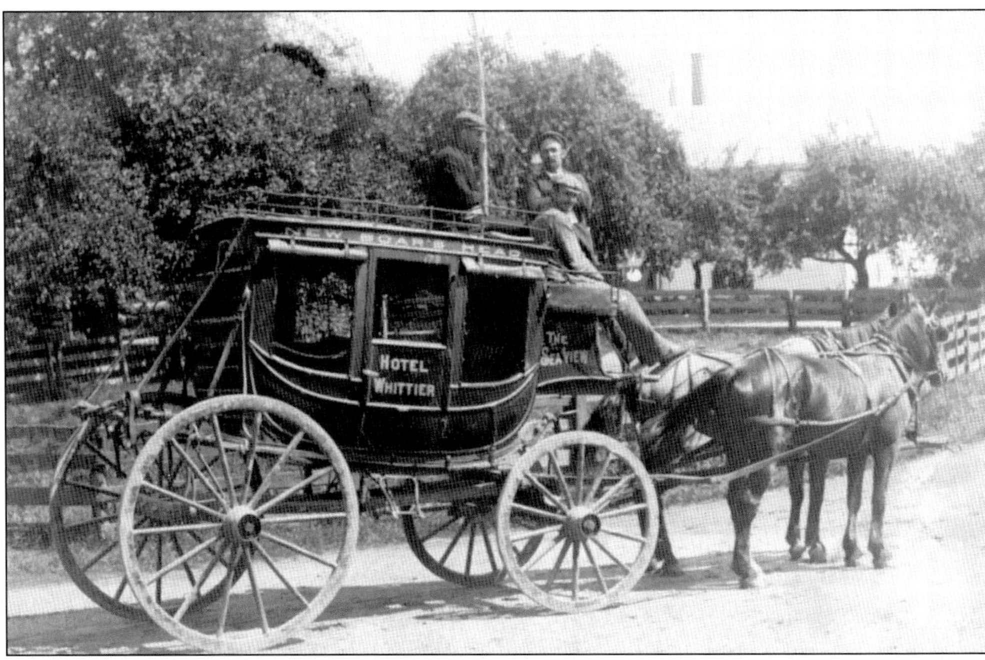

This is one of the stagecoaches that made regular runs from the train station to the various hotels and from those hotels to other attractions. Hotel owners advertised their establishments on the coaches. This *c.* 1895 card shows a stagecoach displaying the names of the Hotel Whittier, in the town center, and the New Boar's Head and Sea View, at the beach.

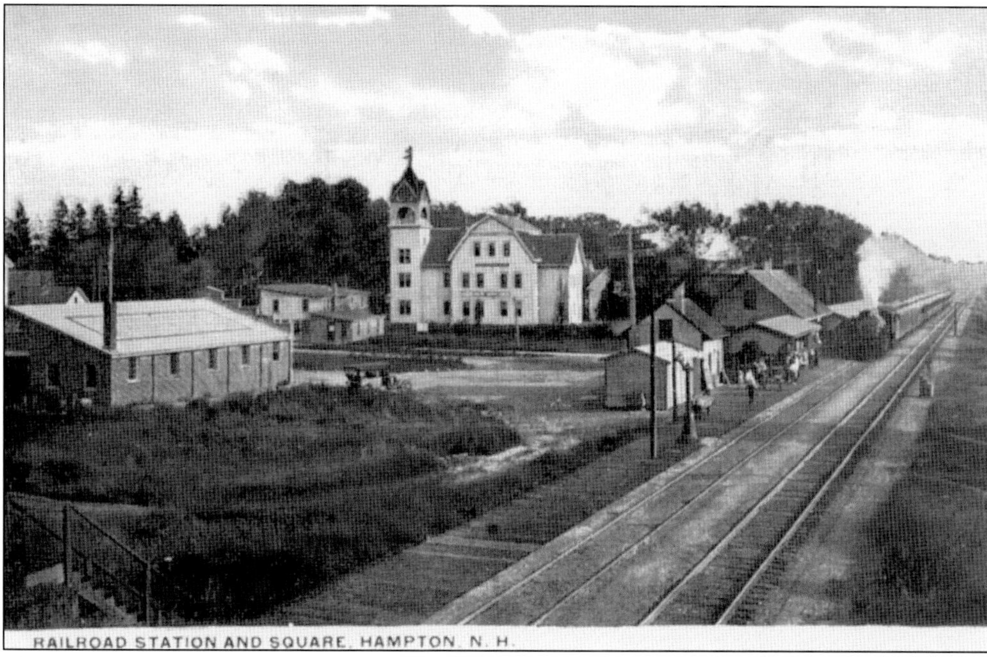

This view of the depot from the railroad overpass on Exeter Road shows a train pulled by a steam locomotive just drawing into the station. The building at left is Brooks Garage, which opened in 1916. In the center is the Odd Fellows hall.

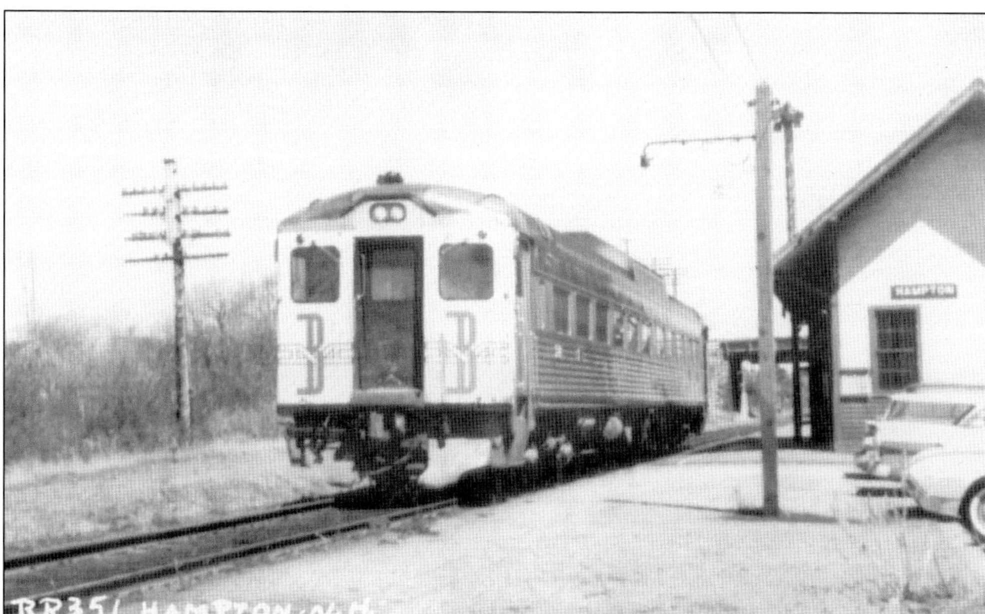

As train travel declined in the mid-20th century, railroad companies experimented with more economical trains. The self-contained diesel Budd cars were the last to carry passengers to Hampton from Boston. The service was discontinued in 1965.

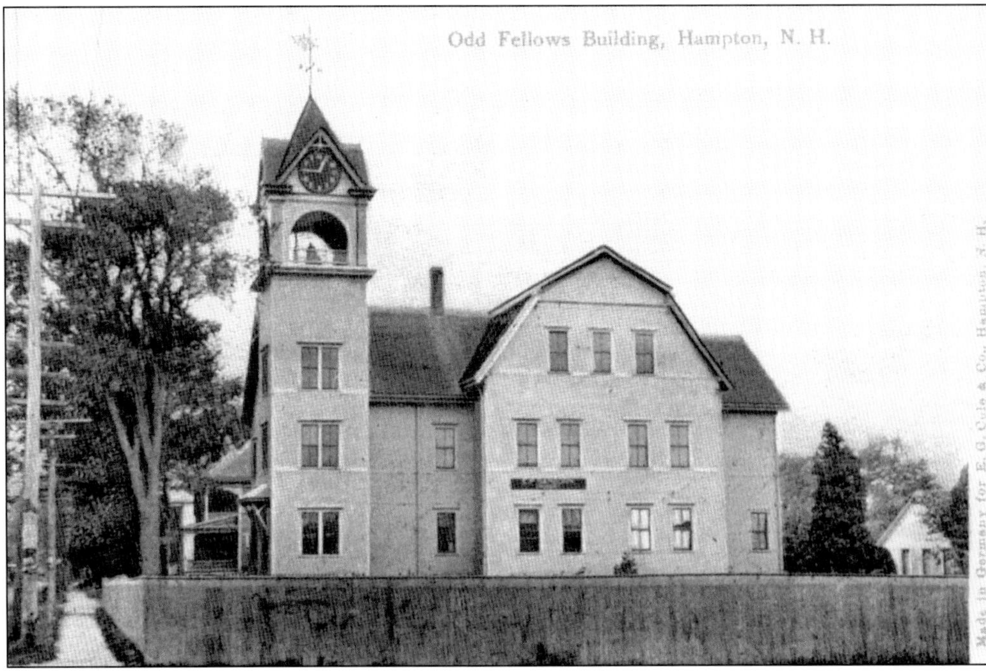

This large building was built in 1896 by the local chapter of the International Order of Odd Fellows. In addition to the Odd Fellows meeting rooms, the building housed a series of businesses. The tower was enlarged in 1898 to house the clock presented to the town by John T. Brown, a wealthy resident of Newburyport, who gave similar clocks to Hampton Falls and Salisbury. This building burned in 1990, but parts of the clock were salvaged.

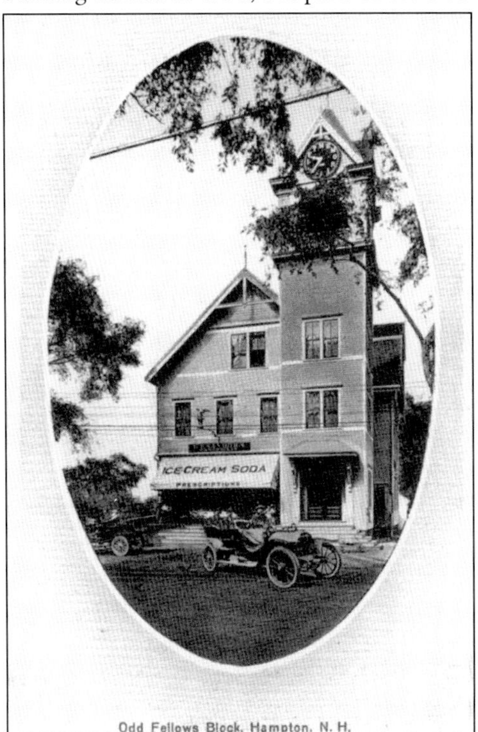

Everett Sanborn started a drugstore in the Odd Fellows hall in 1906 and added a soda fountain in 1911. He published a number of the postcards included in this book.

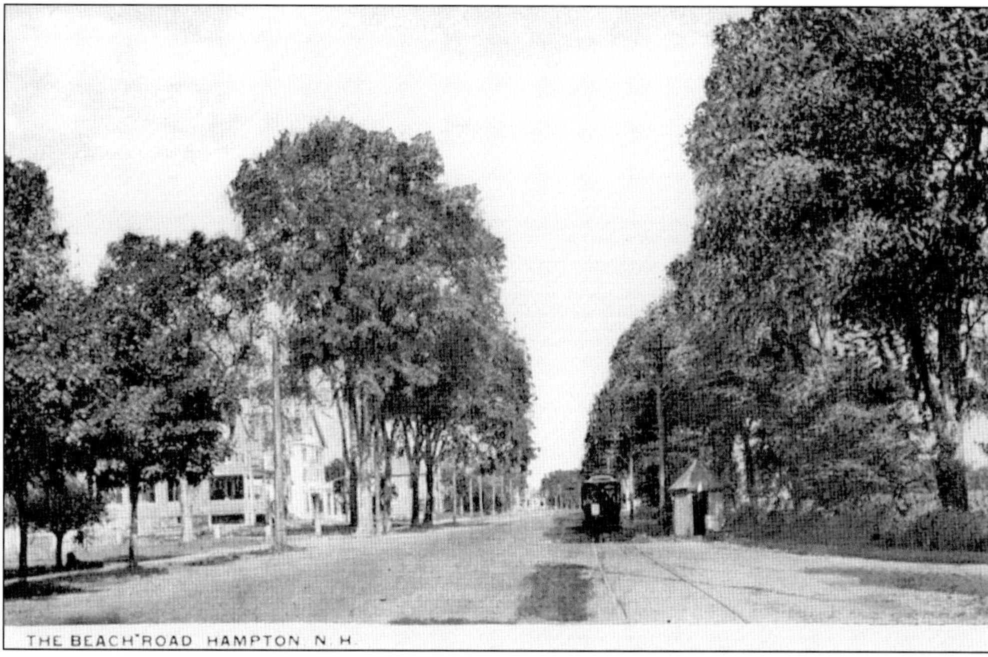

Winnacunnet Road was originally called the Hampton Beach Road or simply the Beach Road. This *c.* 1907 view from the intersection of Lafayette and Winnacunnet Roads is looking toward the east. At right is a small shelter for people waiting for the trolley. The Baptist church can be seen through the trees on the left.

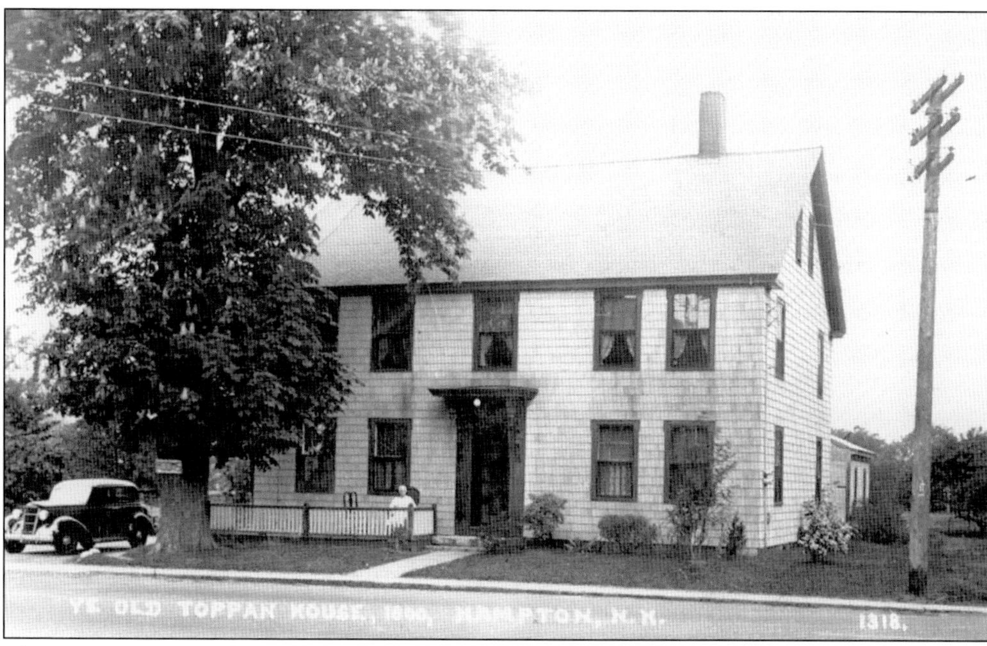

This card, postmarked 1939, shows the front of the Toppan farmhouse, which stood at 340 Lafayette Road until 1971. This angle hides the extensive ell at the back of the house and the large barn that stood behind the ell. The sign on the tree advertises the fact that there are rooms to be let. An apartment complex now occupies the site.

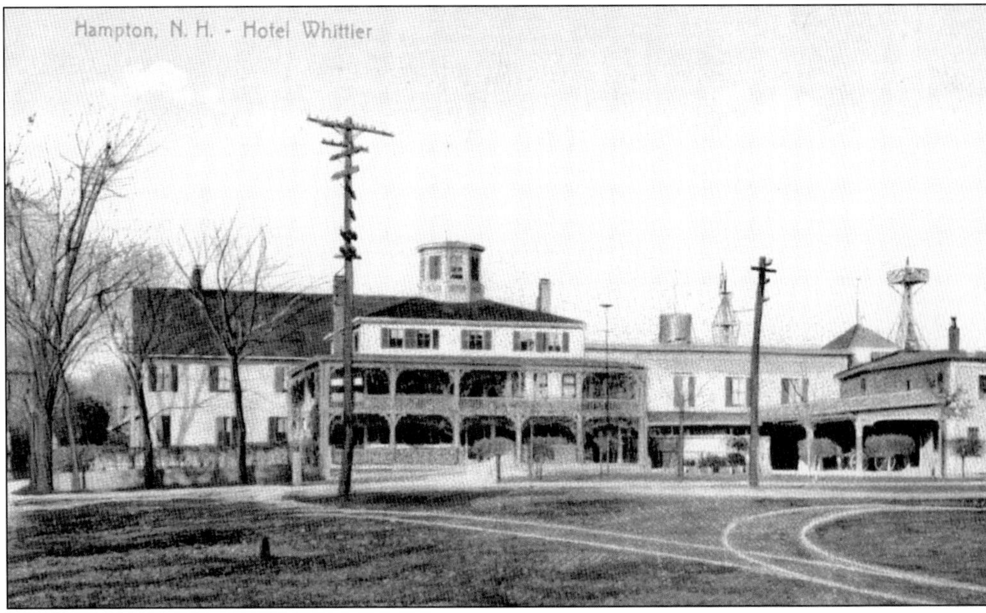

The Hotel Whittier was situated on the corner of Winnacunnet and Lafayette Roads, where taverns had stood since the 18th century. This building was apparently erected early in the 19th century and was remodeled several times by different owners. Although he had owned it for nearly 30 years, Otis Whittier did not give it his name until around 1890. At the turn of the century, it was the most fashionable hotel in town, but it burned in 1916 and was not rebuilt.

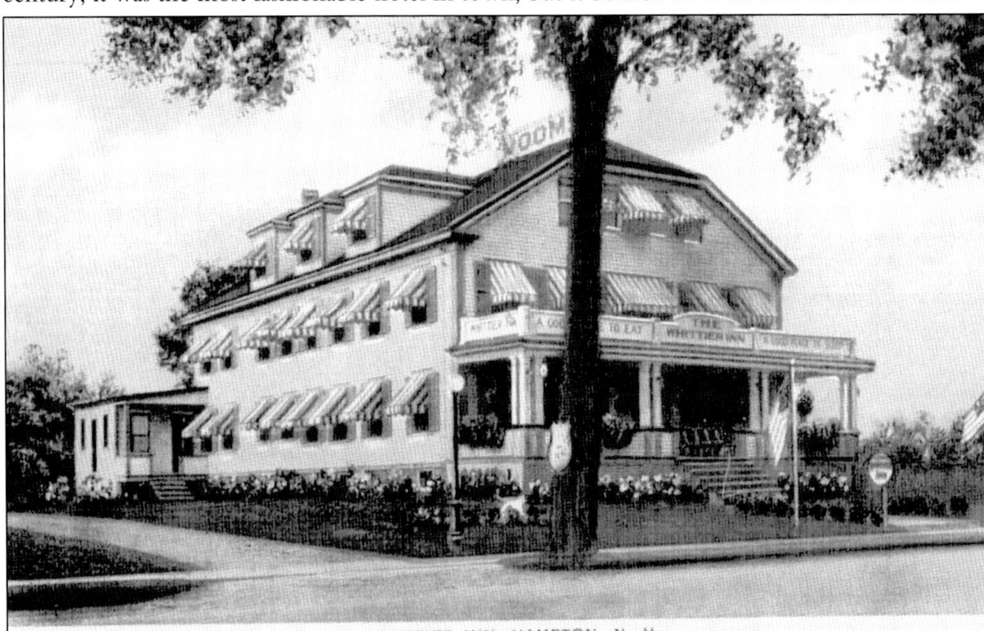

The second hotel to be called the Whittier was located just beyond the site of the first on Winnacunnet Road. It was originally called the Hotel Echo. Built in 1923 to replace a smaller inn that had been located on the site and had burned 10 years earlier, it was later renamed the Whittier Inn after its famous neighbor. It remained in business until Odyssey House took over the building in 1970.

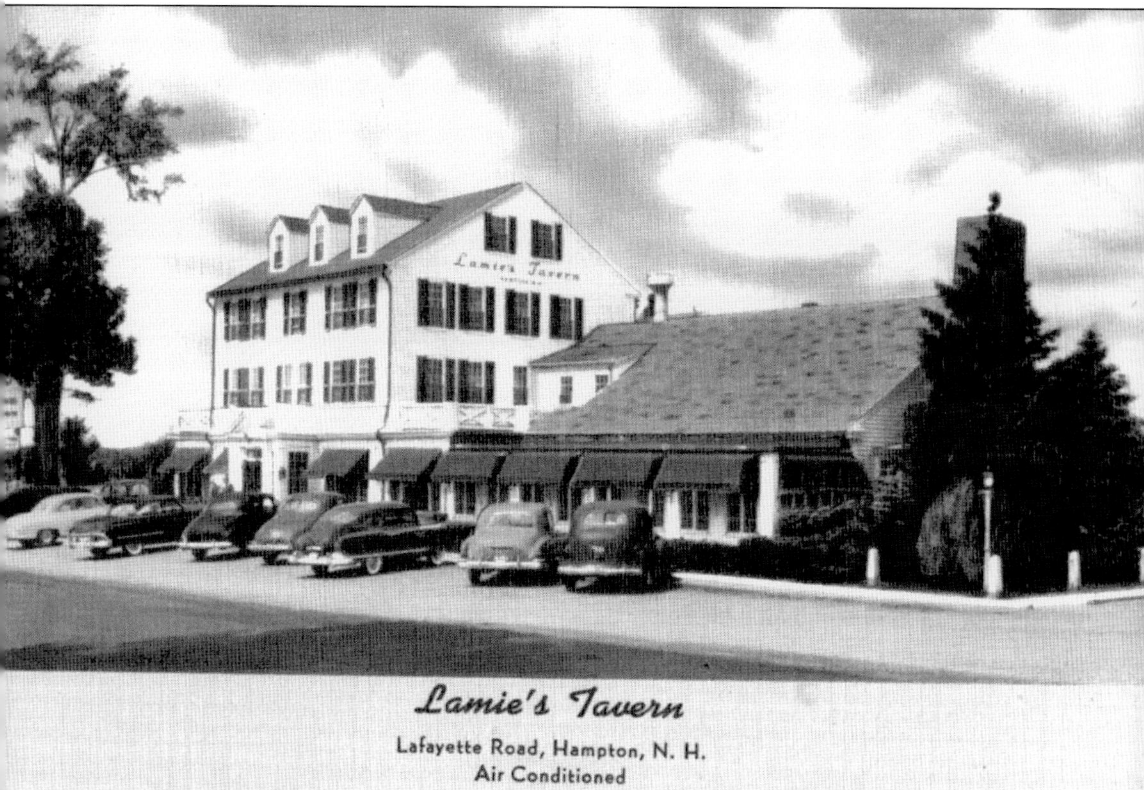

The Ebenezer Lane house, on the corner of Exeter and Lafayette Roads, was purchased in 1931 by Albert Lamie, who turned it into a restaurant called Lamie's Tavern. He raised the house and turned it 90 degrees to face on Lafayette Road, and he built new dining rooms and kitchens on the ground floor. Later owners added motel rooms to the building. The motel is now called Lamie's Inn, but the restaurant is the Old Salt. The building looks much the same today as it does on this card of the 1940s, but parking along Lafayette Road is no longer possible.

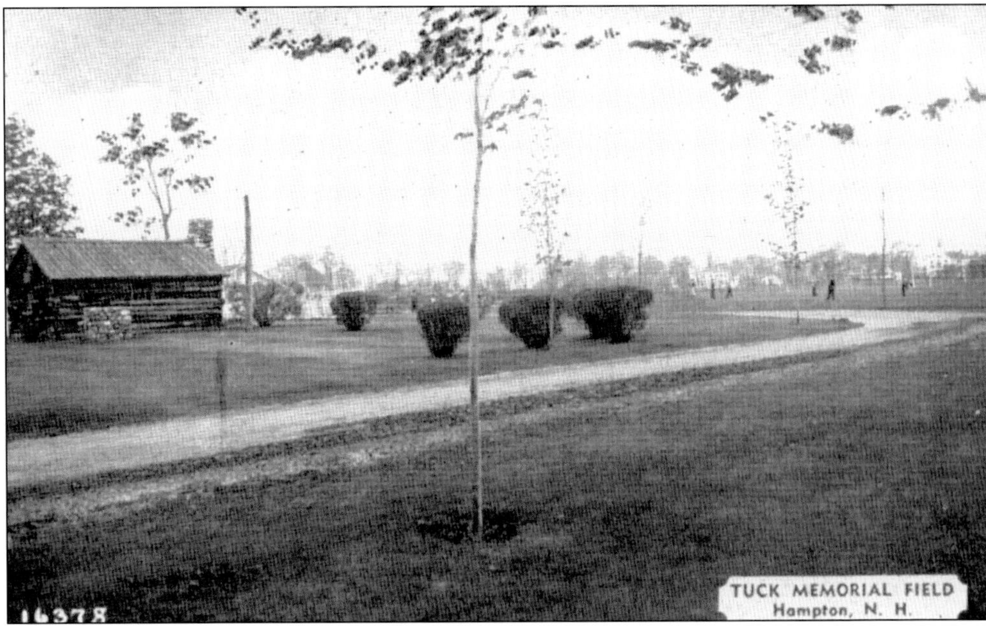

Tuck Field, on Park Avenue, was named for donor Edward Tuck, whose generosity made it possible for the town to build the athletic field in 1930. At the left of this 1930 view is the "log church," a somewhat fanciful representation of the first meetinghouse of 1639, which stood near this spot. This small building was built on the green in 1925 for the newly founded Meeting House Green Memorial Association. The Hampton Historical Society's schoolhouse now stands on the same site and has retained the stone chimney.

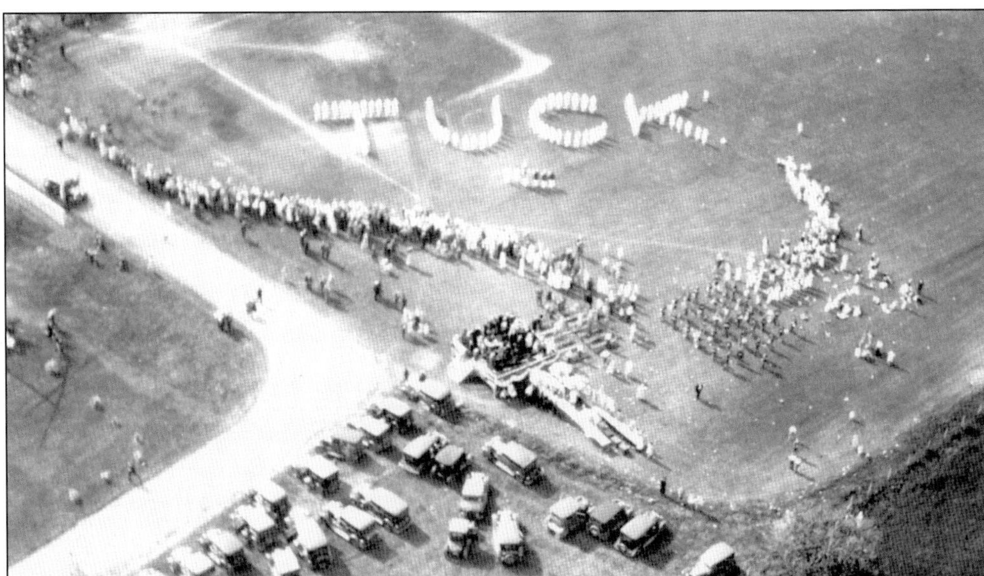

The dedication of Tuck Field on June 4, 1930, called for a daylong celebration, with a parade, sporting events, a concert, and the Tuck Drill, in which 90 "mothers of Hampton," all wearing white, spelled out the word "Tuck." David Colt took aerial photographs of the scene and charged 15¢ for this souvenir postcard.

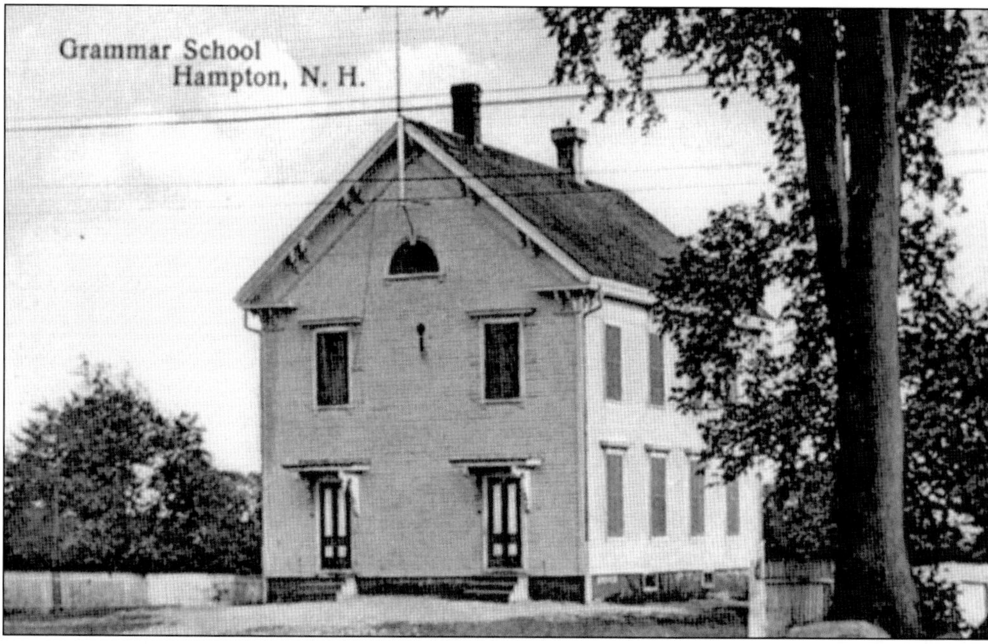

The grammar school was one of two similar schoolhouses built in 1873. This building shared the elementary grades with the East End School at the junction of Locke and Winnacunnet Roads. The grammar school stood on the site of the present Centre School, but it was moved in 1921 to 128 Winnacunnet Road, where it has served as the American Legion hall, the fire station, and the local courthouse.

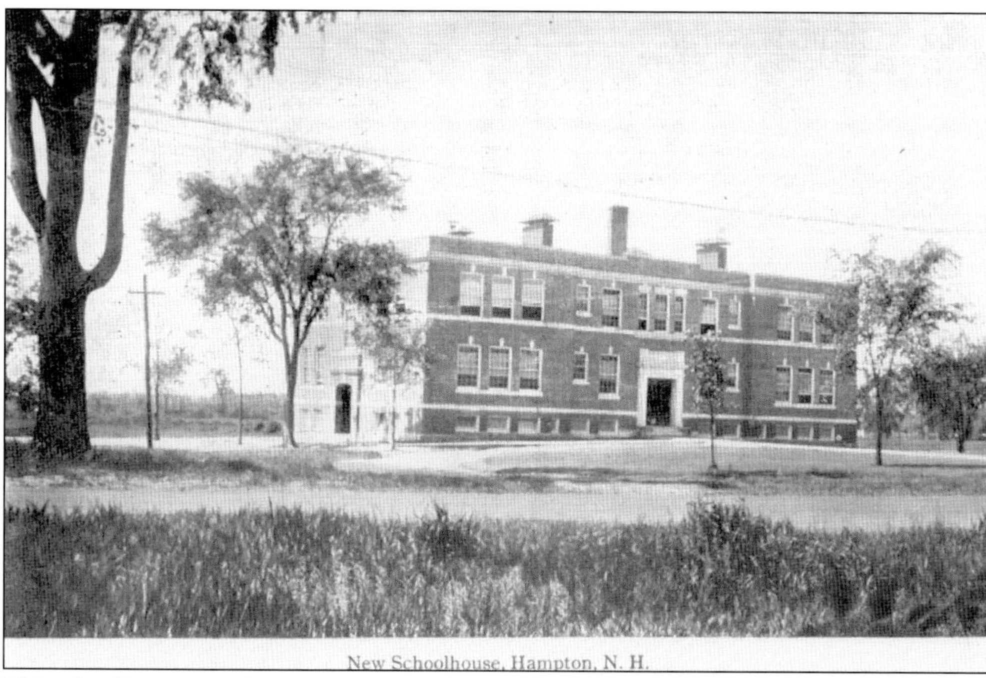

This schoolhouse, now known as Centre School, was built in 1922 on the site of the old grammar school, replacing both the grammar school and the East End School. It originally housed grades one through nine. It is still in use as an elementary school.

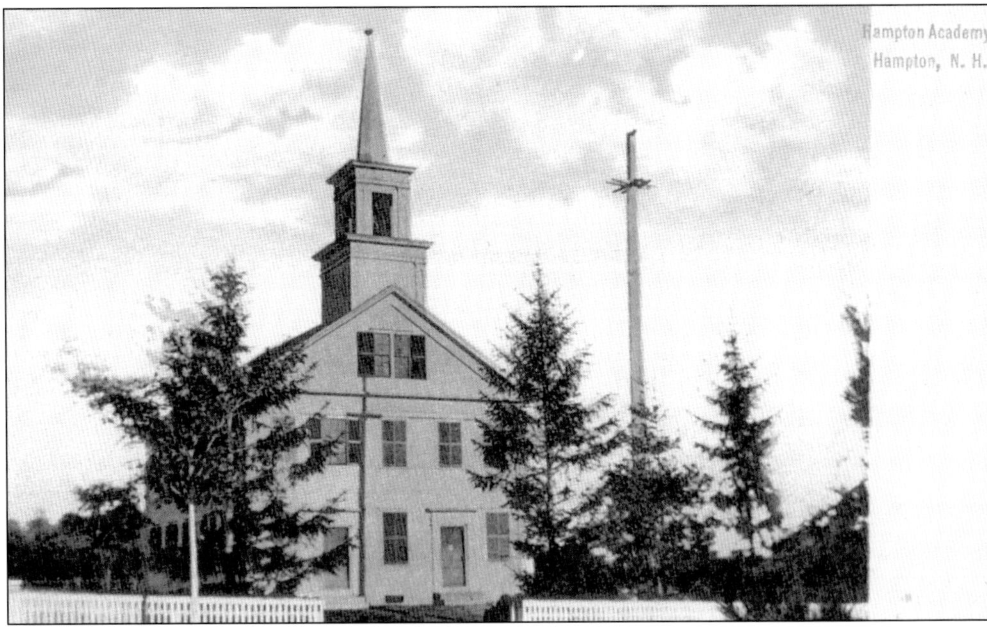

Hampton Academy was founded in 1810 as a private secondary school. The school was originally located on the Meeting House Green on Park Avenue. This schoolhouse, built in 1852 after the first one burned, was moved in January 1883 to a new site on Academy Avenue. The move was a town project for which most of the townspeople turned out. The building was placed on runners, and then 80 teams of oxen and several work horses pulled it across the snowy fields, a task that was accomplished in 17 minutes.

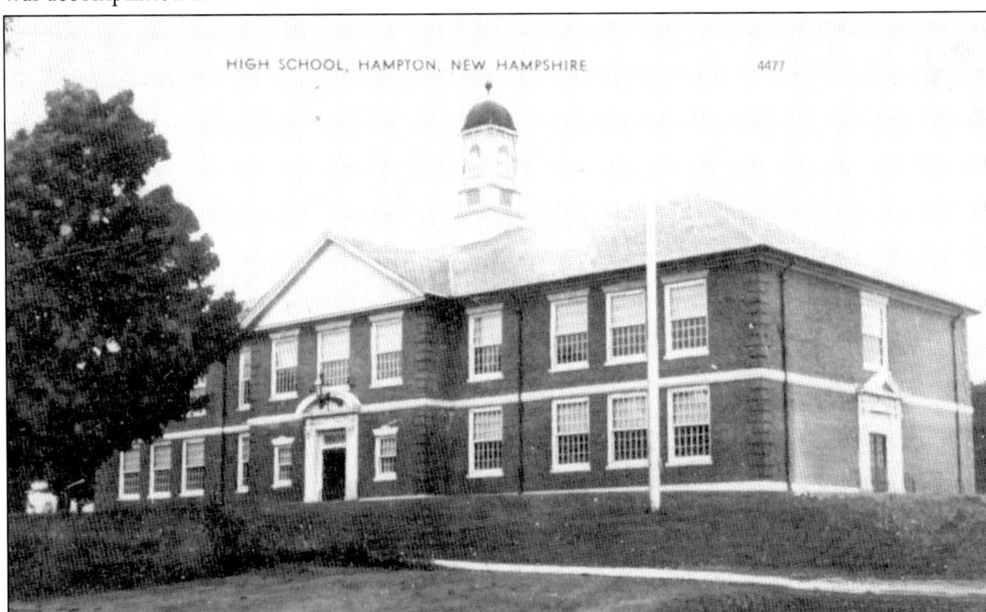

The present Hampton Academy building was erected in 1940 next to the old building, which was then razed. It remained the town's high school until the cooperative Winnacunnet High School was built in 1958 to serve several towns. Hampton Academy is now the junior high school but has retained its name.

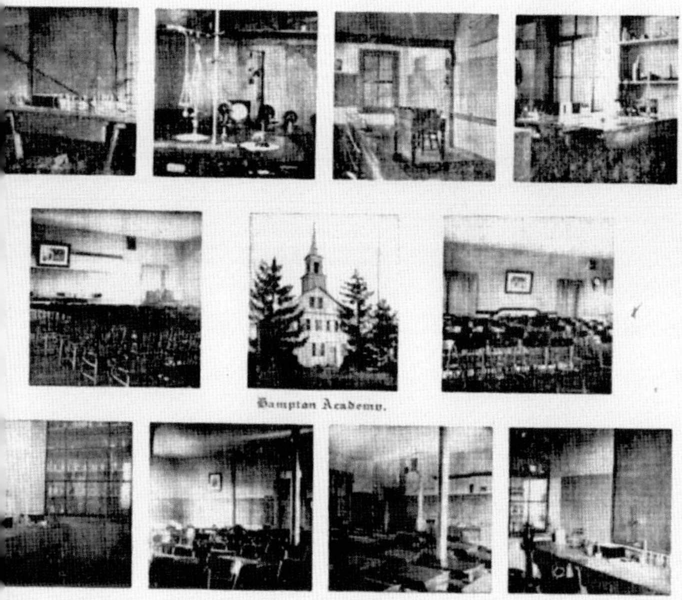

Hampton Academy.

Historical.

THE town of Hampton, settled in 1638, is closely identified with the beginning of New Hampshire and should be of special interest to natives of the Granite State.

In this school, founded in 1810, judges of United States courts, United States senators and representatives, State governors, railroad presidents, noted lawyers, clergymen, members of the other professions, besides many prominent business men and literary women, have gained the foundation for their future greatness or success. The renowned Rufus Choate, Amos Tuck, Lewis Cass, and others of our country's history started here.

The school has full preparatory courses. The completion of each study satisfactorily regardless of time has been one of its unique and important requirements.

In 1885, Hampton Academy became the town's public secondary school and was known as Hampton Academy and High School. Unlike some neighboring towns' schools, this one was coeducational, as it had been since its founding. This and other similar cards showing the classrooms were used to advertise the school, which accepted some students from other towns on a tuition basis.

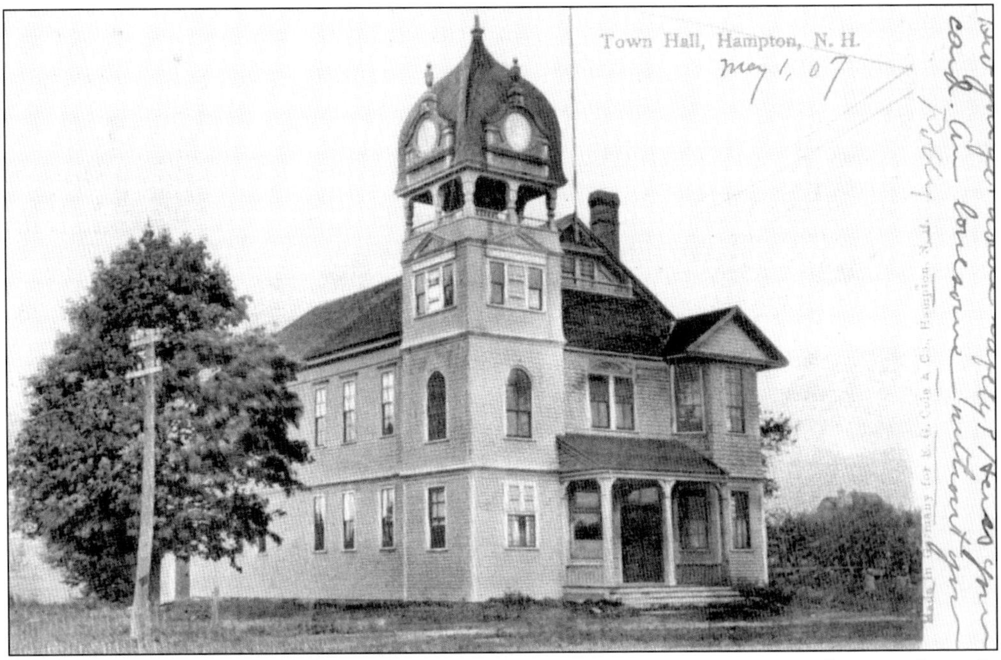

When Hampton was founded, the town and church shared a common meetinghouse. The early buildings were on Meeting House Green, but in 1808 the town abandoned the old building on the green and moved its meetings to the Congregational meetinghouse on Winnacunnet Road. This arrangement lasted until 1844, when the Congregationalists moved to their new church across the road. The town retained the old meetinghouse and, in 1860, made major alterations to it. In this card of 1907, the hall appears to be a grand Victorian building, but in fact it was built in 1797 and was quite plain until its remodeling.

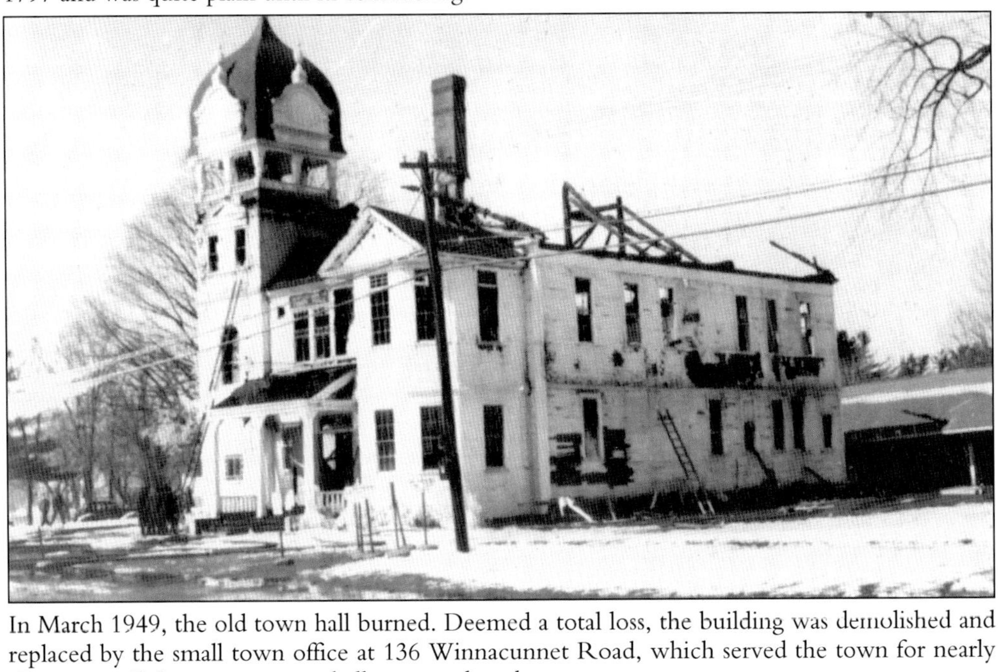

In March 1949, the old town hall burned. Deemed a total loss, the building was demolished and replaced by the small town office at 136 Winnacunnet Road, which served the town for nearly 50 years until the current town hall was purchased.

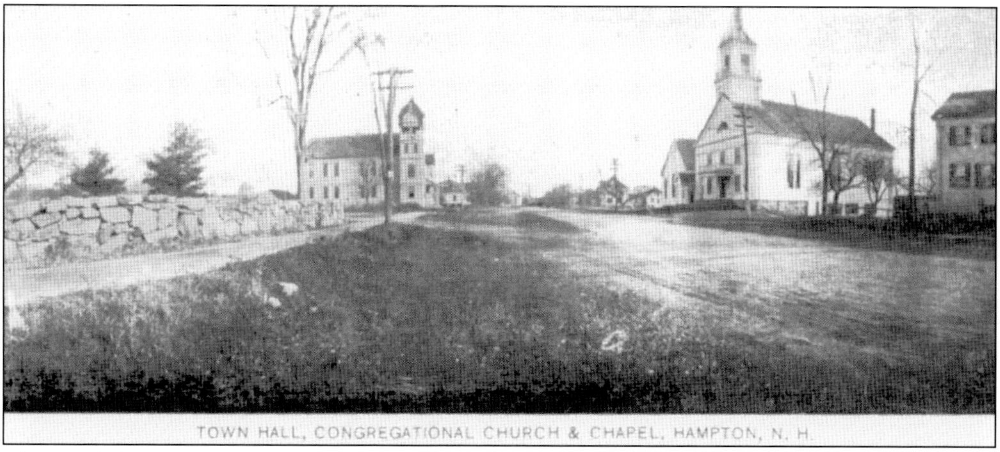

This card shows Winnacunnet Road before 1910. On the left is the town hall, and on the right stands the Congregational church. The Community Bank building is just visible at the right edge. The Lane Memorial Library was later built where the stone wall is in this photograph.

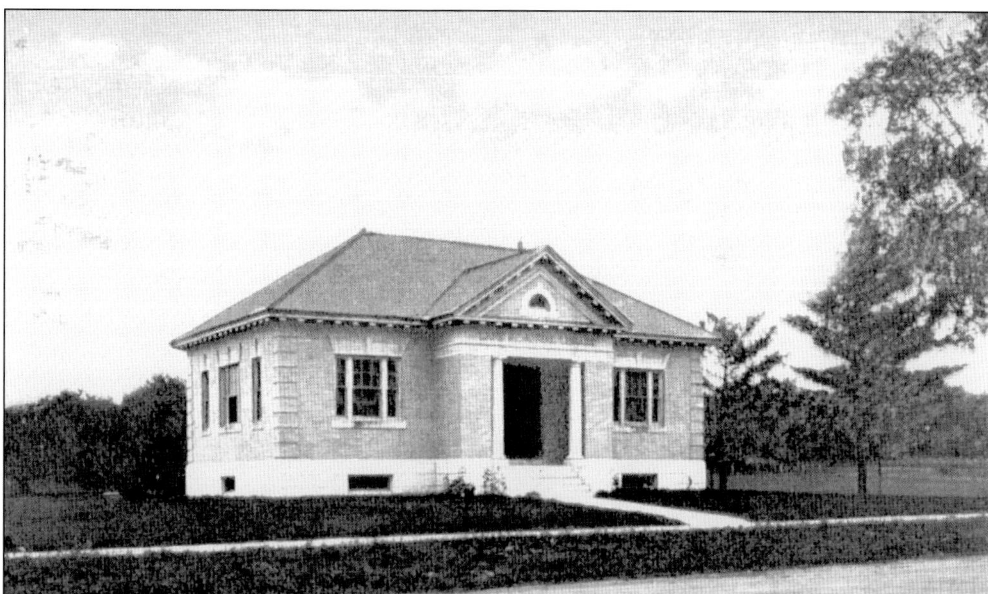

Local merchant Howard Lane gave the Lane Memorial Library to the town in 1910 as a memorial to his father. Until that time, the public library had been housed at a room in the old town hall. This card was produced before 1919, when the bronze tablets listing Civil War and World War I veterans were placed on either side of the front door.

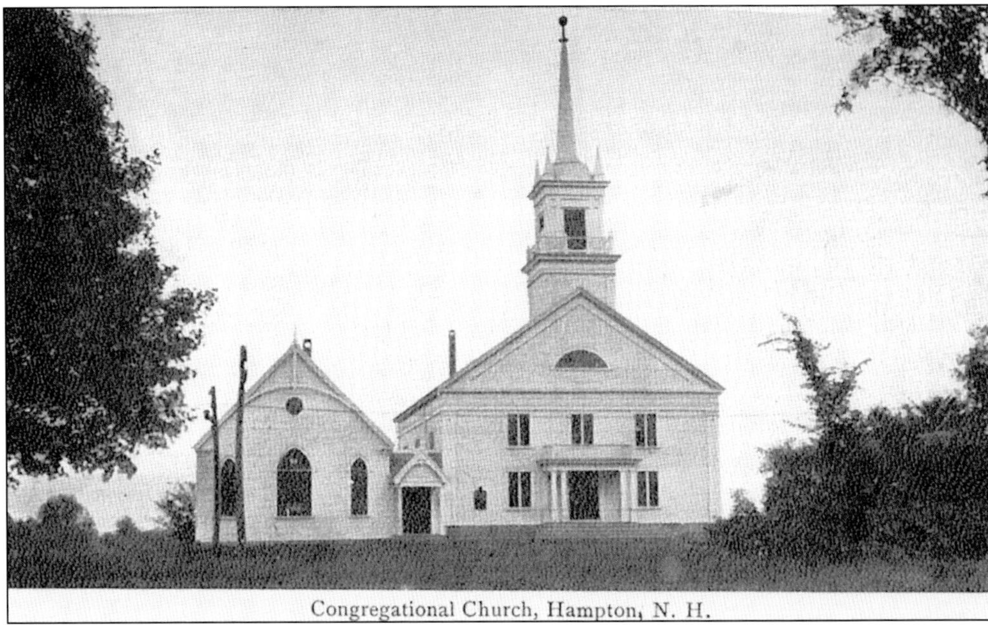

Across the street from the old town hall and the Lane Memorial Library is the Congregational church, which shares its founding date with the town. For 200 years, the town hired and paid the pastors, an arrangement that ended only in 1838. This is the sixth building to serve the congregation: the first four were on Meeting House Green, and the fifth became the old town hall. This building was built in 1844. The chapel at the left was added in 1894.

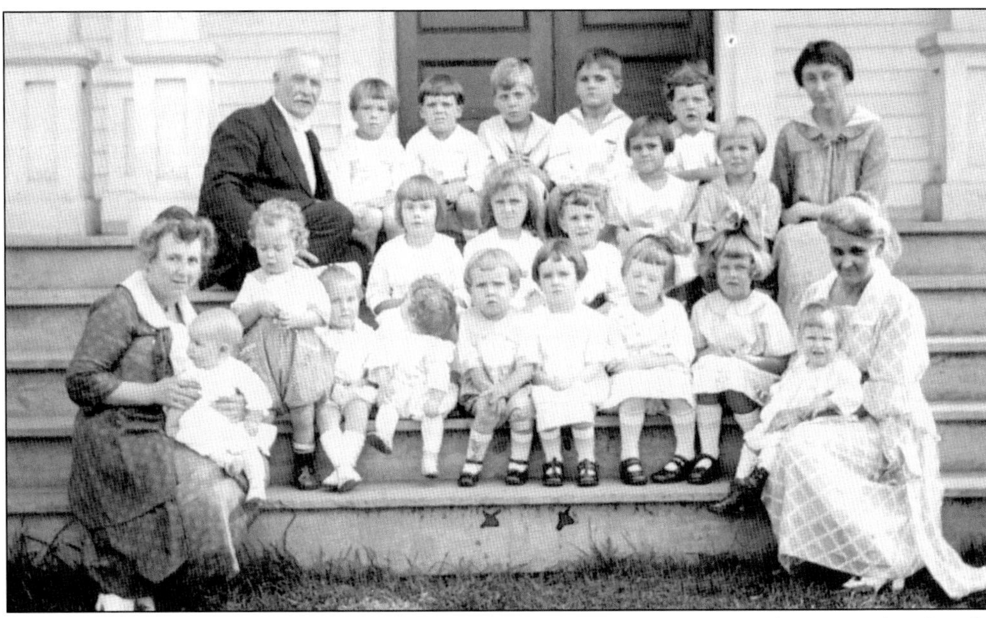

In an effort to divide the Sunday school classes by age, the Congregationalists started a class for very small children around 1920. This postcard, produced for the families of the children, shows the class called the Cradle Roll in 1922 or 1923. Several current senior residents of Hampton are in this photograph.

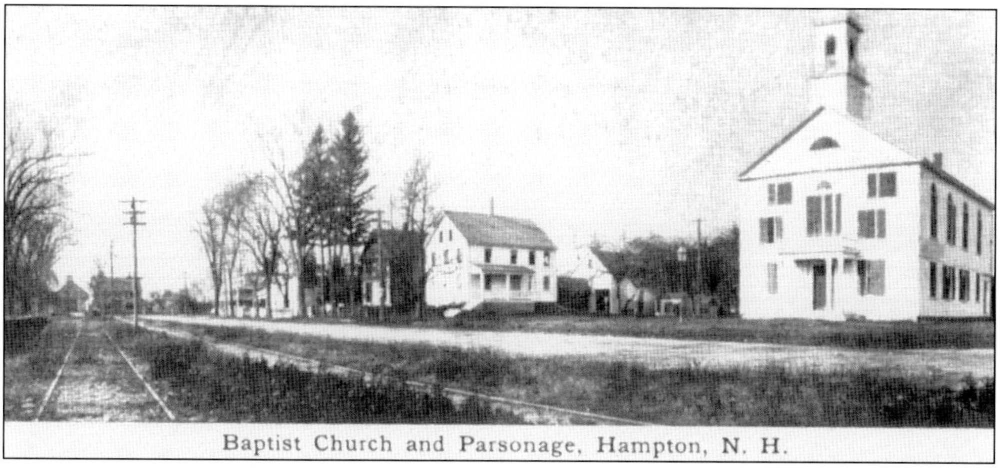

The Baptist church and its former parsonage stand next door to Odyssey House. The church was built in 1834 on land donated by David Towle, and the parsonage was erected in 1854. The church has been remodeled, but it is the oldest church building now standing in Hampton.

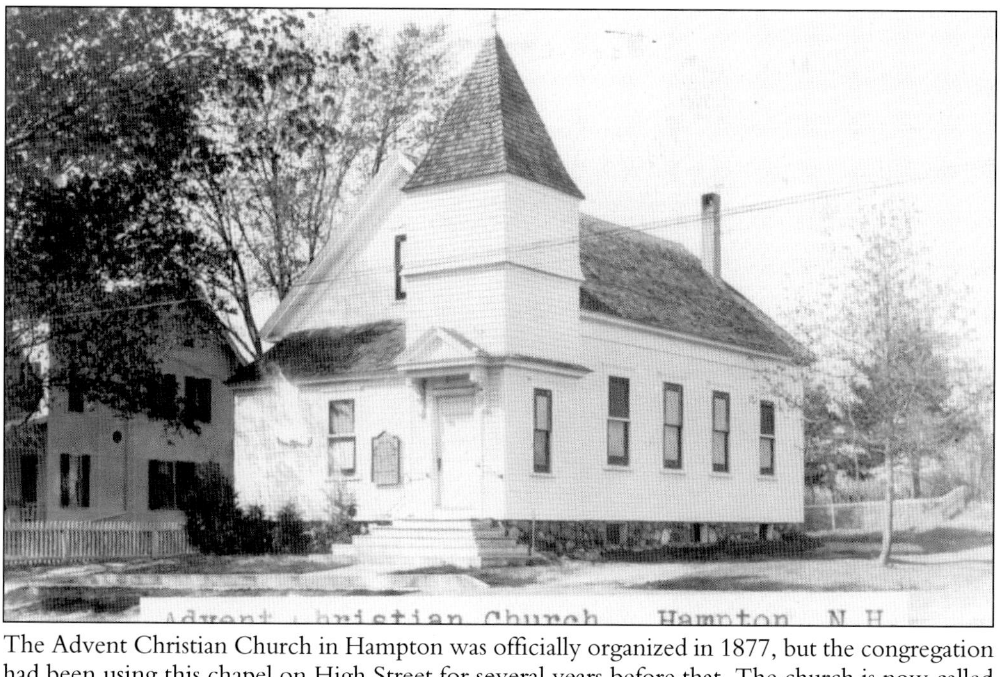

The Advent Christian Church in Hampton was officially organized in 1877, but the congregation had been using this chapel on High Street for several years before that. The church is now called the Faith Community Church.

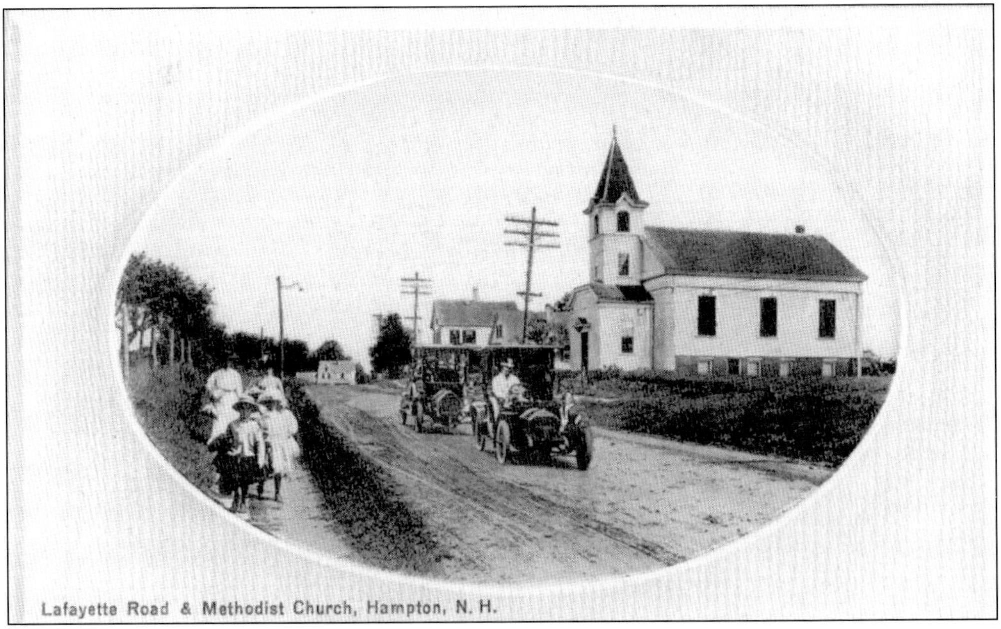

The Methodist church was originally situated on the corner of Ann's Lane and Lafayette Road. Built in 1848, it was moved nearer to the center of town in 1881. The church has had several additions, but the original front of the building has been preserved.

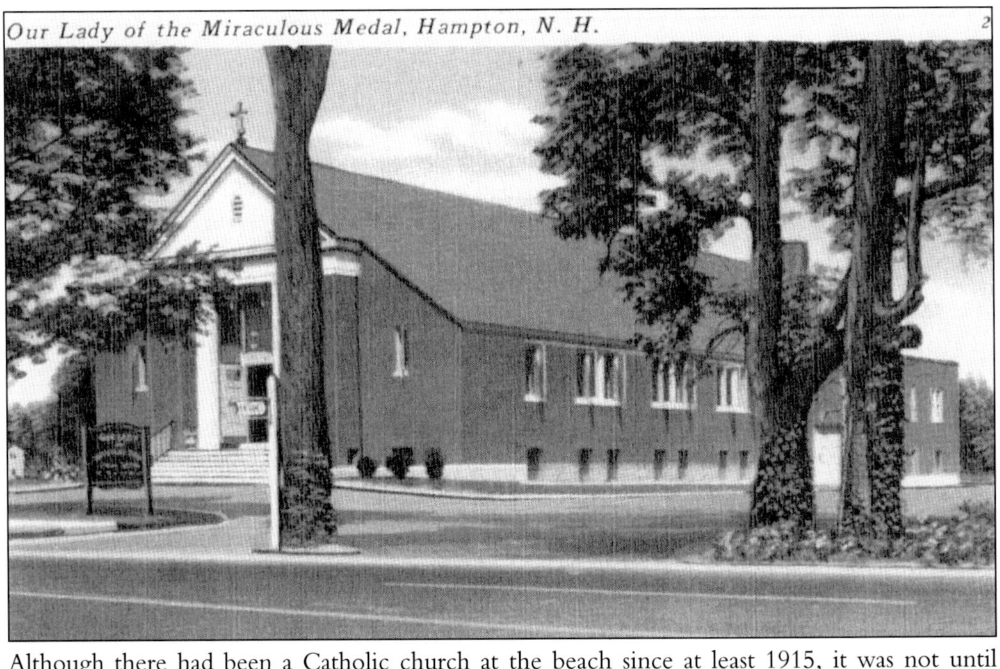

Although there had been a Catholic church at the beach since at least 1915, it was not until 1948 that a church was built in the town center on Lafayette Road. Our Lady of the Miraculous Medal held its first service on Christmas Eve 1948 and has since grown to be the largest church in Hampton. The church also operates the Sacred Heart School.

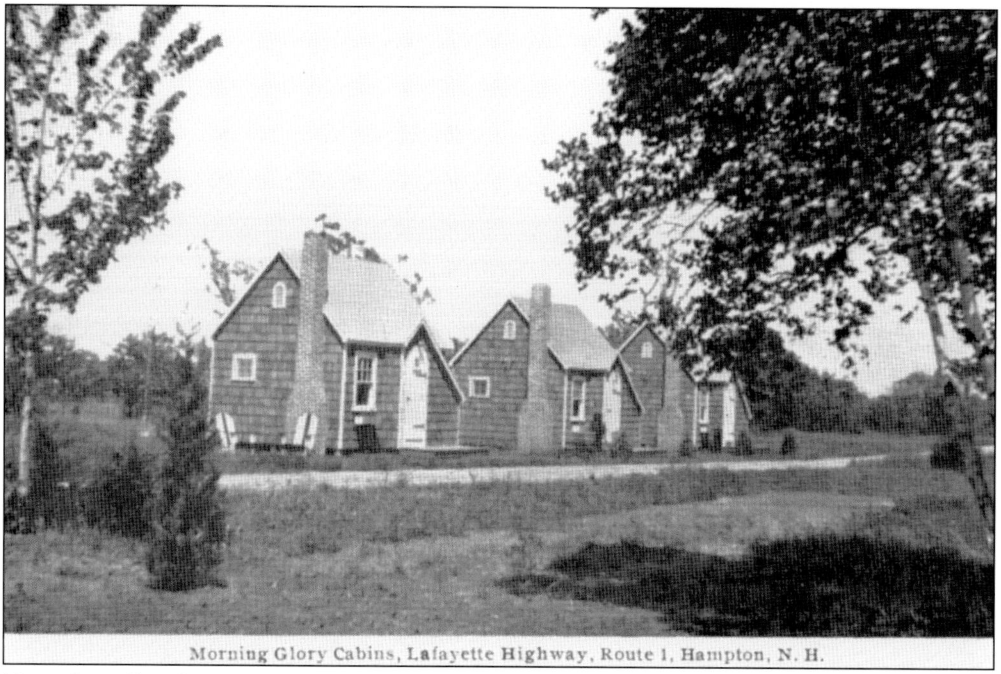

Near the railroad overpass on Lafayette Road at the North Hampton line were the Morning Glory Cabins. The cabins, located at 877 Lafayette Road, were one of several such tourist stops on Route 1 in Hampton in the late 1940s. Almost all have now disappeared.

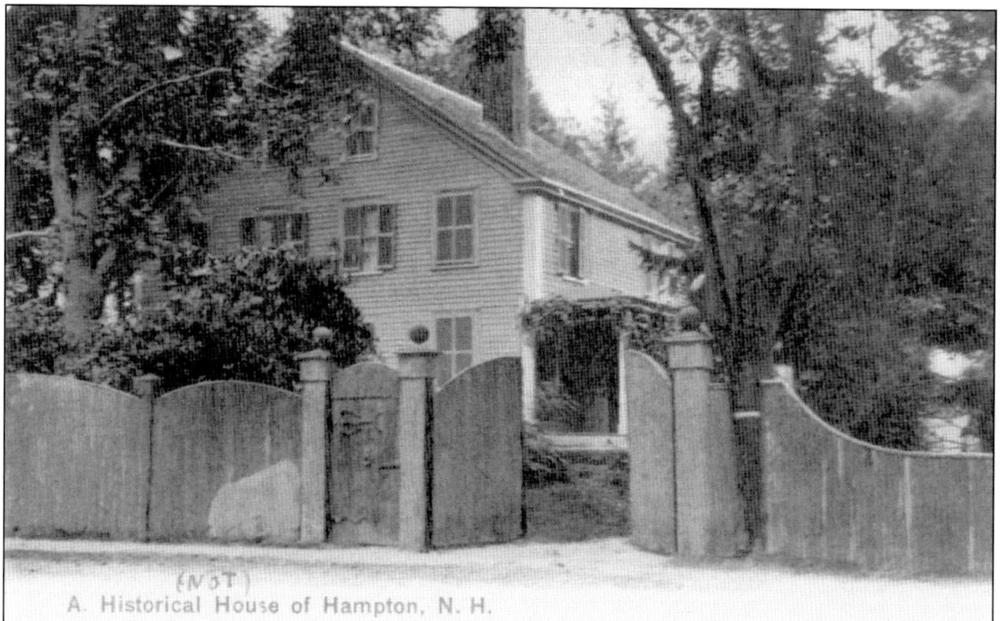

This house seems to be on a rural side road, but it in fact stands at 427 Lafayette Road, which today is in the busy center of town. Although the 1907 card declares the house to be "historical," it was only just over 40 years old. Note that the sender of this card agrees and has added the word "not" before "historical."

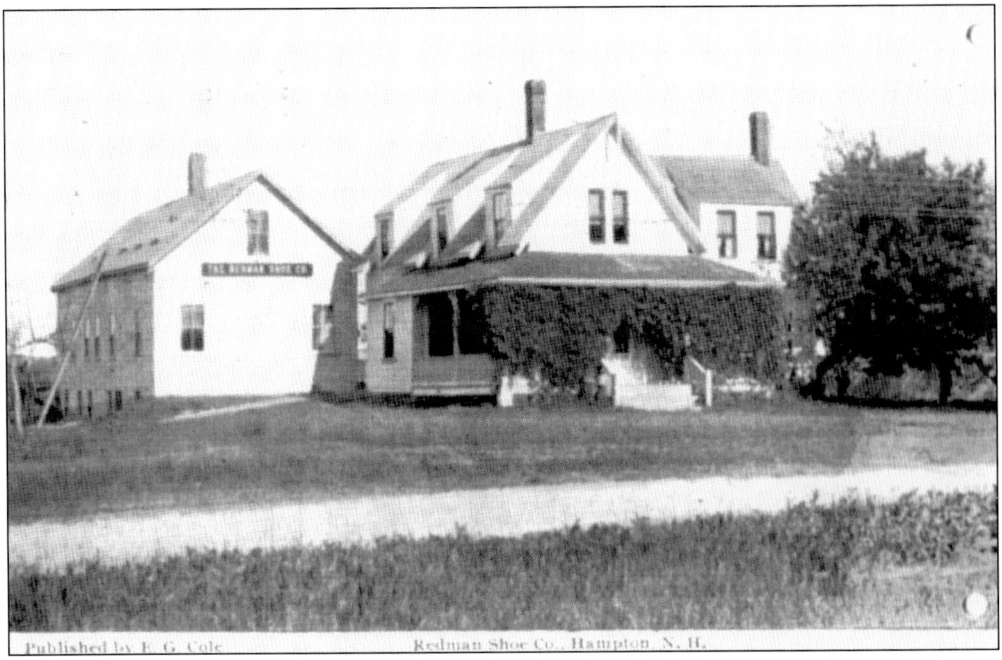

The Redman Shoe Company stood behind the house at 96 Locke Road. The shoe manufactory operated from 1910 to 1935, when it moved to Newburyport. The house still stands, but the factory is gone.

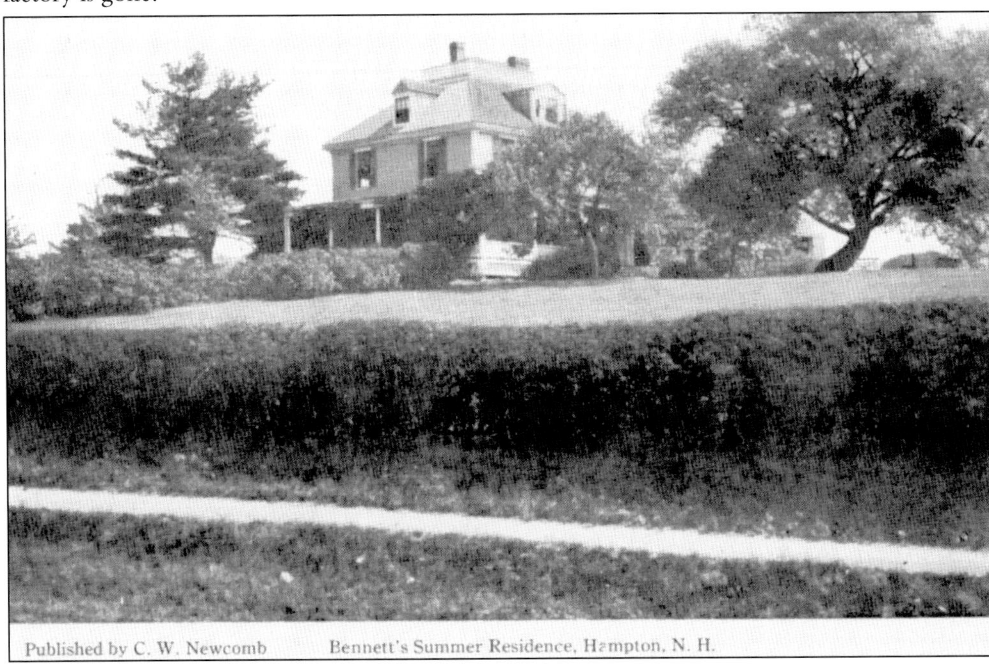

A curving driveway leading from Exeter Road ends at the large white house that Norman Marston built in 1891. Marston was a piano tuner and musician who started Moses Brown on his career as a piano builder, leading to the establishment of Brown's piano factory in Hampton. In 1899, a Boston banker, Josiah Bennett, bought the house for his summer residence. Among later owners was Baron William Frary von Blomberg.

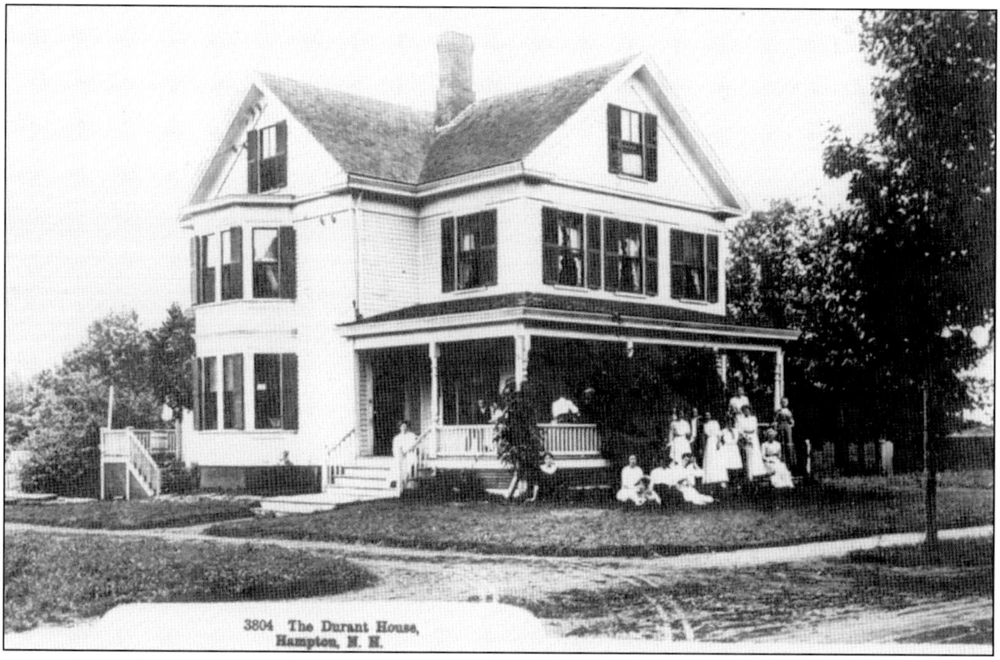

A number of Hampton residents turned their homes into boardinghouses, particularly during the busy summer season. Lena and Joseph Durant operated the Durant House as a tourist home well into the 1930s. The house, although much altered, still stands at 167 High Street.

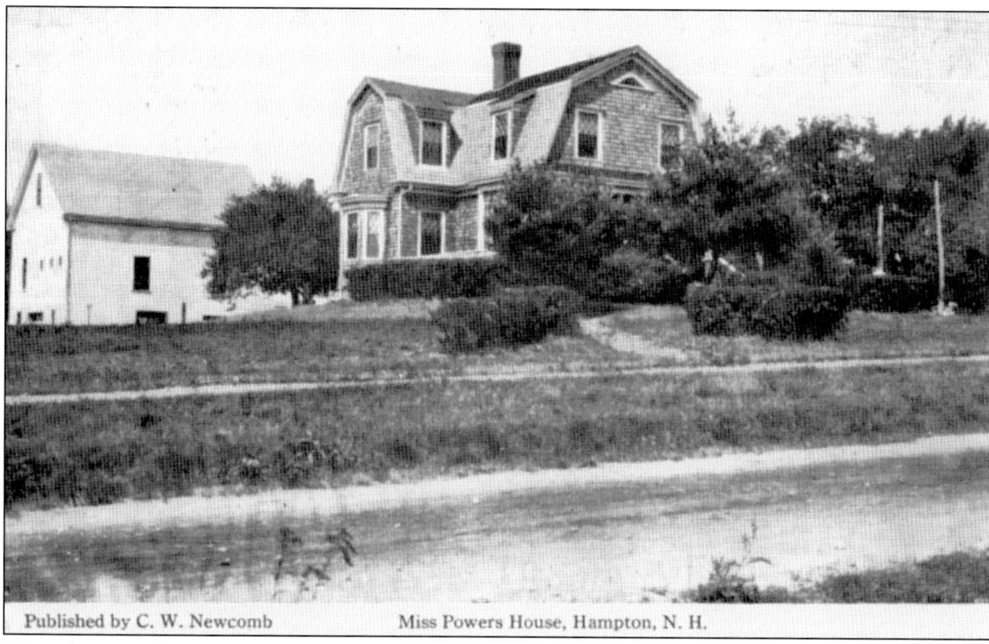

Next door to the Durant House, on the corner of Mill Road, is Clara Powers's guesthouse. This house is unusual for one in the center of town, since its architecture is very much like the beach cottages that were being built in the 1920s. Shingle siding and gambrel roofs were more common along the shore than on the central streets. The house has changed little since the publication of this card around 1930.

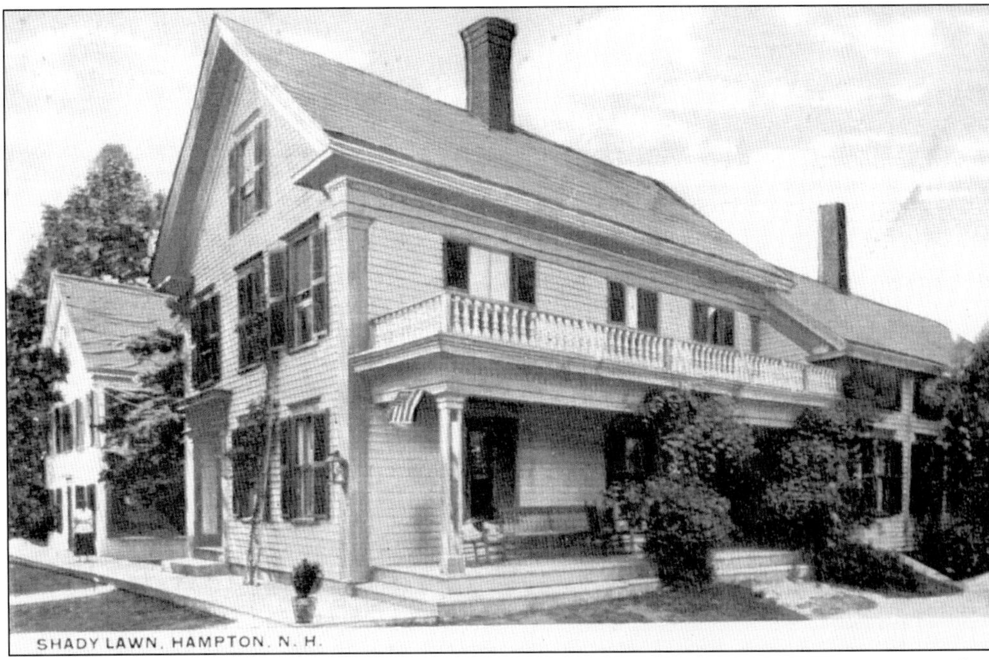

Across High Street from Clara Powers's guesthouse was Shady Lawn, run by John and Lillian Roberts. This boardinghouse could accommodate 45 guests and was frequently a subject of postcards.

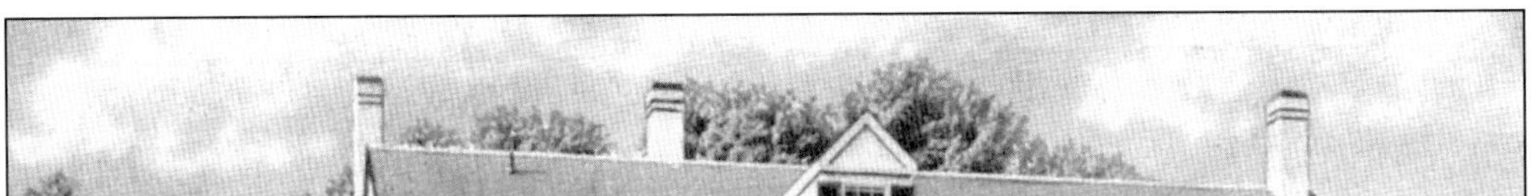

The Ashworth Pines, nearer the beach on High Street, advertised "rooms with and without private bath" for tourists of the 1930s and 1940s. A portion of this house was moved in 1929 from Little Boar's Head in North Hampton, where it had been the occasional summer residence of Pres. Franklin Pierce and his family.

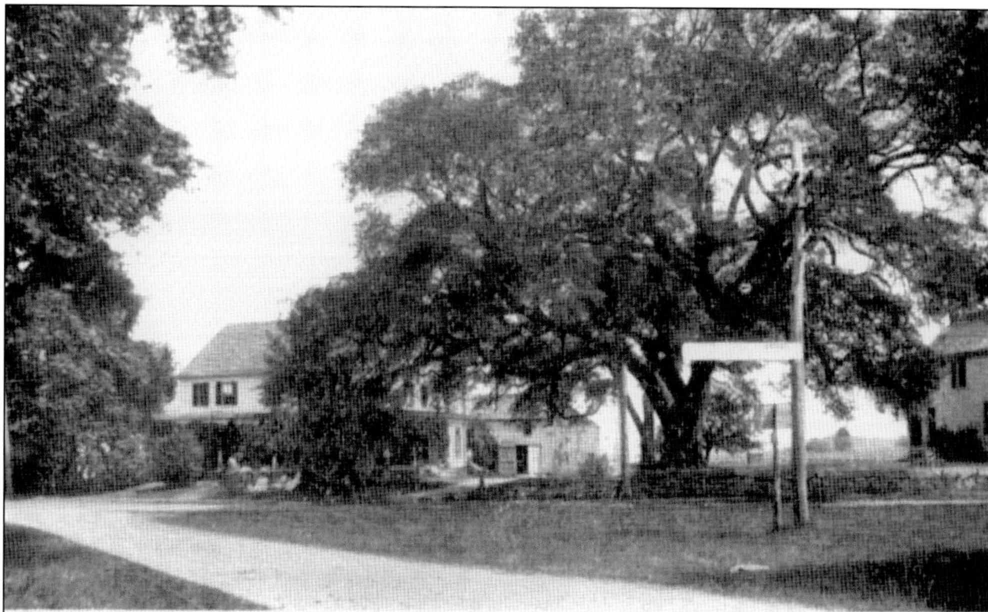

Published by E. P. Sanborn   Elmwood Farm, Hampton, N. H.

Elmwood Farm stands at the junction of Winnacunnet and Landing Roads. It received its name from the magnificent elm tree that is seen on this card. The house originally belonged to the Dow family, one of whom was Joseph Dow (1807–1889), the indefatigable chronicler of Hampton. The house became a boardinghouse in the 1890s, a function it continues to serve to this day.

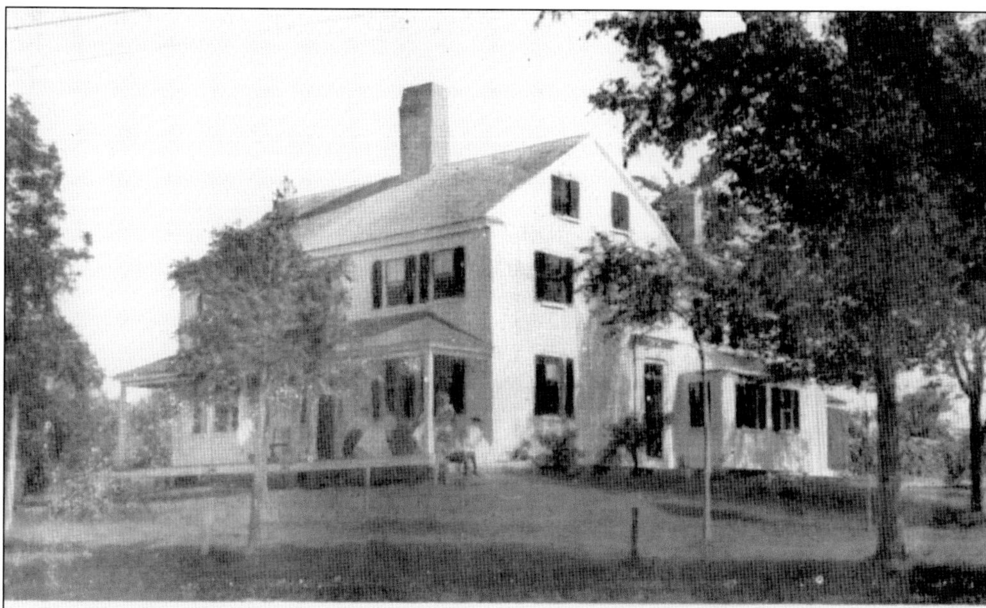

Published by E. P. Sanborn   Garland House, Hampton, N. H.

The Garland house, located on Winnacunnet Road near the end of Locke Road, stands on land first farmed by the Garland family in 1653. In the early 20th century, the house was a boardinghouse run by Lillian Garland, who offered home-cooked meals for as many as 25 guests.

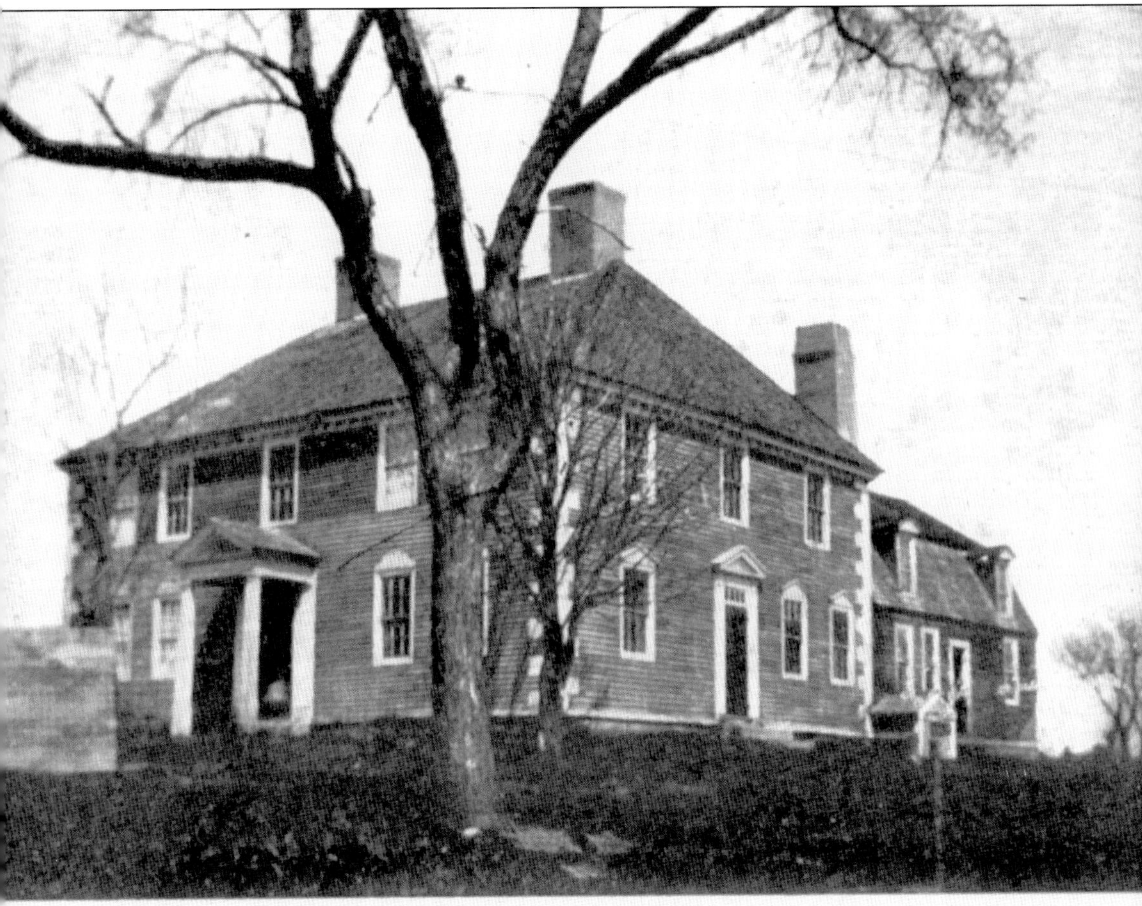

Haunted House, Hampton, N. H.

The most famous house in Hampton is the house at 212 Lafayette Road. It was built in 1769 by wealthy merchant Jonathan Moulton, who served as a general in the Revolutionary War. Moulton, who had worked closely with the merchants of Portsmouth, wanted to emulate his friends, and he built a high-style Georgian house. This display of wealth caused his Hampton neighbors to whisper that he could only have acquired such riches by making a pact with the devil. Other stories involving the ghost of his first wife were repeated by later writers, including John Greenleaf Whittier, giving the house the reputation of being haunted. The building originally stood at a sharp bend in the road, and this corner, now straightened, is still called Haunted House Corner.

Eight

SOUVENIRS OF HAMPTON

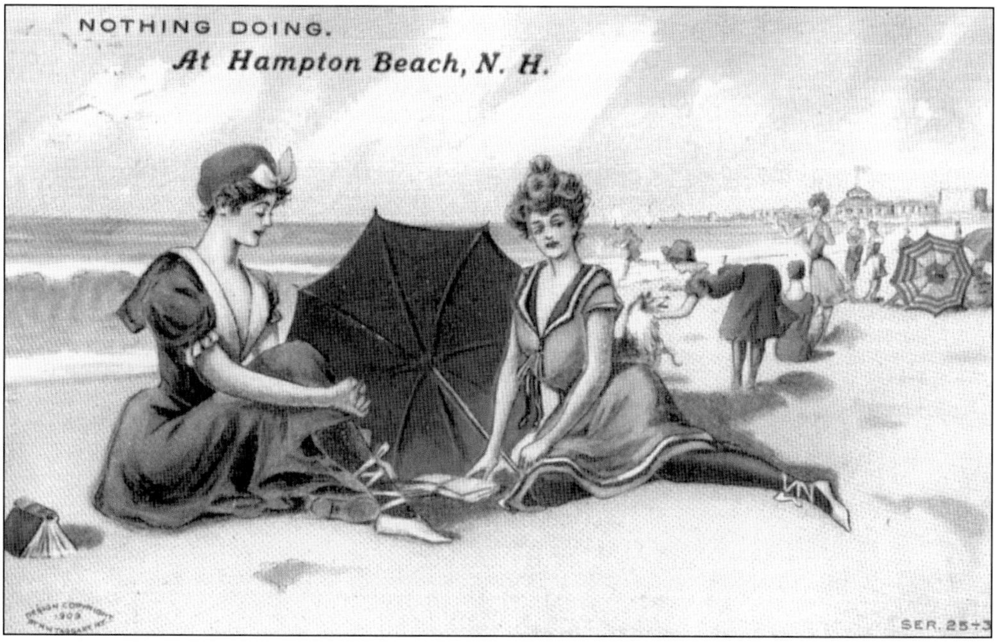

Not all postcards were straightforward pictorial representations of the sights of the town and beach. Publishers liked to put fanciful borders around the images or make visual jokes. Here two young ladies dressed in the height of beach fashion around 1912 sit forlornly on the sand, complaining that nothing is happening here. The card says Hampton Beach, but it could be anywhere.

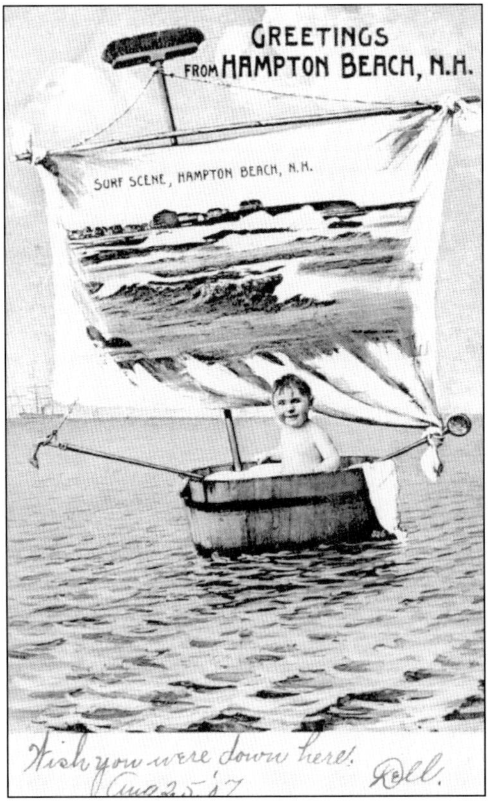

A humorous image of a baby setting sail in a washtub is used to show a scene of Great Boar's Head. The card was mailed in 1907, but the photograph was taken earlier, since the water standpipe does not appear.

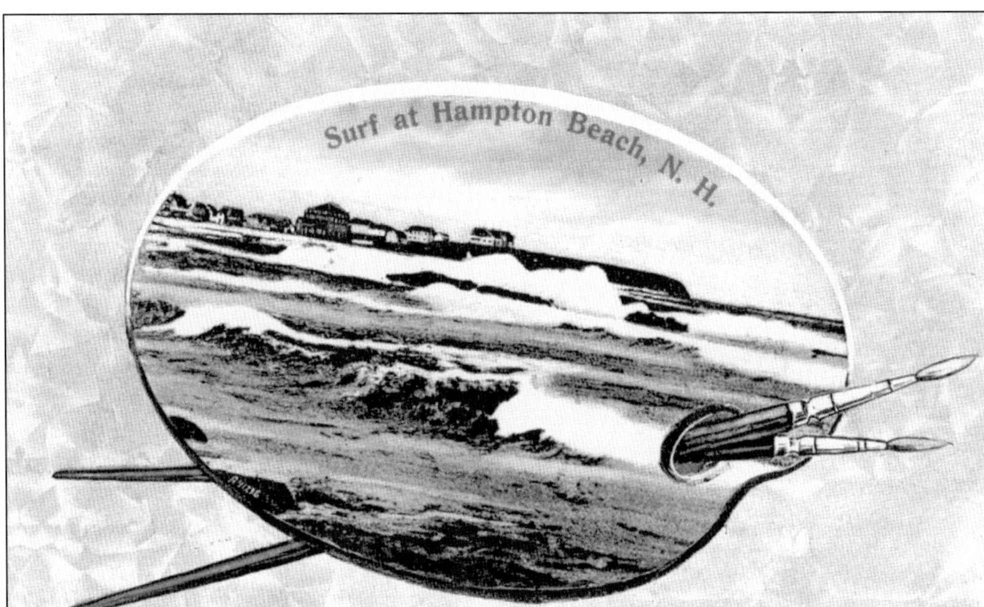

The same scene of Boar's Head is depicted on this card with an artist's palette as the background. Artists of the late 19th century were drawn to the beaches of the area to paint the scenic landscape.

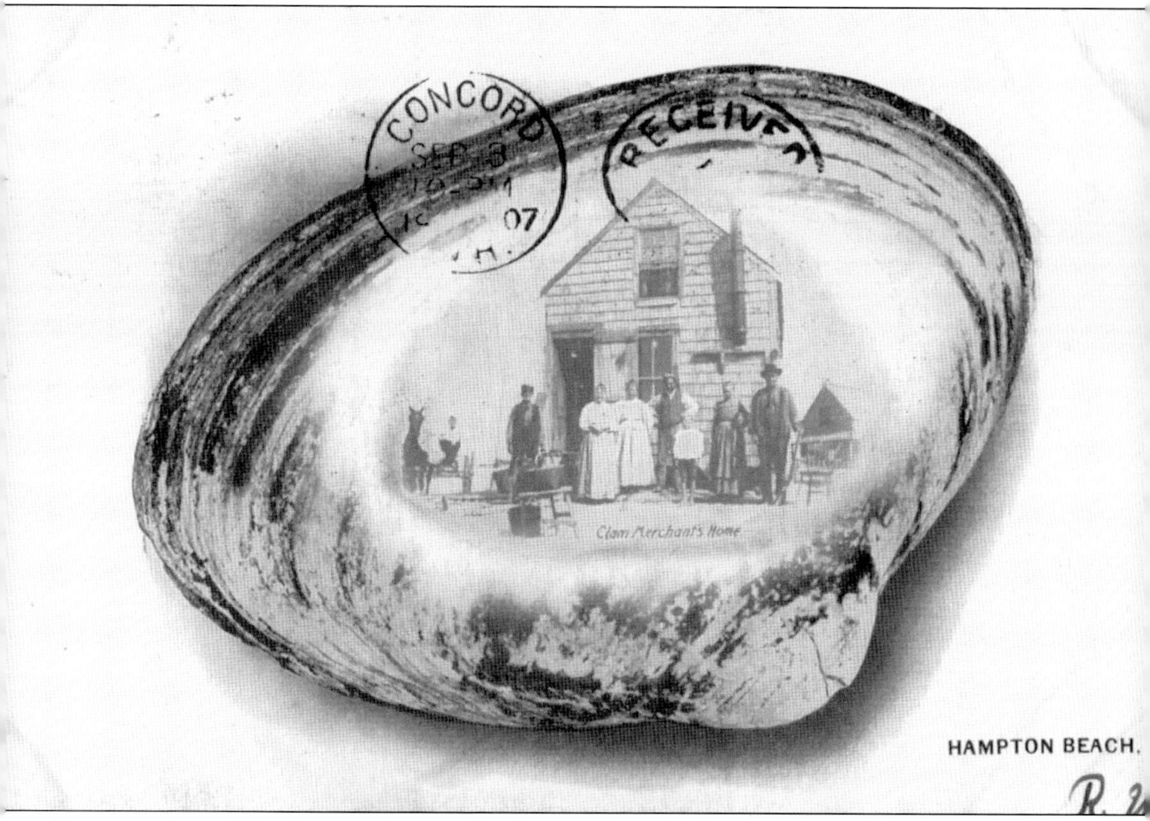

Here members of the Gove and Bragg families are shown before 1900 in front of their beach house on the bank of the Hampton River. The photograph has been superimposed on a drawing of a clam shell to emphasize that the people sold clams (note the clam basket on the stool in the front). The house was later moved to permit construction of the mile-long bridge. The Hampton River was famous for its prolific clam beds.

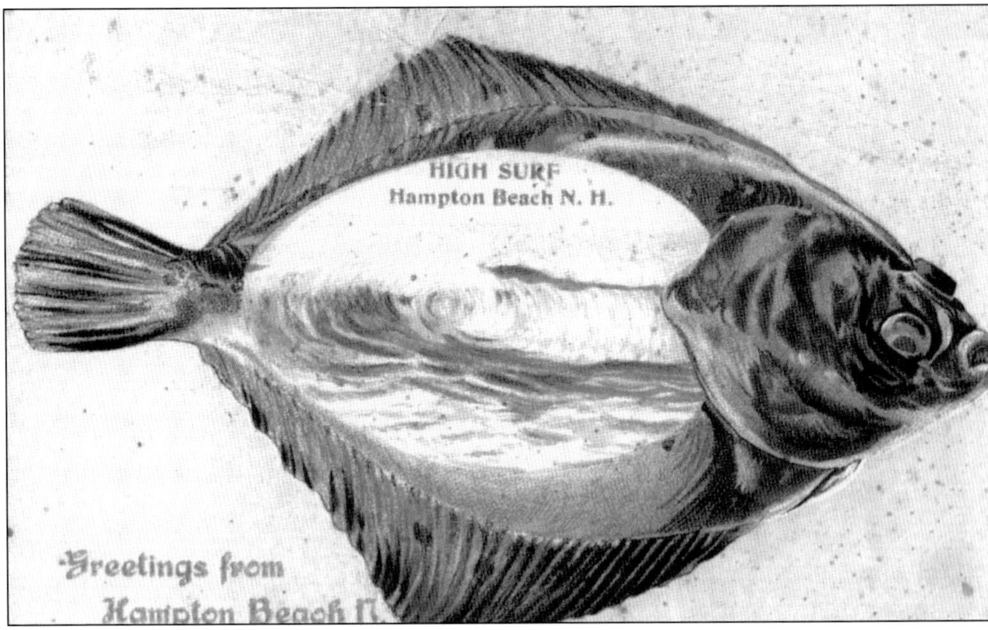

A photograph of the rolling surf of Hampton Beach is superimposed on an image of a flounder, which was one of the most common fish to be found in the local waters.

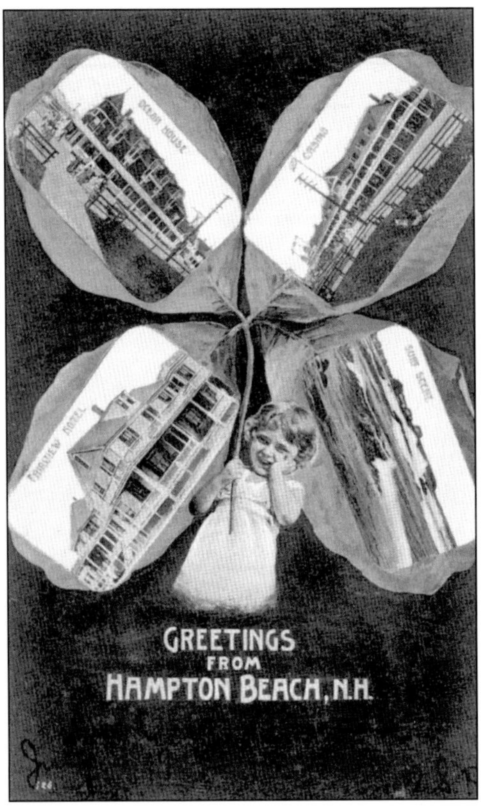

A card showing multiple beach scenes was a popular choice for tourists. This *c.* 1905 card shows the Fairview and Ocean House hotels, as well as the Casino and Boar's Head.

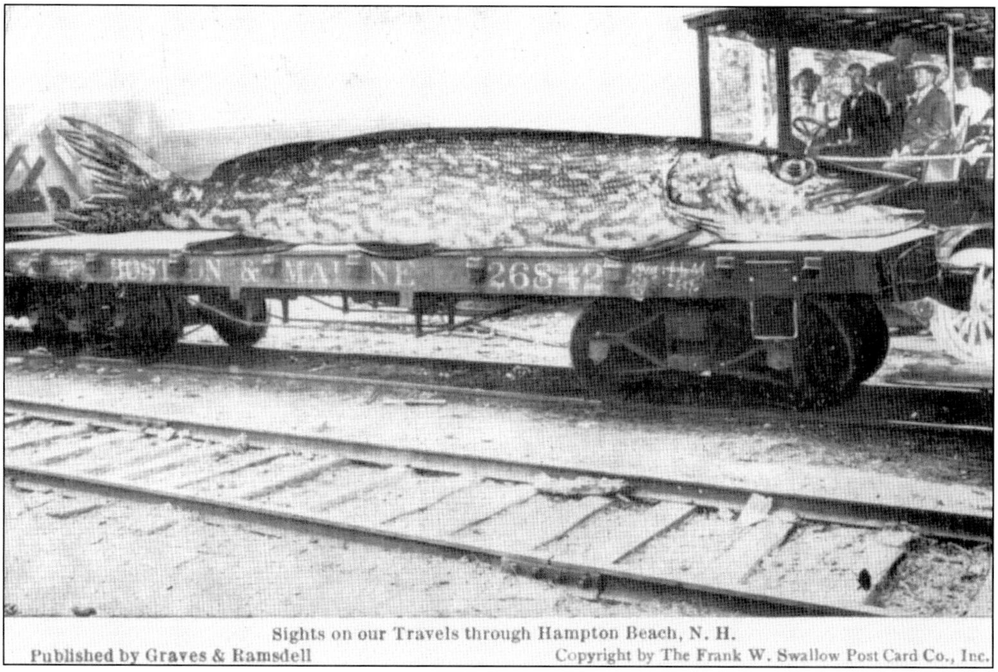

Trick photographs made postcards that were popular with the tourists. Here a mammoth flounder is pictured on a Boston and Maine Railroad flatcar. The publishers of this and the next card were Graves and Ramsdell, who ran the Casino and the Ocean House.

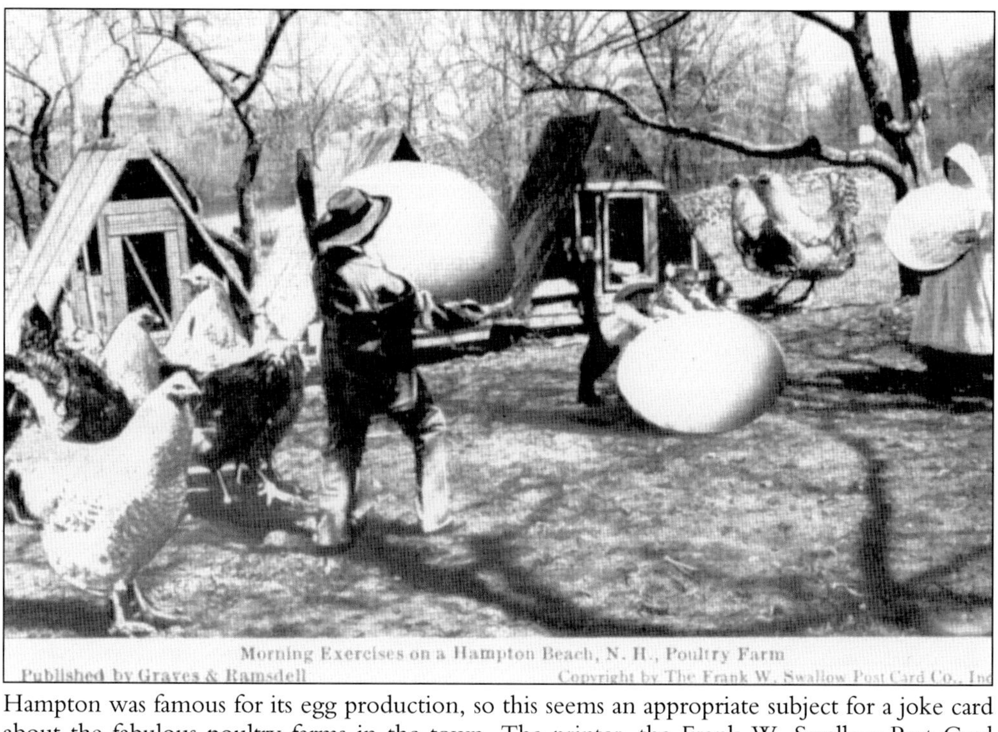

Hampton was famous for its egg production, so this seems an appropriate subject for a joke card about the fabulous poultry farms in the town. The printer, the Frank W. Swallow Post Card Company, was located in Exeter.

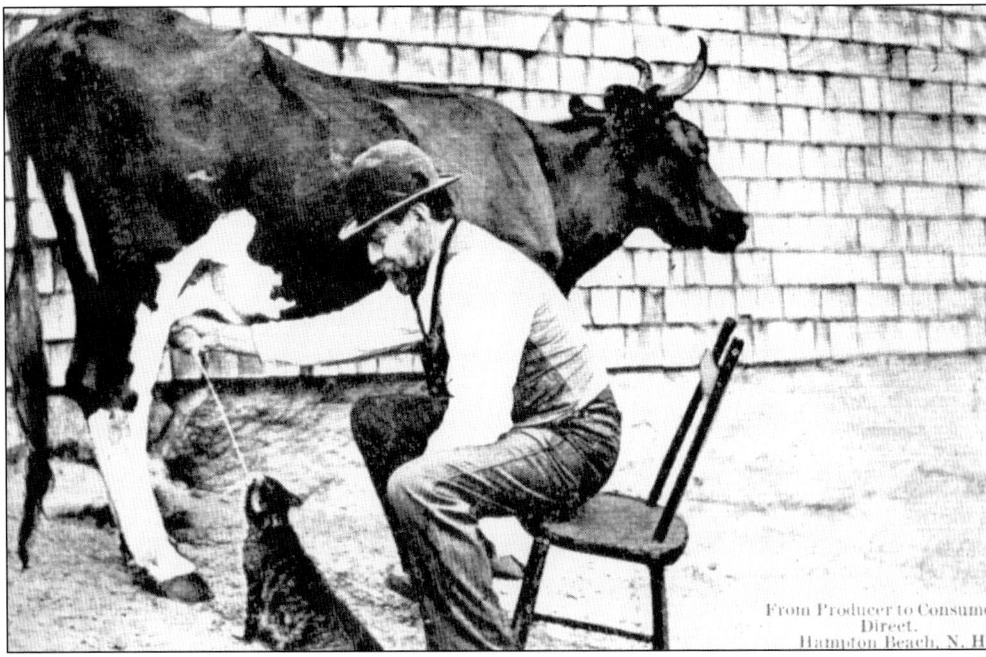

Early in the 20th century, Hampton had a number of dairy farmers who supplied milk to customers in Hampton and other towns, as well as to the farm cats. Christopher Toppan of the Toppan farm was noted for being able to perform this trick.

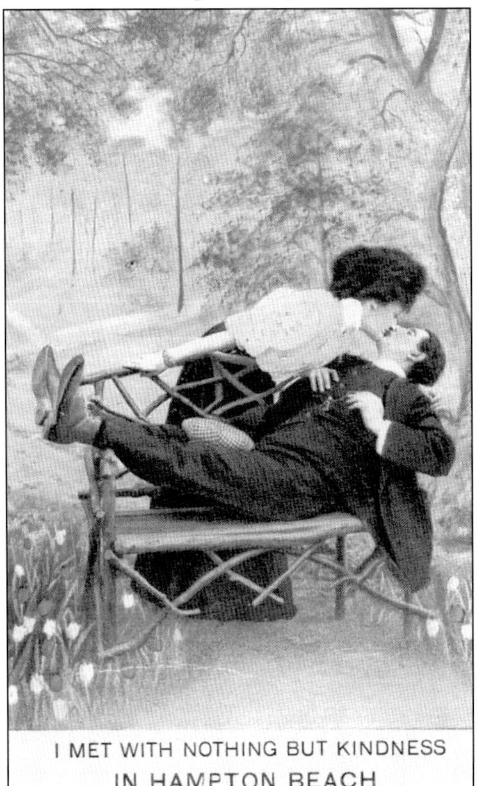

A comic *c.* 1915 card has had "Hampton Beach" added, but the same postcard was undoubtedly made for other places as well.

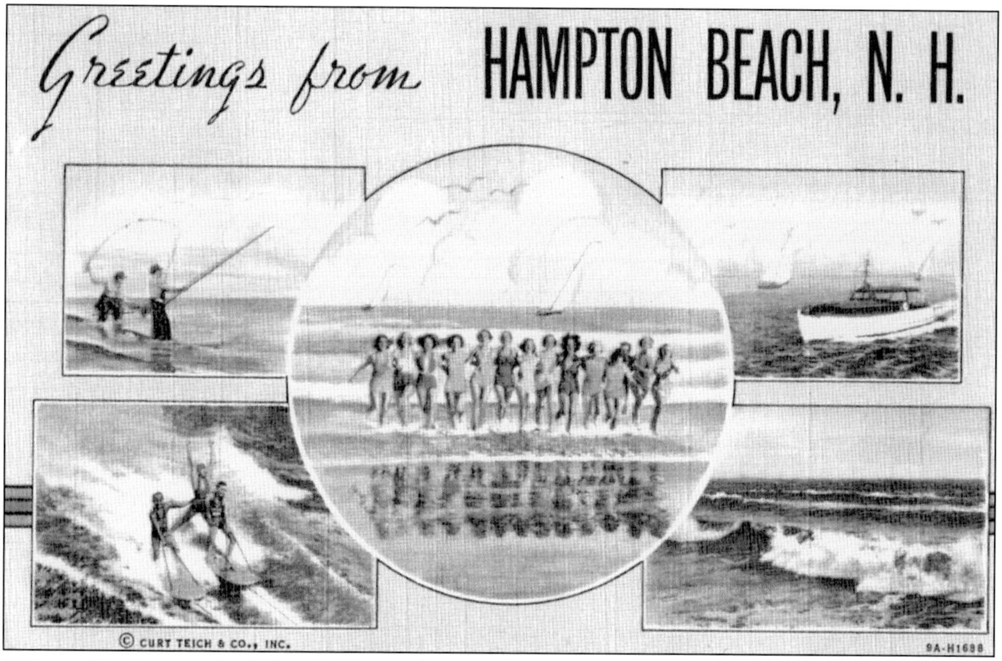

This multi-view card of the 1940s emphasizes the fun to be had at Hampton Beach. Fishing, boating, swimming, and waterskiing, as well as the attractions of pretty girls, made beach vacations memorable.

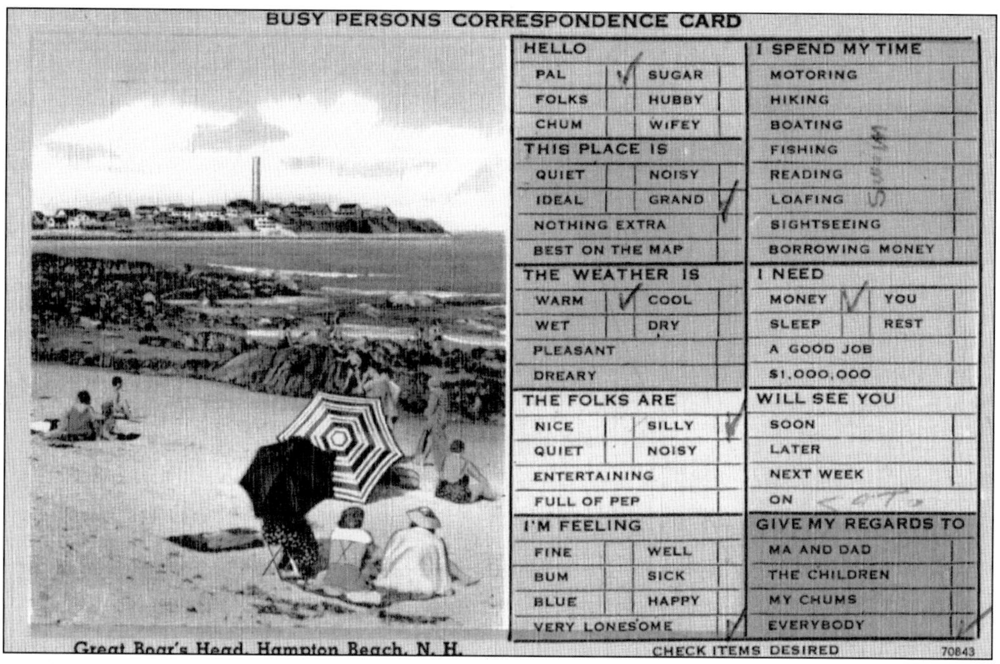

Cards with preprinted messages that could be completed by a choice of endings were popular in the 1940s and 1950s. In 1957, Sue sent this card to her "pal" Janet, commenting on her trip to Hampton Beach. Note the view of Boar's Head.

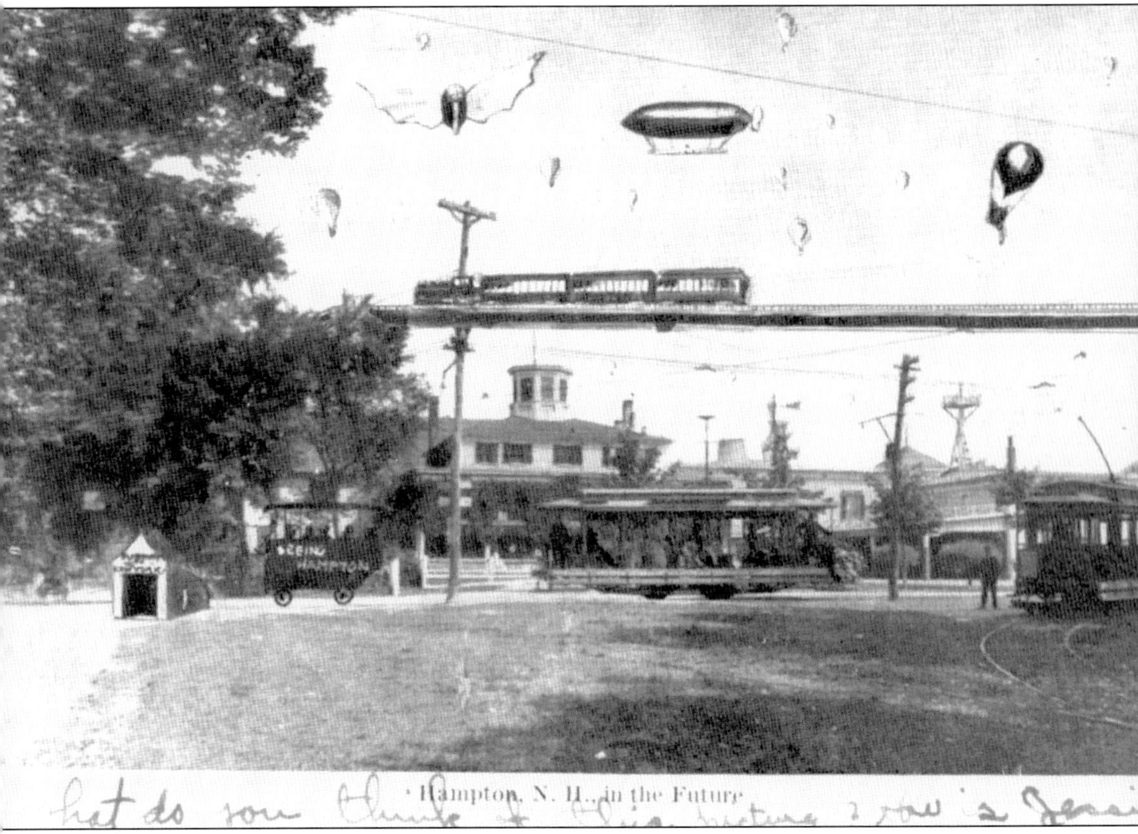

This postcard from the first decade of the 20th century shows the corner at the Hotel Whittier, but the publishers have drawn in what they thought Hampton might look like in the future. At the left is a subway entrance marked "to New York." Apparently travel to the big city was to be as simple as that. Note that none of the objects in the sky resemble the airplane, which may indicate that the card was published before the Wright brothers had had much impact on the public's imagination. The monorail and the dirigible did become a reality, but they were not found in Hampton. What is not included on this card is the automobile, which has transformed Hampton in ways not imagined 100 years ago.